A Professional Approach

Publisher

Bill and Karla Roberts

New York, New York   Columbus, Ohio   Chicago, Illinois   Peoria, Illinois   Woodland Hills, California

Glencoe/McGraw-Hill

*A Division of The **McGraw·Hill** Companies*

Publisher 2002: A Professional Approach
Student Edition
ISBN 0-02-814272-1

1   2   3   4   5   6   7   8   9   10   079/079   07   06   05   04   03   02

Send all inquiries to:
Glencoe/McGraw-Hill
8787 Orion Place
Columbus, OH 43240-4027
Development: settingPace
Production: settingPace

BRIEF CONTENTS

CONTENTS

CONTENTS

Lesson 2:
Working with Text and Graphics 50

CONTENTS

CONTENTS

PREFACE

Publisher 2002, covers the basic features of Publisher 2002. This tutorial and its ancillaries will help you become a knowledgeable, empowered end user. After you complete this tutorial, you will be able to create and modify Publisher publications and use Publisher 2002 to access and explore the World Wide Web, including creating and using hyperlinks and producing a Web site.

STRUCTURE AND FORMAT OF THE *PUBLISHER 2002* TUTORIAL

Publisher 2002 covers a range of functions and techniques and provides hands-on opportunities for you to practice and apply your skills. Each lesson in *Publisher 2002* includes the following:

- **Contents and Objectives.** The Contents and Objectives provide an overview of the Publisher features you will learn in the lesson.

- **Explanations of important concepts.** Each section of each lesson begins with a brief explanation of the concept or software feature covered in that lesson. The explanations help you understand "the big picture" as you learn each new Publisher 2002 feature.

- **Publisher in the Workplace.** This element appears in the margin and provides a brief overview of how the Publisher concepts presented in the lesson can help you succeed in the workplace.

- **New terms.** An important part of learning about computers is learning the terminology. Each new term in the tutorial appears in boldface and italic and is defined the first time it is used. As you encounter these words, read their definitions carefully. If you encounter the same word later and have forgotten the meaning, you can look up the word in the Glossary.

- **Hands On activities.** Because most of us learn best by doing, each explanation is followed by a hands-on activity that includes step-by-step instructions, which you complete at the computer. Integrated in the steps are notes and warnings to help you learn more about Publisher 2002.

- **Publisher Basics.** This element appears in the margin next to Hands On activities. Publisher Basics lists the general steps required to perform a particular task. Use the Publisher Basics as a reference to quickly and easily review the steps to perform a task.

- **Hints & Tips.** This element appears in the margin and provides tips for increasing your effectiveness while using the Publisher 2002 program.

- **Another Way.** This element appears in the margin and provides alternate ways to perform a given task.

- **Did You Know?** Read each Did You Know?, another element that appears in the margin, to learn additional facts related to the content of the lesson or other interesting facts about computers.

- **Illustrations.** Many figures point out features on the screen and illustrate what your screen should look like after you complete important steps.

- **Self Check exercises.** To check your knowledge of the concepts presented in the lesson, a self-check exercise is provided at the end of each lesson. After completing the exercise, refer to Appendix C: Answers to Self Check to verify your understanding of the lesson material.

■ **On the Web.** At the end of each lesson, an On the Web section teaches you how to use Publisher to access the World Wide Web. Various activities show you how to insert a hyperlink into a Publisher Publication, navigate the Web, use the Search page, create a Web page, and more.

■ **Summary.** At the end of each lesson, the Summary reviews the major topics covered in the lesson. You can use the Summary as a study guide.

■ **Concepts Review.** At the end of each lesson, there are five types of objective questions: a true/false exercise, a matching exercise, a completion exercise, short-answer questions, and an identification exercise. When you complete these exercises, you can verify that you have learned all the concepts that have been covered in the lesson.

■ **Skills Review.** The Skills Review section provides simple hands-on exercises to practice each skill you learned in the lesson.

■ **Lesson Applications.** The Lesson Applications provide additional hands-on practice. These problems combine two or more skills learned in the lesson to modify Publisher 2002 publications.

■ **Projects.** The Projects provide additional hands-on practice to apply your problem-solving skills. Each project allows you to create a new publication or modify an existing publication to incorporate one or more skills learned in the lesson. In each lesson, the Projects section contains an *On the Web* project, which reinforces the skills learned in the On the Web section, as well as a *Project in Progress* that builds from one lesson to the next.

■ **Portfolio Builder, Toolbar and Command Summary, and Answers to Self Check.** These appendices provide a wealth of information. The Portfolio Builder gives an overview of portfolios and provides tips on creating your personal portfolio. The Toolbar and Command Summary reviews both mouse and keyboard techniques for completing Publisher 2002 tasks. Answers to Self Check exercises found throughout each lesson are provided in the last appendix.

■ **Glossary and Index.** A Glossary and an Index appear at the back of the tutorial. Use the Glossary to look up terms that you don't understand and the Index to find specific information.

■ **Publisher Data CD.** Attached to the inside back cover of this tutorial you will find the Publisher Data CD. This CD contains Publisher 2002 files for you to use as you complete the hands-on activities and the end-of-lesson activities. You will access files on the Publisher Data CD, but you will need to save the files you create to a folder on the hard drive or network drive, to a Zip disk, to a floppy disk, or to a CD-RW (a read-writable CD).

REVIEWERS

Many thanks are due to the following individuals who reviewed the manuscript and provided recommendations to improve this tutorial:

Michael Perry
Chape Hill High School
Dallas, GA

Randall Schmitz
MSU Billings College
Billings, MT

JoAnne Woods
Duluth High School
Duluth, GA

COPYING FILES FROM YOUR PUBLISHER DATA CD

CD-ROMs can hold hundreds of megabytes of data. As their name implies (Compact Disc-*Read-Only* Memory), you cannot modify the data they contain. Hard and floppy disks are the media generally used as personal data storage devices. To complete the lessons in this tutorial, you may want to copy the files from the Publisher Data CD to a folder on the hard drive or on a network drive, or to a Zip disk.

1. Turn on the computer you are using.

2. Insert the **Publisher Data CD** in the CD drive of your computer.

3. Click **Start** [Start], point to **Programs**, and click **Windows Explorer**.

The Exploring window opens.

4. In the Folders panel of the Exploring window, find and select the drive icon that represents your CD drive.

The contents of the Publisher Data CD will appear in the Contents panel.

5. Click the **Edit menu** and click **Select All**.

6. Click **Copy** [Copy].

7. Scroll up, if necessary, and click the appropriate drive icon (and folder, if necessary) where you want to store your Publisher files.

 If you are copying the Publisher Data CD folders and files onto a Zip disk or a floppy disk, be sure to write Publisher Student Data Disk *on the disk label and insert a blank, formatted disk into the appropriate disk drive. Go to step 8.*

 If you are copying the Publisher Data CD folders and files onto the hard drive or network drive, navigate to the drive and folder where you want to store the files. Then create a folder for the Publisher Data CD folders and files: click the drive icon, click the folder name if necessary, click the File menu, click New, and type Publisher Student Data Disk. *Click this newly created folder in the Folders panel of the Exploring window, and go to step 8.*

8. Click **Paste** [Paste].

A Copying box will appear on the screen to indicate the progress of the copying process.

To use and save changes to the files copied from the CD, you must change the attributes of the files. You must remove the read-only attribute and add the archive attribute to the Publisher Student Data Disk files.

9. In the Folders panel of the Exploring window, click the appropriate drive icon and folder, if necessary, where the files are stored.

10. Click **Edit** and click **Select All**.

11. Right-click one of the highlighted files in the Contents pane, and click **Properties** on the shortcut menu that appears.

12. Click the **General tab** of the Properties dialog box, if necessary.

13. In the Attributes area, click the **Read-only box** until the check mark disappears.

14. Click the **Archive box** until a check mark appears in the white box.

15. Click **OK**.

16. Close Windows Explorer.

17. Remove the disk from the drive, if necessary.

You are now ready to begin working with *Publisher 2002!*

Communicating in Today's World

Print and online communications merge

I n today's increasingly fast-paced business world, the ability to communicate your message clearly and quickly is paramount. Thousands of messages bombard people daily; most are not received or are quickly forgotten. As a publishing professional, your goal must be to get and keep the reader's attention. Software tools such as Publisher 2002 provide the resources you need to create professional print and online publications.

Photo: Photodisc

Advertisers, marketers, and public relations specialists use both print and online media to communicate with the public. Until recently, print publications were a primary medium of communication. These publications include newspapers, magazines, newsletters, brochures, and direct mail pieces. As the use of the Internet grows, so does the importance of planning communication for this medium. Communicators plan Web sites and use banner advertising to supplement, or sometimes to replace, traditional print communications. Communication professionals today consider ways to get people to visit Web sites, as well as ways to get people to read print publications.

The revolution in communication is largely the result of changes in technology. Software tools such as Publisher 2002 allow print pieces such as advertisements, newsletters, brochures, postcards, and flyers to be produced in a fraction of the time required just a few years ago. Software applications allow you to integrate text, graphics, and photographs into a single file. Tasks such as rotating text can be accomplished quickly and accurately by computer, rather than by hand. Changes to layouts and edits to text can be accomplished quickly and easily.

Until recently, print and online publications were planned and executed separately. Although both mediums often conveyed the same information, different software tools were needed to produce the publications. The new generation of software applications such as Publisher 2002 allows you to create dual-purpose publications or to convert print publications for viewing online. By saving a publication as a Web page, the software automatically applies all the special coding needed to create files that can be posted on the Web. Publisher 2002 also allows you to create publications specially designed for the Web. Typical features of online publications such as hyperlinks, sound, and animation can be added quickly and easily in Publisher 2002.

By producing both print and online publications using the same software applications, publishing professionals can maintain a consistent look and feel across all media. Readers more readily identify companies and products that maintain such consistency.

The benefits of improved technology do not come without risks. Layouts that once were crafted by design professionals can now be completed by anyone with the correct software application. However, non-design professionals often do not understand the importance of font selection, visual balance, and effective use of white space. Publisher 2002 provides numerous design templates and color schemes that have been created by design professionals. Nonprofessionals use these templates and color palettes to create professional-looking publications.

Accuracy is often sacrificed in the haste to get a publication to press. Common errors include misspellings, errors in grammar, and incorrect facts. Each time you modify a publication, you may introduce additional errors. Before any publication is sent to the printer or posted online, print and proofread it. At least two people should read every word of the final proof. If you make changes, reprint and re-proof the publication. This step is especially important for printed publications since changes either cannot be made after the publication is printed or are very expensive to make. Online communications can be updated, but an error-free publication should still be the goal.

Careful planning and execution result in professional communications that get and keep the reader's attention—the goal of all communication professionals.

Publisher Basics

CONTENTS

OBJECTIVES

After you complete this lesson, you will be able to do the following:

- Explain desktop publishing.
- Describe the use of frames in publications.
- Use your mouse to point, click, double-click, right-click, select, and drag.
- Start and exit Microsoft Publisher.
- Name the main components of the Microsoft Publisher window.
- Access menus and use Microsoft Publisher commands.
- Get help using the Ask a Question box, the Help window, and the Office Assistant.
- Create and modify personal information sets.
- Use task panes to create publications.
- Create a folder.
- Open, save, print, and close a publication.

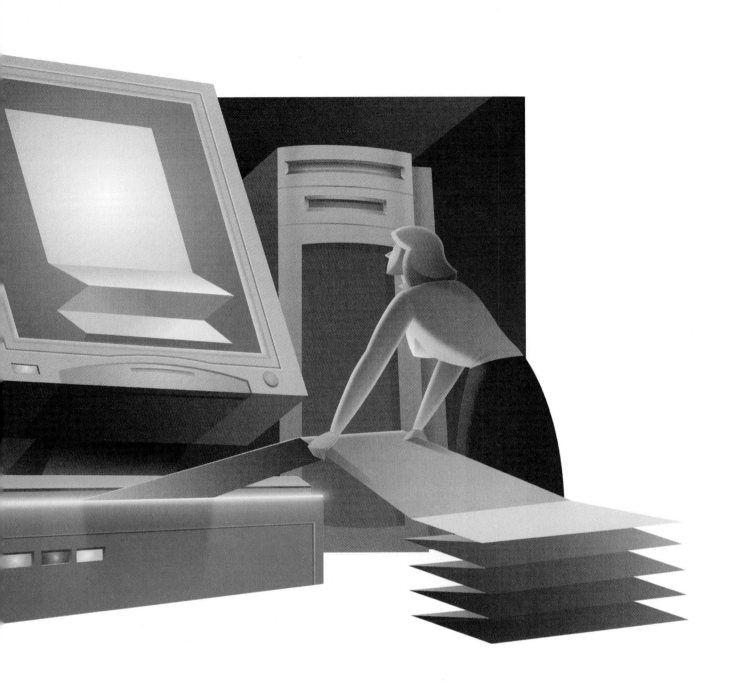

This lesson teaches you basic desktop publishing terms, shows you how to launch Microsoft Publisher, and introduces you to the elements of the Publisher window. You will learn how to open, save, print, and close publications—essential skills that you will use whenever you work with Publisher. You will begin to work with the task panes that help you create interesting, useful, and well-designed publications. You will also explore the online Help system, which you can use to learn more about the features of Publisher and to help you find answers to questions that you may have as you use the program.

INTRODUCING MICROSOFT PUBLISHER

This tutorial teaches you how to use the desktop publishing program Microsoft Publisher. A desktop publishing program enables you to create all kinds of *publications*—from postcard invitations and business cards to multi-page newsletters. Although it is possible to create many of these same kinds of publications using a word processing program like Microsoft Word, desktop publishing programs give you more options and greater flexibility in the layout and design of your publications.

Much of this flexibility is achieved through the use of *frames*. A *frame* holds an object in a publication. Frames can contain text, tables, pictures, clip art—in fact, any object you wish to include in your publication. Frames, such as those shown in Figure 1.1, allow you not only to place text and objects side by side, but also to *layer* objects on top of each other.

Microsoft Publisher allows you to create a professional-looking publication, even if you have little or no training in design, by using one of the many templates provided in the program. A *template* contains the basic layout, formatting, and design elements for a publication. As you learn more about the fundamentals of design, Publisher also gives you the ability to create publications from scratch, incorporating whatever design elements you may choose.

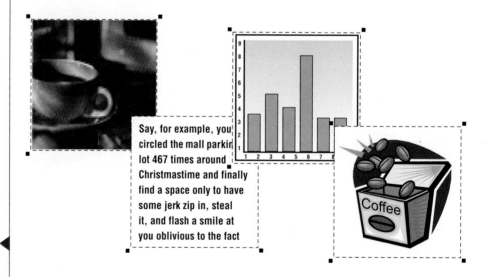

Say, for example, you circled the mall parking lot 467 times around Christmastime and finally find a space only to have some jerk zip in, steal it, and flash a smile at you oblivious to the fact

Figure 1.1
Layered Frames

USING THE MOUSE

You will use the *mouse* extensively in Microsoft Publisher. The mouse is the key to the graphical user interface because it lets you choose and manipulate on-screen objects without having to type on the keyboard. Although the mouse is the most popular pointing device, you may also use several other pointing devices. *Trackballs* have buttons like the mouse, but instead of moving the mouse over the desktop, you spin a large ball. Laptops often employ either a small *joystick* in the middle of the keyboard or a *touch-sensitive pad* below the keyboard. All of these devices perform the same basic functions—they allow you to point to and select items on the screen and click buttons to perform actions on those items.

Your mouse probably has three buttons. Whenever the directions in this tutorial say *click,* use the left mouse button. If you must use the right mouse button, the directions will say *right-click* or *click the right mouse button.*

You can perform several actions with the mouse:

■ On your screen, you should see an arrow pointing toward the upper left. This arrow is called the **mouse pointer,** or more simply, the **pointer.** Moving the mouse to position the pointer on the screen is called **pointing.** Table 1.1 shows several shapes you may notice as you point to objects on the screen.

TABLE 1.1	COMMON POINTER SHAPES
Pointer Shape	**Description**
↗	Normal Select (arrow)
+	Crosshair pointer
↘?	Help Select (What's This? pointer)
↘⌛	Working in Background
⌛	Busy
I	Text Select (I beam pointer)
↘	Drag Text
⌐ RESIZE	Resize
⊘	Unavailable
⛟	Move Object
👆	Hyperlink Select

■ To click the mouse, point to an object and quickly press and release the left mouse button.

■ To work with an object on the screen, you must usually select the item by clicking on the object—pressing and quickly releasing the mouse button.

■ To double-click, point to an object and click the left mouse button twice in rapid succession without moving the pointer.

■ To right click, point to an object, press the right mouse button, and then quickly release it.

■ To drag (or drag-and-drop), point to an object you want to move, press and hold the left mouse button, move the mouse to drag the object to a new location, and then release the mouse button.

Practice using the mouse until you become comfortable using it. Although keyboard alternatives exist for most mouse actions, you will be more efficient if you can use both keyboard actions and the mouse.

STARTING MICROSOFT PUBLISHER

Before you can start Microsoft Publisher, both Microsoft Publisher 2002 and Windows 98, Windows NT 4.0 (with Service Pack 6 or later), Windows 2000 Professional, or Windows Me (Millennium Edition) must be installed on the computer you are using. The figures in this tutorial use Windows Me. If you are using a different version of the Windows operating system, the information appearing on your screen may vary slightly. (If you are unfamiliar with Windows, you may wish to review the Windows features before continuing with this lesson.)

HANDS On

Publisher BASICS

Launching Publisher

1. Turn on your computer.

2. Click the Start button on the Windows taskbar.

3. Point to Programs.

4. Click Microsoft Publisher.

Launching Microsoft Publisher

In this activity, you will start Microsoft Publisher.

1. Turn on your computer.

Note *If you are prompted for a username and/or password, enter the information at this time. If you do not know your username and/or password, ask your instructor for help.*

The Windows operating system boots the computer. Your screen should resemble Figure 1.2. If the Welcome to Windows screen appears, click its Close button ☒ to close the window.

Icons

Start button

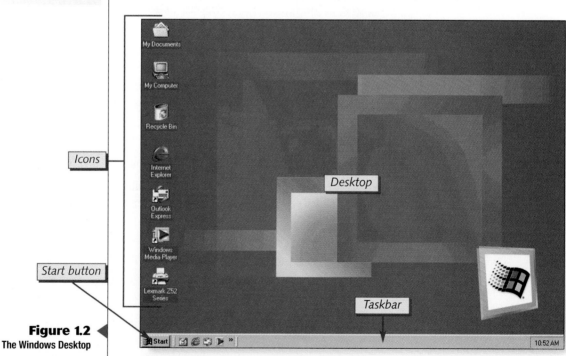

Figure 1.2 ◄
The Windows Desktop

Desktop

Taskbar

2. Click the Start button 🏁Start on the Windows taskbar.

3. Point to Programs.

The Programs menu appears similar to Figure 1.3. Depending on the applications installed on your computer, your Programs menu may be different from Figure 1.3.

Figure 1.3
The Program menu

4. Click Microsoft Publisher.

The Publisher program starts and the initial Microsoft Publisher window appears as shown in Figure 1.4.

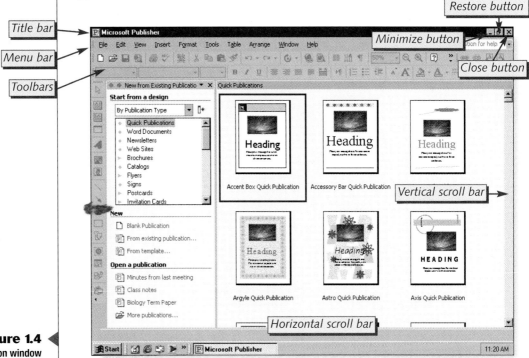

Figure 1.4
Publisher application window

EXPLORING THE PUBLISHER WINDOW

The Publisher *application window* (screen) is shown in Figure 1.4. Your window may look slightly different, because Publisher allows users to customize, or alter, the Publisher window to suit their individual needs. The Publisher window contains many standard Windows elements, including a title bar; the Minimize, Restore, and Close buttons; a menu bar; toolbars; and the scroll bars. These items should be familiar if you have used any other Windows application.

Across the bottom of the screen is the Windows taskbar, including the Start button and other buttons for navigating Windows. Buttons on the taskbar show which applications are open. When the Publisher taskbar icon is displayed, you know that Publisher is ready to use. Across the top, the *title bar* shows the name of the application (Microsoft Publisher) and the name of the current publication, if any.

Identifying Menus and Commands

As shown in Figure 1.4, the Publisher menu bar appears below the title bar. The menu bar displays menu names found in most Windows applications, such as File, Edit, and Help. Publisher also includes menus just for desktop publishing, such as Format and Arrange.

Menus list the *commands* available in Publisher. To display a menu's commands, click a menu name on the menu bar. The menu will display a *short menu,* a list of the most-used commands, with a double arrow at the bottom. If you keep your pointer on the menu for a few seconds or if you click the double arrow at the bottom of the menu, an *expanded menu* appears. This expanded menu shows all commands available on that menu. The most commonly used commands appear when a menu opens; when the list expands, less commonly used commands appear. Figure 1.5 shows both versions of Publisher's View menu—a short menu and an expanded menu.

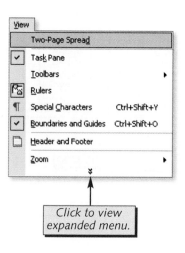

Click to view expanded menu.

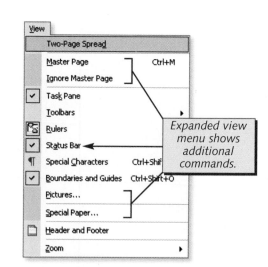

Expanded view menu shows additional commands.

Figure 1.5
Initial View menu

As you can see in Figure 1.5, eight commands appear on the initial View menu. These eight commands are the commands used most often from this menu. The expanded menu shows five additional commands that are not used as frequently. After you use one of these additional commands, it will be added to the short menu. This ***adaptive menu*** feature allows each user to customize the menus. Publisher will automatically customize the menus as you work, placing the commands you use often on the short menu.

An ellipsis (…) after a command indicates that clicking the command will display either a dialog box or a new task pane. Pointing to a command with an arrow to the right displays another list of commands called a submenu.

Note   *In this window, many features are not yet available because you have not yet opened a publication. For example, note that if you click Edit on the menu bar, all of the options beneath are grayed (meaning that they are currently disabled). As you will soon discover, the available Publisher options change depending on what you are doing at the moment.*

To close a menu, click the menu name again or click anywhere outside the menu.

Table 1.2 provides a brief description of the menus available on the Publisher menu bar.

TABLE 1.2	PUBLISHER MENU BAR
Menu	**Contains Commands that Let You...**
File	Control your publication files by opening, closing, saving, and printing them.
Edit	Rearrange text and other elements of publications by locating, copying, moving and deleting them. Also contains the personal information set dialog box.
View	View publications different ways; display and hide toolbars.
Insert	Insert various elements, such as pictures, symbols, and objects, into your publications.
Format	Determine the appearance of text and objects in your publications, such as the font size and style or the color scheme.
Tools	Use Publisher's special desktop publishing tools, such as Design Checker, Mail Merge, and the Commercial Printing Tools.
Table	Insert, fill-in, and format an arrangement of columns and rows as tabular information.
Arrange	Rearrange the position of objects in a publication. Also contains the layout and ruler guides.
Window	Work in multiple publications at once, in one or more windows.
Help	Access Publisher's Help system and the Microsoft Office Home page on the Internet for desktop publishing assistance and support.

Note   *Although the lessons in this tutorial emphasize the mouse method for performing most commands, the Command Summary in Appendix B lists the keyboard actions for all commands discussed in this tutorial.*

Exploring Menus

In this activity, you will explore some of the menus available in Microsoft Publisher.

1. Click **File** on the menu bar.

The short File menu opens displaying common Windows commands and other options for controlling your publications.

2. Click the **double arrow** at the bottom of the short menu.

The expanded menu, showing all the options available on the File menu appears.

If you point to the short menu for several seconds, the expanded menu will automatically appear (and the double arrow at the bottom of the menu will disappear).

3. Click outside the File menu to close the menu.

4. Click **Edit** on the menu bar and review the commands listed. Expand the menu and view the additional options available on the Edit menu.

5. Explore the View, Insert, Format, Tools, Table, Arrange, Window, and Help menus.

You will notice in each menu that the expandable menu contains more options. Remember, as you use commands, Publisher adjusts the options that appear on your short menu.

Identifying the Standard Toolbar and Buttons

Below the menu bar is Publisher's Standard toolbar, as shown in Figure 1.4, on page 9. A ***toolbar*** contains a row of buttons for many of the most frequently used commands. Although you can access these commands on one of the menus, clicking a toolbar button is often more convenient. You can quickly identify any toolbar button by pointing to it and reading the name. The name appears in a small text box called a ***ScreenTip.***

When this tutorial mentions a toolbar button, a picture of the button is displayed within the text. For instance, when a step instructs you to click the Open button, the button will be illustrated as shown here.

The icon on each toolbar button symbolizes the command. For example, on Publisher's Standard toolbar, the New button ⬜ is symbolized by a piece of paper. Table 1.3 displays each button available on the Publisher Standard toolbar and explains the function. The Standard toolbar, like Publisher's menus, is adaptive. The most common buttons appear on the main toolbar, while buttons used less often are accessible by clicking the Toolbar Options button ⬚ at the end of the toolbar. When you click on one of these seldom-used buttons, Publisher adds it to the main toolbar.

TABLE 1.3	THE PUBLISHER STANDARD TOOLBAR	
Button	**Name**	**Action**
	New	Creates a new blank publication.
	Open	Opens a publication.
	Save	Makes a permanent copy of a publication to a file on a disk or drive.
	E-mail	Opens a header to send your publication as an electronic mail message.
	Search	Opens the Basic Search task pane, which allows you to find files by specifying search text and where to search.
	Print	Prints the entire publication.
	Print Preview	Previews the publication before printing.
	Spelling	Checks for spelling errors.
	Cut	Removes the selected item(s) from the publication to the Clipboard—a temporary storage place for information that is used by all Windows applications.
	Copy	Copies the selected item(s) and places a copy of the item(s) on the Clipboard.
	Paste	Pastes the selected item(s) from the Clipboard into the current location.
	Format Painter	Copies the formatting from the selected item(s) to another item(s).
	Undo	Reverses the last command.
	Redo	Repeats the last command.
	Bring to front...	A group of selections that allows for the placement of objects in the same area of the page layout. Objects can be moved from the foreground to the background.
	Free rotate...	A group of selections that allows the orientation of an object to be changed in various ways.
	Insert Hyperlink	Inserts a link from the current publication to another part of the current publication, another publication, or an Internet site.
	Web Page Preview	Generates pages as a web site and opens them in the default web browser.
	Columns	Adjusts text to a column format.
	Special characters	Shows or hides the formatting markers.
36%	Zoom box	Increases or decreases the displayed size of the publication.
	Zoom out	Decreases the displayed size of the publication by small amounts.
	Zoom in	Increases the displayed size of the publication by small amounts.
	Help	Displays various help options.

(continues)

To move a toolbar to a different location, point to the
handle on the left end. When
the four-way arrow appears
drag the toolbar to its new
location.

TABLE 1.3		THE PUBLISHER STANDARD TOOLBAR	*(continued)*
	Close all	Closes all open publications.	
	Save all	Saves all open publications.	
	Date	Inserts the current date into the publication.	
	Time	Inserts the current time into the publication.	
	Align top	Aligns an object with the top of the object with which it is linked.	
	Align bottom	Aligns an object with the bottom of the object with which it is linked.	
	Align left	Aligns an object with the left edge of the object with which it is linked.	
	Align right	Aligns an object with the right edge of the object with which it is linked.	
	Align center	Aligns an object precisely between the left edge and the right edge of the object with which it is linked.	
	Align middle	Aligns and object precisely between the top edge and the bottom edge of the object with which it is linked.	

In addition to the Standard toolbar, Publisher includes many other toolbars, each arranged for a different purpose. The View menu includes the
Toolbars command. The Toolbars submenu allows you to control which
toolbars are displayed as you work. A check mark next to a toolbar name
indicates that toolbar is displayed. Clicking a check mark will ***deselect,*** or
hide, that toolbar.

Displaying and Hiding Toolbars

In this activity, you will display and hide toolbars.

Displaying and Hiding Toolbars

1. Click the View menu; point
to Toolbars.

2. Click the toolbar name you
want to display or the check
mark beside the toolbar you
want to hide.

1. Click the View menu and point to Toolbars.

The Toolbars submenu displays, as shown in the Figure 1.6

> *Note*   *If the Standard toolbar is not selected, select it now. If any other toolbars are selected, deselect them now.*

2. On the Toolbars submenu, click Formatting.

The Formatting toolbar displays below the standard toolbar.

3. Click the View menu, point to Toolbars, and click Connect Frames.

The Connect Frames toolbar displays at the right end of the Standard toolbar.

4. Click the View menu, point to Toolbars, and click Objects.

The Objects toolbar displays along the left edge of the screen.

5. Click the View menu, point to Toolbars, and click Task Pane.

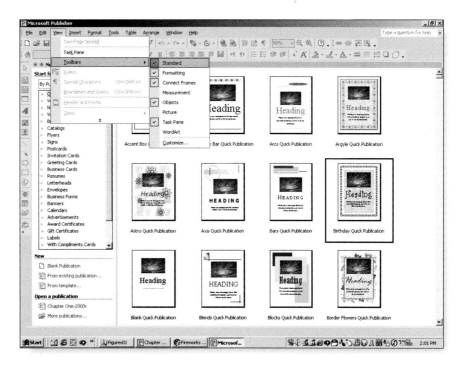

Figure 1.6
Toolbar submenu

The Task Pane appears to the right of the Objects toolbar. Your screen should now display the Task Pane and the Standard, Formatting, Connect Frames, and Object toolbars. It should look similar to the screen shown in Figure 1.7

The number of buttons that appear on a toolbar varies depending on the size of the computer screen.

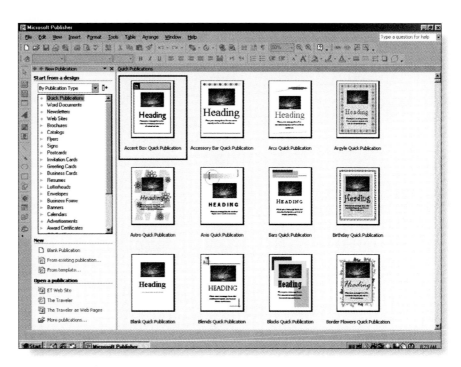

Figure 1.7
Toolbar turned on

Identifying More Toolbars and Buttons

The Formatting toolbar appears directly below the Standard toolbar, as shown in Figure 1.7. The commands available on the Formatting toolbar are listed in Table 1.4 and include commands for controlling the appearance of text and objects. The Formatting toolbar, like the Standard toolbar is adaptive. The most common buttons appear on the main toolbar, while buttons used less often are accessible by clicking the Toolbar Options button ⬚ at the end of the toolbar. When you click one of these seldom-used buttons, Publisher adds it to the main toolbar.

 If your Standard and Formatting toolbars share one row below the menu bar, you can display them as two separate toolbars by clicking Customize on the Tools menu. On the Options tab, select Show Standard and Formatting toolbars on two rows and click Close.

TABLE 1.4	THE PUBLISHER FORMATTING TOOLBAR	
Button	**Name**	**Action**
𝐴	Styles and Formatting	Displays the Styles and Formatting task pane.
Normal	Style	Applies a specific style to the selected text.
Times New Roman	Font	Lists the typeface options available.
10	Font Size	Lists the size of the selected text.
B	Bold	Bolds the selected text.
I	Italic	Italicizes the selected text.
U	Underline	Underlines the selected text.
	Align Left	Aligns the selected text on the left margin.
	Center	Centers the selected text between the margins.
	Align Right	Aligns the selected text on the right margin.
	Justify	Aligns the selected text on the left and right margins.
	Numbering	Inserts auto numbering.
	Bullets	Inserts bullets.
	Decrease Indent	Decrease the indent on the selected text.
	Increase Indent	Increases the indent on the selected text.
A	Decrease Font Size	Decreases the font size on the selected text.
A	Increase Font Size	Increases the font size on the selected text.
	Fill Color	Changes the color of the selected area.
	Line Color	Changes the color of the selected line.
A	Font Color	Changes the color of the selected text.
	Line/Border Style	Changes the size of the selected line or border.
	Dash Style	Changes the style of dashed lines.
	Arrow Style	Changes the style of the selected arrow.
	Shadow Style	Changes the style of shadow on selected objects.
	3-D Style	Applies various 3-D effects to objects.
ABC	Small Caps	Changes the selected text to small capital letters.

(continues)

TABLE 1.4		THE PUBLISHER FORMATTING TOOLBAR	*(continued)*
All Caps		Changes the selected text to all capital letters.
x²	Superscript	Changes the font style to superscript for the selected text.
x₂	Subscript	Changes the font style to subscript for the selected text.
Outline	Outline	Applies the outline feature to selected text.
Emboss	Emboss	Applies the embossing feature to selected text.
Engrave	Engrave	Applies the engraving feature to selected text.
≡	Single Spacing	Changes the line spacing for the selected text to single spaced.
≡	1.5 Spacing	Changes the line spacing for the selected text to 1.5 lines.
≡	Double Spacing	Changes the line spacing for the selected text to double spaced.

Immediately to the right of the Standard toolbar is a short bar called the Connect Frames toolbar. As its name implies, this toolbar is used specifically to connect and disconnect frames and text boxes. Table 1.4 describes the buttons available on the Connect Frames toolbar. This toolbar can be customized by clicking the Toolbar Options button ▯ at the end of the toolbar.

 If your Connect Frames toolbar does not share a row with the Standard toolbar, point to the left edge of the Connect Frames toolbar and drag it to the end of the Standard toolbar.

TABLE 1.5		THE PUBLISHER CONNECT FRAMES TOOLBAR	
Button	**Name**	**Action**	
🔗	Create Text Box Link	Creates a link between text frames (boxes) that allows text to overflow from one text box to another.	
🔗	Break Forward Link	Disconnects the link between text frames.	
▯	Previous Text Box	Selects the previous linked text box.	
▯	Next Text Box	Selects the next linked text box.	

At the far left of the window is a vertical toolbar called the Objects toolbar. Table 1.6 lists the buttons on the Objects toolbar and explains their functions. The Objects toolbar, like the Connect Frames toolbar, can be customized. Buttons can be added and deleted by clicking the Toolbar Options button ▯ at the bottom of the toolbar.

TABLE 1.6	THE PUBLISHER OBJECTS TOOLBAR	
Button	**Name**	**Action**
	Select Objects	Selects objects that you indicate with the pointer and lets you move them as a group.
	Text Box	Creates a frame for text.
	Insert Table	Creates a frame and places a table within that frame.
	Insert WordArt	Opens the WordArt program.
	Picture Frame	Creates a frame for importing pictures.
	Clip Organizer Frame	Opens the Microsoft Clip Organizer and the Insert Clip Art task pane.
	Line	Draws lines.
	Arrow	Draws arrows.
	Oval	Draws ovals and circles.
	Rectangle	Draws rectangles.
	AutoShapes	Inserts common shapes, such as triangles, hearts, and arrows.
	Hot Spot	Draws a frame over part of an object and inserts a hyperlink.
	Form Control	Inserts form elements, such as check boxes and option buttons.
	HTML Code Fragment	Creates a frame for an HTML code fragment so that special objects, such as animation, can be inserted in a publication.
	Design Gallery Object	Inserts objects from the Microsoft Publisher Design Gallery.

Understanding Task Panes

Below the Formatting toolbar and to the right of the Objects toolbar is the *task pane.* A task pane is a menu box that provides options for designing your publication and previews of those options. The task pane that appears when Publisher is first opened is the New Publication task pane. Other task panes can be selected by clicking the down arrow ▼ next to the New Publication heading. In this lesson, you will be starting from the New Publication task pane.

The New Publication task pane provides three ways to create publications— **Start from a design, New,** and **Open a publication.**

Under **Start from a design,** a drop-down menu lists three options that allow you to create professional-looking publications quickly and easily. These options are shown in Figure 1.8. The first option, **By Publication Type,** is displayed when Publisher is first opened. When this option is selected, a list of publication types is displayed in the box below the drop-down menu. As you click on each publication type, thumbnail previews of the available designs for that publication type are displayed in the

Publication Gallery—the box to the right of the task pane. To view all of the available designs for that publication type, use the scroll bar on the right side of the Publication Gallery. It is also possible to close the Publication Gallery by clicking on the Hides Publication Gallery button ⬚ to the right of the drop-down menu. Clicking on this button causes the Publication Gallery to be replaced by a single page. Clicking on this button again causes the Publication Gallery to reappear.

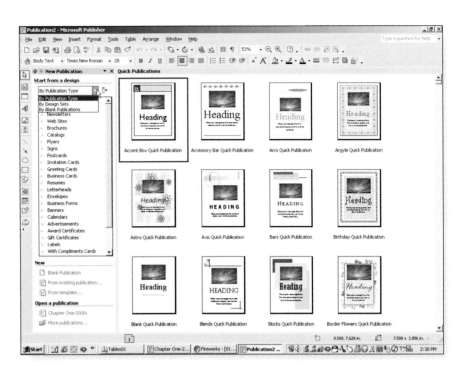

To see the other options under **Start from a design,** click the down arrow on the right side of the drop-down menu. The second option that is displayed is **By Design Sets.** Design sets, as the name implies, are sets of publications that have been designed to go together. Using these design sets, you can create several publications for the same business that will have consistent design elements. For example, a design set may include publications such as a business card, a calendar, a catalog, an envelope, and a newsletter. The third option, **By Blank Publications,** allows you to create publications from blank page layouts.

Three additional options for creating a new publication are listed on the task pane under the heading **New—Blank Publication, From existing publication,** and **From template.** When you click on **Blank Publication,** the task pane disappears and a blank page is displayed as shown in Figure 1.9. In this window, you can create publications from scratch once you have learned the basics of design and layout. (To return to the task pane from this window, click Task Pane on the View menu.) After you have created a publication, you can use the **From existing publication . . .** or **From template . . .** options to make your publication the basis for a new publication.

The final option on the New Publication task pane allows you to find and open publications that you have already created. You will learn more about **Open a publication** later in this lesson.

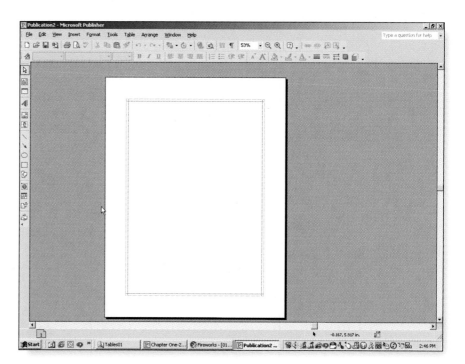

Figure 1.9
New blank design page

GETTING HELP WITH PUBLISHER

While you are using Publisher, you may need to reference Help. Like many application programs, Publisher provides an extensive ***online Help system***—an electronic manual that you can open with the press of a key or the click of a mouse. You can get an overview of the Help system by clicking Microsoft Publisher Help on the Help menu or by clicking the Help button [?] on the Standard toolbar. As you can see, the Help system includes tutorials, as well as links to Web sites that can provide additional Help. The Help system also provides five different tools that you can use to get help without using the Web: the Ask a Question box, the Contents tab, the Index tab, the Answer Wizard, and the Office Assistant.

The Ask a Question box is located in the upper right corner of the Publisher window at the end of the Menu bar, as shown in Figure 1.10. When you type a question, a list of topics that may answer your question appears in a box below the Ask a Question box. When you select a topic, the Publisher Help window appears and gives you information on your topic or additional choices. The Publisher Help window can also be expanded to include three tabs: Contents, Index, and the Answer Wizard. You can use the Contents tab to view a listing of general Help topics. This method can be useful if you don't know the name of a feature. The Index tab can find instances of specific keywords within a Help window. The Answer Wizard can answer specific questions, similar to the Ask a Question box.

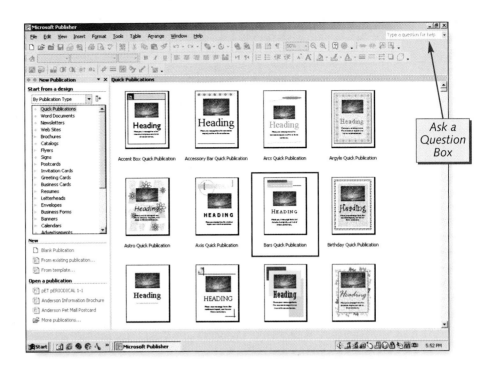

Ask a
Question
Box

Figure 1.10
Ask a Question box on menu bar

Using the Ask a Question Box

In this activity, you will explore the Publisher Help system, starting with the Ask a Question box.

1. **In the Ask a Question box, type** find specific text **and press the** Enter key Enter◄─┘ .

Topics that may answer your question appear in the box under the Ask a Question box, as shown in Figure 1.11.

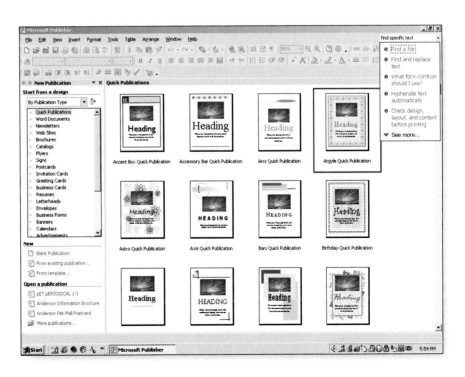

Figure 1.11
Ask a Question topics

2. Click Find and replace text.

The Publisher Help window appears, as shown in Figure 1.12. The Help system gives you two choices: Find text and Find and replace text.

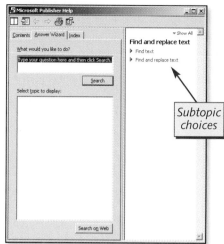

Figure 1.12
Microsoft Publisher
Help window

3. Click Find text.

4. Text appears that explains how to find specific text, as shown in Figure 1.13.

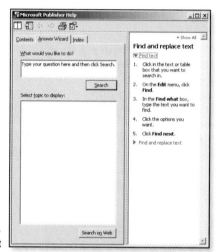

Figure 1.13
Steps to find text

Using the Contents and Index Tabs and the Answer Wizard

In this activity, you will continue to explore Publisher help, using the Contents and Index Tabs and the Answer Wizard.

1. Click the Contents tab, **if it is not on top.**

2. Click the plus sign **in front of Microsoft Publisher Help to expand the topic, if not already expanded.**

3. Click the plus sign **in front of the Text topic.**

The topic expands to show subtopics, and the closed-book icon changes to an open-book icon, as shown in Figure 1.14. The pane on the right continues to show the previous search results.

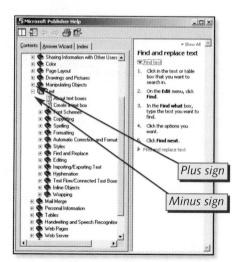

Figure 1.14
Contents tab

Using the Contents Tab

1. If the tabs are not displayed on the Help window, click the Show button.

2. Click the Contents tab, if it is not on top.

3. Click the plus sign in front of the topic you wish to open.

4. Double-click the subtopic you wish to read.

5. If more specific subtopics appear, click the one you wish to read.

Using the Index Tab

1. If the tabs are not displayed on the Help window, click the Show button.

2. Click the Index tab, if it is not on top.

3. Type or click one or more keywords.

4. Click the Search button.

5. In the Choose a topic box, click the topic you wish to read.

Using the Answer Wizard

1. If the tabs are not displayed on the Help window, click the Show button.

2. Click the Answer Wizard tab, if it is not on top.

3. Type a question or phrase in the What would you like to do? box.

4. Click the Search button.

5. In the Select topic to display box, click the topic you want to read.

---

4. **Double-click the Formatting subtopic.**

A list of even more specific subtopics appears, as shown in Figure 1.15.

5. **Double-click the Spacing subtopic.**

6. **Click on Adjust tracking and Kerning.**

Information about this topic appears in the pane on the right. You will notice that some of the text is in black and some is in blue. The blue text is *hypertext* (also called *hyperlinks*), which provides links to additional topics. When you point to hypertext, the pointer changes to the shape of a hand.

7. **Click the Adjust tracking hyperlink.**

Text that explains how to adjust tracking appears below the hyperlink.

Another way to obtain help is to type and/or choose keywords at the Index tab.

8. **Click the Index tab, and in the Type keywords box, type** print. **Then click the Search button.**

As you type each letter, the highlighted word within the Or choose keywords box jumps to the next word that contains the letter you just typed. The search results in many topics listed in the Choose a topic box.

9. **In the Or choose keywords box, scroll to the word** *copy* **and double-click it so that both** *print* **and** *copy* **appear in the Type keywords box.**

A two-word search results in fewer topics than a one-word search. The list of topics that contains both keywords appears in the Choose a topic box. The first topic is displayed in the right pane, as shown in Figure 1.16.

10. **Click the Print more than one copy topic, and read the Help information in the right pane.**

A third way to obtain help is to use the Answer Wizard.

11. **Click the Answer Wizard tab.**

12. **In the What would you like to do? box, type** change paper size **and click the Search button.**

Topics that may answer your question appear in the Select topic to display box.

13. **Click the Change the paper size topic, and read the Help information in the right pane.**

14. **Click the Close button on the Help window.**

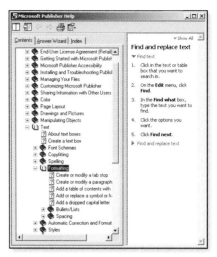

Figure 1.15
Specific list of subtopics

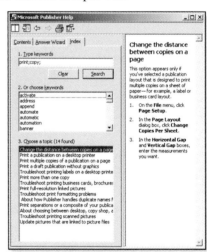

Figure 1.16
Results of two-word search

Using the Office Assistant

1. If the Office Assistant isn't already displayed, click Show the Office Assistant on the Help menu.

2. Click the Office Assistant character.

3. In the What would you like to do? box, type a question or search topic.

4. Click the Search button.

5. Click the topic that best answers your question.

Using the Office Assistant

Another way to get help is to use the Office Assistant, an animated character that can answer specific questions. The Office Assistant is hidden by default. To use the Office Assistant:

1. **Click** Show the Office Assistant **on the Help menu.**

2. **Click the** Office Assistant character.

The Office Assistant asks what you would like to do. (It continues to show the latest question that you asked and topics related to that question.)

3. **In the question box, type** preview before printing **and click the** Search button.

The Office Assistant provides a list of topics that may answer your question, as shown in Figure 1.17. It also gives you the option of looking for more help on the Web, if none of the topics answers your question.

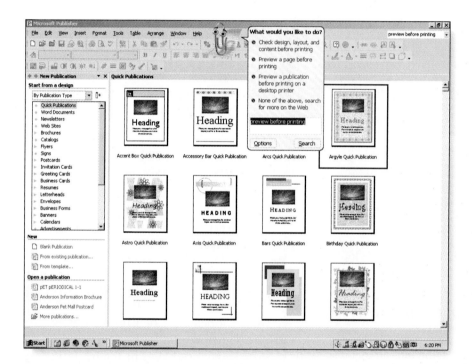

Figure 1.17 ◀
Office Assistant

4. **Click the** Check design, layout, and content before printing topic.

The Help window appears, and provides information on your topic as well as links to related topics.

PERSONAL INFORMATION SETS

In many of the activities in this tutorial, you will be creating publications for Anderson Pet Mall, a pet food and supply store. The name, address, phone number, and other information about Anderson Pet Mall will be used again and again. Microsoft Publisher allows you to create ***personal information sets*** to store this information so that it does not have to be re-entered for each new publication you create. In the following activity, you will create a personal information set for Anderson Pet Mall.

Creating a Personal Information Set

1. Click the Edit menu; then click Personal Information…

2. Select an information set to edit.

3. Edit the default information in each of the boxes.

4. Click the Update button.

Creating a Personal Information Set

In this activity, you will create a personal information set for Anderson Pet Mall.

1. **Click** Edit **on the menu bar.**

If all of the commands on the Edit menu are grayed, click Edit again to close the menu, and then click the Hides Publication Gallery button [◄] *to activate the Edit menu. Repeat step 1.*

2. **Click** Personal Information… **in the drop-down menu.**

The Personal Information dialog box appears as shown in Figure 1.18.

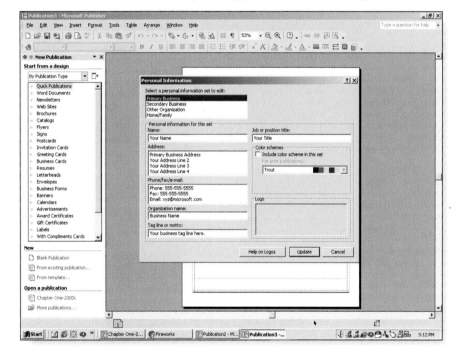

Figure 1.18
Personal Information dialog box

3. **Click** Primary Business.

4. **Press** [Tab] **to move to the Name box.**

5. **Type** Pat Germann **in place of the highlighted text.**

6. **Press** [Tab] **to move to the Address box.**

7. **Type** 1111 Church Street **and press** [Enter ←].

8. **Type** Anderson, IN 46012-9012.

9. **Press** [Tab] **to move to the Phone/fax/e-mail box.**

The default information in the box will be highlighted.

10. **To change the phone number, click at the end of the phone number and drag to the left to highlight the number.**

11. **Type** 765-555-1234.

12. **To change the fax number, click at the end of the fax number and drag to the left to highlight the number.**

13. **Type** 765-555-1235.

14. **To change the e-mail address, click at the end of the e-mail address and drag to the left to highlight the address.**

15. **Type** ruffmeow@anderson.net.

16. **Press** Tab **to move to the Organization name box.**

17. **Type** Anderson Pet Mall.

18. **Press** Tab **to move to the Tag line or motto box.**

19. **Type** Your Best Friend's Favorite Store.

20. **Press** Tab **to move to the Job or position title box.**

21. **Type** Marketing Assistant.

For now, you can ignore Color schemes and the Logo box.

22. **Your dialog box should contain the information shown in Figure 1.20. Click the Update button** Update **in the lower right corner to save your information and exit the Personal Information dialog box.**

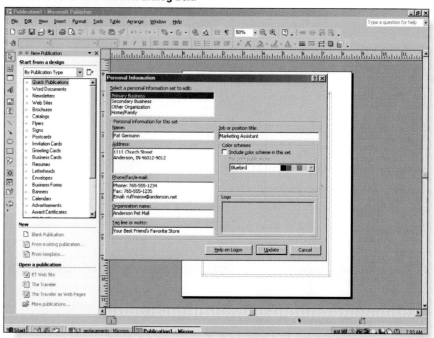

Figure 1.19
Personal information completed

CREATING PUBLICATIONS USING DESIGN TEMPLATES

Design templates are pre-set formats for publications. Microsoft Publisher includes a wealth of design templates that can assist you in creating your publications. By using design templates, you do not need to become a graphic artist to produce attractive and professional-looking publications. Design templates include frames for the common elements of a publication. These frames are already set up on the base publication. Text format, including fonts, sizes, and styles, have already been selected. Even the color scheme to be used for text, graphic elements, and borders are included.

Although you may start with a blank publication, most Microsoft Publisher users choose to begin from one of the design templates. Using the templates saves time and ensures consistency. As you become a skilled Microsoft Publisher user, you will learn to make wise design template choices. You will evaluate the goals of the publication and consider the audience to whom the publication is addressed. For example, if you need to announce a corporate merger to the stockholders who own the company, you will likely select a very conservative template to create the announcement. On the other hand, if you are sending sale invitation postcards through the mail to thousands of potential customers, you will choose a template with bold colors and large print to attract your readers to look more closely at the invitation.

To use design templates, you first select the type of publication in the task pane. Designs that match your selection appear on the right in the Publication Gallery. Use the scroll bars to examine the various designs available. Select the one that most closely matches the look and feel that is appropriate for your publication. Remember that you can make changes to the template; the template simply gives you a good starting point.

HANDS On

Publisher **BASICS**

Creating a Postcard from a Design Template

1. Click the down arrow under Start from a design and select By Publication Type.

2. Select Postcards from the menu under By Publication Type.

3. Select one of the types of postcards.

4. Click one of the designs shown in the Publication Gallery.

5. Enter the information to customize the postcard to your needs.

Creating a Postcard from a Design Template

In this activity, you will create a postcard invitation to the grand opening of Anderson Pet Mall.

1. In the **New Publication** task pane, click **By Publication Type** in the drop down menu, if it is not already displayed.

2. Click **Postcards** in the menu under **By Publication Type**.

A list of the kinds of postcards appears as shown in Figure 1.20.

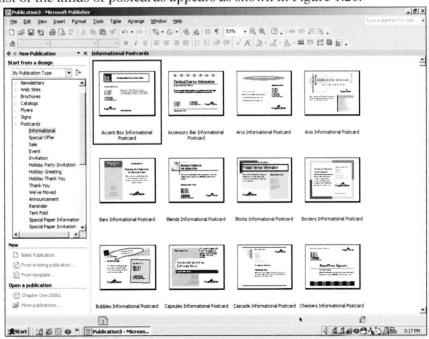

Figure 1.20 ◀
Postcards in Publication Gallery

3. **Click Invitation.**

Pictures of several kinds of postcard invitations appear in Publication Gallery to the right as shown in Figure 1.21.

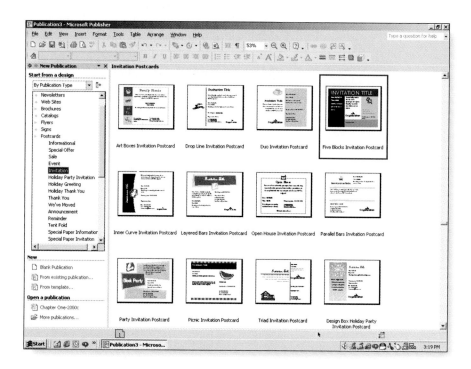

Figure 1.21
Invitation Postcards in Publication Gallery

4. **Click the picture for the Five Blocks Invitation Postcard.**

The template for the Five Block Invitation Postcard appears, replacing the Publications Gallery as shown in Figure 1.22.

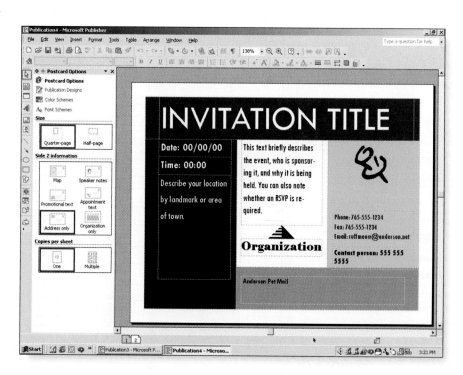

Figure 1.22
Five Blocks Invitation Postcard template

Note *If you are completing this activity immediately after creating the personal information set for Anderson Pet Mall, some of the information that you entered in that personal information set automatically appears in the invitation postcard. If the information that has been inserted is not the information for Anderson Pet Mall, you will need to repeat the steps under Creating Personal Information Sets (pages 25 to 26) before continuing with this activity.*

5. **Click on Invitation Title and type** Grand Opening. **(This replaces the words Invitation Title.)**

Note *The style of the invitation title is set for all uppercase letters. Even if you type a mix of uppercase and lowercase letters, Publisher will display all uppercase letters. You will learn how to create and change styles in a later lesson.*

6. **Click on 00/00/00 and type** 12/22/02.

7. **Click on the 00:00 and type** 6 to 9 p.m.

8. **Click on Describe your location… and type** We're located on the south side of the Courthouse square at 1111 Church Street.

9. **Click on This text briefly describes… and type** Come join us for our grand opening celebration! Your pets will love our brand new store. Great discounts will be available, so be sure to visit us on December 22.

10. **Click on Contact person and type** Call Pat:

11. **Click on the telephone number (555 555 5555) and type** 765-555-1234 for more details.

You have now entered all of the text for the front of the invitation postcard. You will notice that the name of the store, Anderson Pet Mall, has been inserted in the frame at the bottom of the postcard. To improve the appearance of the postcard, you will need to enlarge this text.

12. **Click to the right of Anderson Pet Mall and drag to the left to select the text.**

Notice that the Formatting toolbar, which was previously disabled (grayed), is now activated.

13. **Click the down arrow to the right of the Font Size box** `10` **in the Formatting toolbar. A drop-down menu appears, giving various font sizes. Click the down arrow until the number 28 appears. Click 28.**

The text Anderson Pet Mall increases in size. This change emphasizes the name of the store.

Note *There are other ways to increase the size of this text. You will learn some of these other methods in later lessons.*

Inserting a Logo from a CD

You have now completed the front of the invitation postcard, except for the logo in the middle of the postcard. Anderson Pet Mall already has a logo that is used on their signs and letterhead. This logo is included on the Publisher Data CD that accompanies this tutorial. In the next few steps, you will learn how to insert this logo in place of the default (Organization) logo on the postcard.

1. Insert the Publisher Data CD in the CD-ROM drive of your computer, if it is not already there.

2. Click on the Organization logo on the postcard.

The wizard icon appears below the logo.

3. Click the Wizard icon.

The task pane to the left changes to the Logo Designs task pane.

4. Click Logo Options.

5. Under the heading New or existing, click Inserted picture.

The Choose picture... button | Choose picture... | becomes active.

6. Click Choose picture... | Choose picture... |.

The Insert Picture dialog box appears as shown in Figure 1.23.

Figure 1.23
Insert Picture dialog box

7. Click the down arrow to the right of the Look in: box.

8. Click on the drive that contains the Publisher Data CD.

9. Click on the file named Anderson Logo.

10. Click the Insert button [Insert ▾] in the lower right corner of the dialog box.

The logo for Anderson Pet Mall appears in the middle of your postcard. The front side of postcard is now complete. It should appear as shown in Figure 1.24.

Figure 1.24 ◄
Completed front of postcard

HANDS On

Publisher **BASICS**

Creating the Back of the Postcard

1. Click page 2 in the status bar.

2. Click the desired option under side 2 information on the Postcard Options task pane.

3. Change text or other elements in the frames as desired.

Creating the Back of the Postcard

Now that you have finished the front of the postcard, you will view and make changes to the back of your postcard.

Near the bottom of the window, above the taskbar, is another bar called the status bar. In the status bar, you will see two small icons that look like pages with folded corners. These represent page 1 and page 2 of the publication—in this case, the front and back of the postcard.

1. Click .

The back of the postcard appears as shown in Figure 1.25. The task pane has changed to the Postcard Options task pane, and the name and address of the store have been automatically inserted as the return address of the postcard. An area for the mailing address and the stamp have also been provided. The postcard could be used without making any further changes, but Anderson Pet Mall would like to use the back of the postcard to describe the discounts that are mentioned on the front of the postcard. In the last few steps of this activity, you will make changes to the back of the postcard to include information about these discounts.

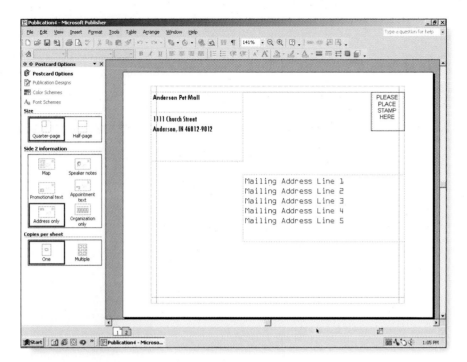

Figure 1.25
Postcard Options task pane

2. **Click** Promotional text **under** Side 2 information.

The return address changes to include the Anderson Pet Mall logo, and additional frames appear on the left side of the postcard, as shown in Figure 1.26.

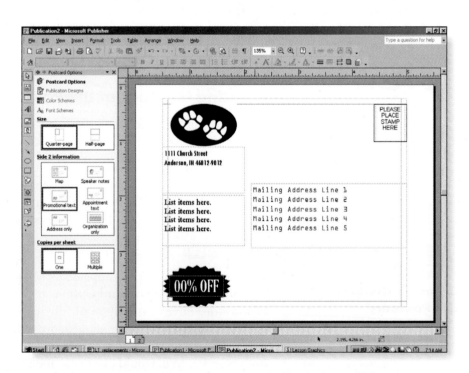

Figure 1.26
Promotional text frame inserted
on back of postcard

3. **Click on** List items here **and type** Pet food. **The default text in the frame disappears. Press** Enter← **twice to create a blank line before the next item.**

4. **Type** Collars and leashes **and press** Enter← **twice.**

5. **Type** Kennels and accessories **and press** Enter← **twice.**

Figure 1.27
Completed back of postcard

6. Type Toys of every variety.

7. Click on 00% OFF and type 20% OFF.

The back of the postcard is now complete. Pat, the marketing assistant at the Anderson Pet Mall, will be sending many of these postcards, so she will take the postcard to a print shop to have copies made. She will then put addresses on the postcards using address labels, so you do not need to type an address in the address area.

8. To delete the default address information, click on any of the address lines and press the Delete key [Delete].

The completed back of the postcard should appear as shown in Figure 1.27.

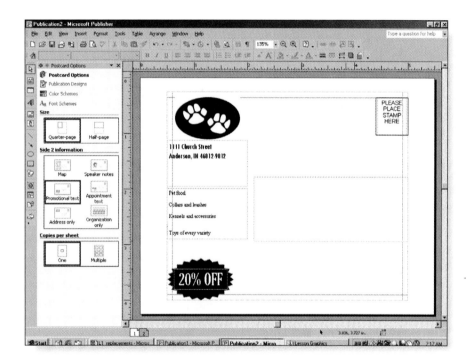

SAVING PUBLICATIONS

After creating your publication, you should *save* it. Saving a publication transfers all the text from computer memory to your disk or drive, and you can open the publication later. Saving your work is important in case something goes wrong with the computer. For example, if you have not saved your publication and your computer malfunctions or someone kicks the power cord, all your work may be lost.

When you are working on a new publication that you have not saved, Publisher gives the file a default name, such as Publication1 or Publication2. When you save the file, you should give the file a more meaningful name, so you can see at a glance what information the file contains. To save a file for the first time, click the Save button 🔲 on the Standard toolbar. Because the file has not been saved before, the Save As dialog box appears. Besides naming your file, you also must specify where to store the file (the drive and path). A file name, including the drive and path, can contain up to 255 characters, including spaces. The file name may not include any of the following characters, however: \ / * ? " ; : or |.

You can also create a new *folder* in which to save the file. A folder is a named location where you store and organize your files. If you will be saving your publications to a network drive, you will need to create a folder on the network drive to keep your work separate from other students' work. This will be particularly important if you and the other students in your class are working on the same projects and are giving them the same names. If you do not save your work to your own folder, you may inadvertently save your work in place of the work of another student who has used the same name for a publication. To create a folder for your work, click the Save As command on the File menu. When the Save As dialog box appears, select the drive (and folder, if appropriate) for the location of your new folder. Then click the Create New Folder button 🗀. Type a name for your folder, following the guidelines provided by your instructor, and click OK. You can then save your files to this folder.

HANDS
On

Naming and Saving a Publication

1. Click the Save button [icon] on the toolbar.

2. Select the drive and folder in the Save in box.

3. Type a name for the publication in the File name box.

4. Click the Save button.

Another Way

■ To save your work, press Ctrl+S.

Naming and Saving a Publication

To save the Anderson Pet Mall Invitation Postcard:

1. Click the Save button 🖫 on the Standard toolbar.

The Save As dialog box appears.

2. Locate your folder in the drop-down menu next to Save in: and double-click on its name.

3. Type Anderson Invitation Postcard in the File name: box.

4. Click the Save button in the lower right corner of the dialog box.

Because you modified the logo in this publication, Publisher asks if you want to save the logo to the Primary Business personal information set.

5. Click Yes.

The logo is now part of the personal information set and will be inserted in future publications for Anderson Pet Mall.

After you name and save a file, clicking the Save button 🖫 on the Standard toolbar replaces the file on your disk or drive with the version currently in memory, without displaying the Save As dialog box. If you want to save the file in a different place or under a new name, click the Save As command on the File menu. The Save As dialog box appears, and you can type a new file name and/or location. When you use the Save As command, you are not renaming a file. Instead, you are saving a copy of the file under a different name or in a different place. The original file with the original name will not be deleted.

Save your files often—especially after making any changes. Even if you have saved a file, unsaved changes will be lost if your computer malfunctions or a power outage occurs.

PRINTING A PUBLICATION

Printing a proof copy of a publication is a simple task in Publisher. Clicking the Print button  on the Standard toolbar prints one copy of all pages of your publication. To print more than one copy or to print only some of the pages, click Print… on the File menu. In the Print dialog box, specify how many copies you want to print and whether you want to print all pages, selected pages, or just the current page. If you are printing a double-sided publication, such as the postcard that you created in this lesson, clicking the Print button will cause the two sides to print as separate sheets unless your printer supports duplex printing. (If you do not know whether your printer supports duplex printing, ask your instructor.) For most business publications, however, you will want to print the two sides as separate sheets, so that you can take the sheets to a print shop to have copies made. The print shop will copy the sheets back-to-back to create a two-sided publication.

HANDS On

Printing Selected Pages

In this activity, you will print page 1 of your postcard.

1. **On the File menu, click Print…**

2. **In the Print range box of the Print dialog box, select the Pages option.**

3. **Type 1 in the From box and 1 in the To box.**

4. **Verify that Number of copies is set to 1, as shown in Figure 1.28. If not, click the down arrow until 1 appears in the list box. Then click OK.**

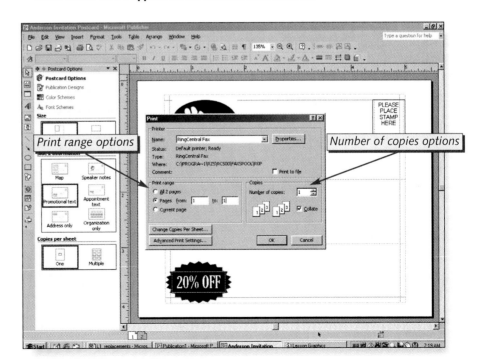

Figure 1.28
Print dialog box

Publisher will print the first page, or front, of the postcard.

CLOSING AND OPENING PUBLICATIONS

When you are finished working with a publication, you should **close** the file. You do not need to close your publication file to open another publication, however. Publisher lets you keep several files open at the same time. To have more free memory, though, you should close files that you are no longer using. When you close a publication, you remove that publication from memory but leave Publisher operating.

To close a publication, click the Close command on the File menu. (If you have made changes to your publication since you last saved it, Publisher will ask you if you wish to save your changes.) If more than one publication is open, closing the current publication will cause the next publication to be displayed. Once you have closed all open publications, Publisher displays the New Publication task pane, with a blank publication in the working area to the right of the task pane.

Publications that you have opened recently are added to the list under Open a publication in the task pane. If you need to reopen a publication you just closed, you can select the publication quickly from that list. Publisher lists the last three publications that you opened and then allows you to locate other publications by clicking More Publications.... You can also open a publication by clicking the Open button 📂 on the Standard toolbar or by clicking the Open command on the File menu. All three of these methods cause a dialog box to be displayed, where you specify the drive, folder, and file that you want to open.

Closing and Reopening a Document

In this activity, you will close and reopen a file.

1. On the File menu, click Close.

2. Click the File menu.

The file name appears near the bottom of the menu with the file closed most recently listed first, as shown in Figure 1.29.

3. To reopen the file, click the file name near the bottom of the menu.

The file is reopened and the first page of the postcard appears.

File name and location of most recently used files

Figure 1.29
File menu

ENDING A WORK SESSION

When you are finished with the Publisher program, you should exit the program properly. Failure to close Publisher can lead to problems the next time you want to start the application. Exiting the program closes any open Publisher files and removes Publisher from the computer's memory. You can exit Publisher by clicking the Close button **X** on the title bar or by clicking the Exit command on the File menu. After exiting Publisher, you will see the desktop if you have no other programs running. From there, you may choose to shut down your computer.

Exiting Publisher

1. Click the Close button on the title bar or click Exit on the File menu.

2. Remove your Publisher Data CD from the drive, if necessary.

Another Way

■ To exit Publisher, press Alt+F4.

Exiting Publisher

In this activity, you will exit the application.

1. Click the **Close button** **X** on the title bar.

Publisher disappears from the screen and the desktop reappears.

2. Remove your Publisher Data CD from the drive, if necessary.

Test your knowledge by answering the following questions. See Appendix C to check your answers.

T F 1. A template provides formatting, layout, and basic design elements.

T F 2. The Office Assistant appears automatically when you start Publisher.

T F 3. The Publication Gallery allows you to view all the available designs for the selected publication type.

T F 4. Personal information sets remember information such as name, address, and phone numbers, and insert the information into a publication.

T F 5. The first time a publication is saved, the file is automatically placed in the Publisher directory.

ON*the*WEB

ACCESSING THE WEB THROUGH PUBLISHER

Every day, computer users around the world use the Internet for work, play, and research. The **Internet** is a worldwide network of computers that connects each Internet user's computer to all other computers in the network. Vast quantities of infinitely varied information—from simple text in the form of an e-mail message to extremely complex software—can pass through these connections. An Internet tool, the **World Wide Web** (the Web), organizes information into small parcels, or pages. Therefore, a page (parcel) of information is called a **Web page.** Because a page holds a specific place on the Web, it is also called a **Web site.**

Visiting a Web page requires an Internet connection. Companies called **Internet service providers,** or **ISPs,** provide access to the Internet for a monthly or annual fee. Most schools also provide Internet connections for their students. To access the Web, you must also have a **Web browser** installed on your computer. A Web browser is a software tool used to navigate the Web. Publisher accesses the Web through **Internet Explorer,** the Microsoft Web browser. In this activity, you will open the Internet Explorer window from within Publisher, connect to the Internet, and locate a specific Web site.

1. **Start Publisher, if it is not currently running.**

2. **Click Blank Publication on the New Publication task pane.**

A blank publication appears and the task pane disappears.

3. **Click the Web Page Preview button on the Standard toolbar.**

The Internet Explorer window is displayed, as shown in Figure 1.30. As you can see, the Internet Explorer window has its own toolbar.

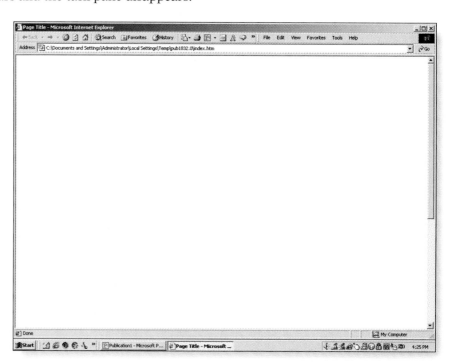

Figure 1.30
Internet Explorer window

38 Publisher 2002
LESSON 1

Note   *If you click the Web Page Preview button with a completed publication displayed, Publisher not only opens the Internet Explorer window but also shows you how your publication would look as a web page.*

Below the Explorer toolbar is the ***Address bar.*** If you know the address of a particular Web site, you can type the address in the Address bar and press Enter◄— to go directly to that site. As you navigate the Web, the text in the Address bar changes to display the address of the current page.

4. In the Address bar, type www.glencoe.com **and then press Enter.**

If you are not already online (connected to the Internet), Internet Explorer connects to the Internet using your Internet Service Provider.

Note   *If necessary, type your user name and password. If you do not know your user name and password, ask your instructor for assistance.*

After you are successfully connected, the Glencoe/McGraw-Hill Web home page is displayed as shown in Figure 1.31. The first of several pages at a Web site is commonly called the ***home page.***

5. Scroll slowly to the bottom of the page.

You will notice that some of the text is a different color from the rest of the text and is underlined. This text is called ***hypertext*** and provides links (also called *hyperlinks*) to other pages on the same Web site or to other Web sites. Buttons, pictures, and even graphic elements, such as bars and buttons, can be hyperlinks. If you're not sure if text or another element on a page is a hyperlink, point to it. If the pointer takes the shape of a hand, you're pointing to a hyperlink.

6. Scroll back to the top of the page.

7. Point to various text and graphics on the page to determine which are hyperlinks and which are regular text and graphics.

8. Click the Home button 🏠 on the Internet Explorer toolbar.

Figure 1.31
Glencoe home page

Explorer connects you to the Web page designated as *your* home page (also called a ***start page***). Your Internet service provider or your instructor probably designated the start page. Start pages usually provide links to other links that allow you to explore the Web.

9. To close Internet Explorer, click the Close button ⊠.

10. Exit Publisher.

11. Disconnect from the Internet if your instructor tells you to do so.

Lesson Summary & Exercises

SUMMARY

Microsoft Publisher is a desktop publishing program that enables you to create all kinds of publications by using pre-designed layouts, called templates, or by starting from a blank page. In Lesson 1, you learned how to start and exit Publisher, and you explored menus, toolbars, task panes, and other objects in the Publisher window. You also learned how to open, close, save, and print publications. In addition, you learned how to create personal information sets to store information, such as names, addresses, and phone numbers, so that this information can be used again and again in different publications. You also created your first publication, a postcard invitation, using one of Publisher's pre-designed templates.

Now that you have completed this lesson, you should be able to do the following:

■ Start Microsoft Publisher and name objects in the application window.

■ Provide a brief description of each menu on the Publisher menu bar.

■ Provide a brief description of each button on the Standard, Formatting, Connect Frames, and Objects toolbars.

■ Get help using the Ask a Question box, the Help window, and the Office Assistant.

■ Display ScreenTips for various screen elements.

■ Explain task panes and how to select a design in the New Publication task pane.

■ Create personal information sets for businesses and individuals.

■ Create a postcard invitation using one of Publisher's templates.

■ Insert a logo in a publication.

■ Save a publication for the first time or under a different file name, and create a folder where you can save your files.

■ Print a proof copy of your publication.

■ Close a publication and reopen it.

■ Exit Publisher.

Lesson Summary & Exercises

CONCEPTS REVIEW

1 TRUE/FALSE

Circle T if the statement is true or F if the statement is false.

T F **1.** A desktop publishing program gives you greater flexibility in the design and layout of publications than a word processing program.

T F **2.** Frames in a publication are only used to hold text.

T F **3.** To display a list of the toolbars in Publisher, click View on the menu bar and point to Toolbars.

T F **4.** The Standard toolbar is the only toolbar that can be customized.

T F **5.** An ellipsis after a command indicates that clicking the command will display a dialog box or a task pane.

T F **6.** The task pane that is displayed when Publisher is first opened is the New Publication task pane.

T F **7.** You open and close the Publication Gallery by clicking on the Open button on the Standard toolbar.

T F **8.** When you use the Save As command, the original file with the original name is deleted.

T F **9.** To print one copy of all pages of a publication, click the Print button on the Standard toolbar.

T F **10.** You must close the current publication before you can open another publication.

2 MATCHING

Match each of the terms on the left with the definitions on the right.

TERMS

1. design sets

2. folder

3. layering

4. Office Assistant

5. personal information set

6. task pane

7. taskbar

8. template

9. title bar

10. toolbar

DEFINITIONS

a. Placing objects on top of each other in a publication

b. An animated character that answers questions and provides Help

c. Contains the Start menu and buttons for navigating Windows

d. Contains a row of buttons for frequently used commands

e. Displays the name of the application and the current publication name

f. A menu box that provides options for designing your publication and previews of those options

g. Sets of publications that have been designed to go together

h. Contains names, addresses, phone numbers and other information for insertion in related publications

i. Contains the basic layout and formatting for a publication

j. A named location where you store and organize your files

Lesson Summary & Exercises

3 COMPLETION

Fill in the missing word or phrase for each of the following statements.

1. A _____ holds an object in a publication.

2. The initial Microsoft Publisher window is called the _____ window.

3. The name that appears when you point to a toolbar button is called a _____.

4. Thumbnail previews of the available designs for a publication type are displayed in the _____.

5. The _____ menu is used to save a publication.

6. The New Blank Publication button on the Standard toolbar is symbolized by _____.

7. The short bar to the right of the Standard toolbar is called the _____.

8. The vertical toolbar at the far left of the Publisher window is the _____ toolbar.

9. After you have created a publication, you can use the From existing publication or the From _____ option to make your publication the basis for a new publication.

10. When a file has not been saved before and you click on the Save button, the _____ dialog box appears.

4 SHORT ANSWER

1. Describe how to start and exit Publisher.

2. Describe three ways to open a publication that you have just closed.

3. In the status bar, what do pages with folded corners represent?

4. In the Toolbars submenu, what does a check mark next to a toolbar name indicate?

5. What are the three options provided by the drop-down menu under Start from a Design?

6. In a network environment, what could happen if you do not save your work to your own folder?

7. How do you save a file in a different place or under a different name?

8. If an option on a menu is grayed, what does that indicate?

9. What are the characters that cannot be used in a file name?

10. What are four different tools that you can use to get Help information?

5 IDENTIFICATION

Label each of the elements of the Publisher window in Figure 1.32.

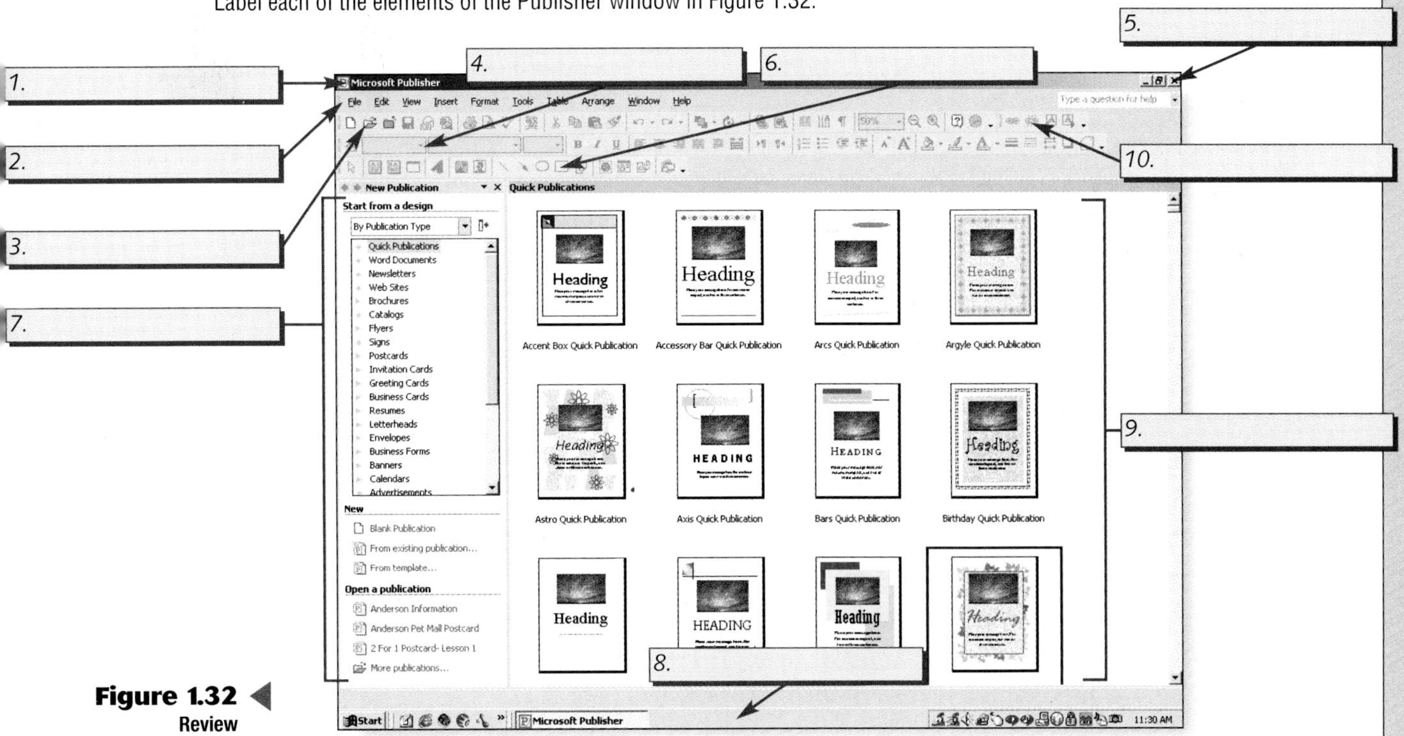

Figure 1.32
Review

SKILLS REVIEW

Complete each of the Skills Review problems in sequential order to review your skills to start Publisher; identify objects in the application window; use the Help system; create personal information sets; create publications using design templates; save, print, close, and open publications; and exit Publisher.

1 Starting Publisher

1. Click the **Start button** 🔲**Start**.
2. Point to **Programs** and click **Microsoft Publisher.**

2 Exploring the Publisher Window

1. Under **Start from a Design** in the **New Publication** task pane, click the down arrow to the right of the drop-down menu and select **By Design Sets.**

2. Click on any of the design set choices and preview the designs in the **Publication Gallery.**

3. Click the **Edit menu** and read the short list and expanded list of commands.

4. Click anywhere outside the menu to close it.

5. Point to any command on the **Insert menu** that will display a submenu.

6. Display the **View menu** and point to **Toolbars.**

7. Hide the **Standard toolbar** by clicking on the check mark next to its name.

8. Display the **WordArt toolbar** by clicking on the box in front of its name.

9. Hide the **WordArt toolbar.**

10. Display the **Standard toolbar.**

11. Point to the first five buttons on the **Standard toolbar** and read their ScreenTips.

12. Click on the **Toolbar Options button** at the end of the **Standard toolbar,** point to **Add or Remove buttons,** and then point to **Standard.**

13. Add any button that is not already on the toolbar (does not have a check mark) by clicking on it.

3 Using Help

1. In the **Ask a Question box,** type How do I change colors and press ⌷Enter⏎⌷.

2. Click the **Change the color of text** topic.

3. Read the Help window and explore the **How?** link.

4. Click the **Show button,** if necessary.

5. Click the **Contents tab,** if it is not on top.

6. Click the **plus sign** in front of the **Microsoft Publisher Help.**

7. Double-click the **Managing Your Files** subtopic and then click **About protecting files from macro viruses.**

8. Click the **Index tab.**

9. In the **Type keywords box,** type frame.

10. Click the **Search button.**

11. Click the **Create an empty picture frame** topic and read the information in the right pane.

12. Click the **Answer Wizard tab.**

13. In the **What would you like to do? box,** type move objects and click the **Search button.**

14. Click the **Move an object** topic and read the information in the right pane.

15. Click the **Hide button** and close the Help window.

4 Creating a Personal Information Set

1. Click **Personal Information** on the **Edit menu.** (If the commands on the Edit menu are grayed, click on one of the publications in the Publication Gallery before clicking the Edit menu.)

2. Click **Home/Family.**

3. Press ⌷Tab⌷ to move to the **Name box.**

4. Type your name.

5. Press ⌷Tab⌷ to move to the **Address box.**

6. Type 2222 University Circle and press ⌷Enter⏎⌷. (Note: To protect your privacy, do not enter your own street address.)

7. Type your city, state, and zip code.

8. Press ⌨Tab to move to the **Phone/fax/e-mail box.**

9. Type 765-555-2234 for the phone number and 765-555-2235 for the fax number. Enter your own e-mail address.

10. Press ⌨Tab to move to the **Organization Name box.**

11. Press ⌨Delete to delete the default information.

12. Press ⌨Tab to move to the **Tag line or motto box.**

13. Press ⌨Delete to delete the default information.

14. Press ⌨Tab to move to the **Job or position title box.**

15. Type Student.

16. Press the **Update button** ⌈ Update ⌉ in the lower right corner to save this information and exit the Personal Information dialog box.

5 Creating a postcard using a design template

1. In the **New Publication** task pane, click **By Publication Type** in the drop-down menu.

2. Click **Postcards,** and then click **Sale.**

3. Click on the picture for the Garage Sale postcard.

4. To change the default information, click **Personal Information** in the **Edit** menu.

5. Click **Home/Family** in the Personal Information dialog box, and then click the **Update button** ⌈ Update ⌉.

6. Click on **00/00/00** and type 8/10/2002.

7. Click on **00:00** and type 8:00 A.M. to 5 P.M.

8. Click on **Describe your location...** and type Our house is on the northwest corner of Williams Street and University Circle.

9. Click on **To spark interest...** and type Vintage Clothing ⌈Enter⌉ ⌈Enter⌉ Classic Rock Albums ⌈Enter⌉ ⌈Enter⌉ Framed Posters ⌈Enter⌉ ⌈Enter⌉ Sports Equipment ⌈Enter⌉ ⌈Enter⌉ And much, much more!

10. Check to make sure that the rest of the information for the front of the card has been supplied from the personal information set.

Note: If your information does not appear, click Personal Information on the Edit menu, edit the Home/Family information, and click the Update button.

11. Switch to the back side of the postcard by clicking the **Page 2 button** ⌈2⌉.

12. Click the empty box (frame) above the return address and type your name.

13. Click the address box and press ⌨Delete to remove the default information.

6 Saving and printing a publication

1. Click the **Save button** 💾 on the **Standard toolbar.**

2. Locate your folder in the *Save in:* box and click on it.

3. In the **File name: box,** type Garage Sale Invitation.

4. Click the **Save button** in the lower right corner.

5. Click **Print** on the **File menu.**

6. In the **Print range box,** click on *Pages from* and type 1 *to* 1.

7. Click **OK.** (Only the front of your invitation will print.)

7 Closing and reopening publications and exiting Publisher

1. With the Garage Sale Invitation open, click **Close** on the **File menu.**

2. Click **Garage Sale Invitation** under **Open a publication** on the New Publication task pane.

3. Click **Close** on the **File menu** to close the Garage Sale Invitation again.

4. Click the **Close button** on the title bar to exit Publisher.

LESSON APPLICATIONS

1 Start Publisher and open a publication

Launch the Publisher program and open a publication stored on the Publisher data CD.

1. Using the Start button  and the Programs menu, launch Publisher.

2. Insert the Publisher Data CD in your CD-ROM drive, if it is not already there.

3. Click the Open button.

4. Select the CD drive and open the 2 For 1 Postcard on the Publisher Data CD.

2 Edit and save a publication

Update an existing publication and save it under a new name.

1. Edit the 2 For 1 Postcard to match the illustration in Figure 1.33.

2. Click on Save As in the File menu.

3. Locate and click on your folder in the drop-down menu.

4. Type 2 For 1 Postcard in the File Name box and click Save.

3 Print a proof copy and close a publication

Print the updated publication and close and exit Publisher.

1. Click the Print button.

2. Click Close on the File menu.

3. Click the Close button **X** on the title bar.

Your Best Friend's Favorite Store

2 for 1

Just to say "Thank You" for making us your place to buy your pet supplies, we are extended to you a limited time offer. For the first part of March, you can bring in this card and receive 2 items for the price of 1. All food and supply items are included in this offer.

ANDERSON PET MALL

Date of Sale: March 1-15, 2003

Time of Sale: 12 noon to 9 p.m.

We're located on the south side of the Courthouse square at 1111 Church Street.

Remember bring this card with you to receive the 2 for 1 special offer.

Expiration date: 3/15/03

Figure 1.33
Completed postcard

Lesson Summary & Exercises

PROJECTS

1 Can Help help?

You want to print a draft of a postcard you're working on so that you can proof-read it, but you don't want to waste ink by printing the graphics. Is it possible to print a copy of the postcard without the graphics? Use the Help tools to find the answer. Then print a copy of the Anderson Pet Mall Invitation Postcard without the graphics.

2 What's Available in the Publication Gallery?

Explore the designs available in the Publication Gallery, by clicking on each category and subcategory under By Publication Type. Also try scrolling through the designs, using the scroll bar to the right of the Publication Gallery. To view each design in greater detail, click on its picture in the Publication Gallery. To return to the Publication Gallery, change the task pane back to the New Publication task pane, and then click on the Shows Publication Gallery button 🖃.

Click on the down arrow next to By Publication Type and select By Design Sets. Explore each of these designs as well, by clicking on each category or by scrolling through the designs.

Make a list of the ten designs or design sets that you found most interesting or appealing. List two things that you like about each of the ten designs.

3 She Changed Her Mind

After you completed the postcard invitation for Anderson Pet Mall's grand open-ing, the owner decided to expand the hours to 5:00 to 10:00 P.M. She also decided to increase the discount to 25%. She has asked you to revise the post-card before it goes to the print shop.

Locate the original postcard invitation (Anderson Invitation Postcard) that you saved in your folder. Edit both sides to show the updated hours and discount. Save the revised postcard under the name *Anderson Invitation Postcard - Revised*. Print both sides of the revised postcard to take to the print shop.

4 The Response Was Overwhelming

Anderson Pet Mall's grand opening was a huge success. The owner had a draw-ing for a door prize during the grand opening, so she now has a list of the cus-tomers who came. She wants to send each of them a thank you card, which they can bring to the store for a one-time discount on the purchase of selected mer-chandise.

Use the *High Spot Thank You Postcard* template under Postcards/Thank You to cre-ate this card. (If Anderson Pet Mall's personal information is not inserted auto-matically, you may need to edit the Primary Business personal information set again, following the steps under Creating Personal Information Sets earlier in this lesson.)

Change the text under Thank You to read: Thank you for coming to our grand opening! `Enter⏎` It was a huge success! `Enter⏎` Bring this card with you on your next visit `Enter⏎` and receive a 20% discount `Enter⏎` on toys and pet food.

Select (highlight) the text you just typed and change the font size to 12.

Print both sides of the thank you postcard.

5 Thanks, Aunt Mary!

Your favorite aunt just sent you a sweater for your birthday. You want to show her what you've been learning, so you decide to create a thank you card using Publisher.

Choose any of the templates under Postcards/Thank you. Edit the front side only. Thank your aunt for her gift, and tell her any other personal or family news that you may wish to include. If the personal information that is inserted in the template is not your own information, either edit the information on the postcard itself, or edit the Home/Family personal information set to reflect your own information and click Update.

Print only the front side of the thank you card.

6 Out of this World on the World Wide Web

You will be writing a report about the planet Venus, and you have read about a Web site that you think may be helpful. Open a blank publication and then click the Web Page Preview button. When the Internet Explorer window appears, type the following Web address in the Address bar:

http://seds.lpl.arizona.edu/nineplanets/nineplanets/venus.html

Press Enter to connect to the Internet and search for this Web page. Read the information on the Web page and explore the links for additional information about Venus. Make a list of the five links that you think would be most helpful. Close the Explorer window and disconnect from the Internet.

Project in Progress

7 Project in Progress

You were recently elected secretary of your local Friends of the Library group. The Friends of the Library organization supports the local public library through fundraising and volunteer activities. Each year, during the last week in June, the Friends of the Library holds a used book sale to raise money for special needs at the library.

You have been asked to send a postcard announcing the book sale to everyone on the Friends of the Library's mailing list. Using the Blackboard Event Postcard, or another appropriate postcard, create an invitation to this event. Use the Other Organization personal information set and edit it to include the following information:

Name: [Your name]
Job or position title: Secretary
Address: 101 Main St.
         [Your City, State, and Zip Code]
Phone: [Your Area Code]-555-BOOK
Email: [Your E-mail address]
Organization name: Friends of the Library of [Your city]

If the logo for Anderson Pet Mall (or another logo) is inserted on your postcard, delete it. Indicate the dates and times of the book sale, and list prices for various kinds of books. (For example, adult paperback fiction $0.50, children's hardbacks $1.00, etc.) Emphasize that the purpose of the book sale is to raise funds to purchase special non-budgeted items for the library. Save the postcard as Friends Postcard.

Working with Text and Graphics

CONTENTS

OBJECTIVES

After you complete this lesson, you will be able to do the following:

- Create a tri-fold brochure using a Publisher template.
- Select text and objects in a publication.
- Insert text files and pictures into a publication.
- Move and resize frames around text and objects.
- Create and change bulleted lists.
- Choose appropriate fonts and styles for each part of your publication.
- Change fonts, font sizes, and font styles, and apply colors to text boxes.
- Use AutoCorrect and Publisher's Spelling feature to correct typos and other misspellings.
- Use the Format Painter and apply and change Publisher styles.

As you learned in Lesson 1, Publisher provides templates that you can use to create publications. The large number of templates available in Publisher gives you a variety of options for creating publications, but you can expand the options greatly by learning to modify the design elements within the templates. In Lesson 2, you will learn how to identify and change some of these elements. You will also learn how to use Publisher tools to correct and prevent misspellings in your publications.

Hints & Tips

It is often easier to select text by dragging from right to left than from left to right.

Publisher BASICS

Moving and resizing objects

To move an object:

1. Select it.

2. Move the mouse pointer over the frame until the MOVE pointer appears.

3. Click and drag the object to a new location.

To resize an object:

1. Select it.

2. Move the mouse pointer over a handle until the RESIZE pointer appears.

3. Click and drag the handle toward the center of the frame to make it smaller; or

4. Click and drag the handle away from the center of the frame to make it larger.

SELECTING TEXT AND OBJECTS

Before text and objects in publications can be modified, they must be *selected.* Selecting text causes it to be highlighted. There are several different ways to **select text:**

TABLE 2.1	SELECTING TEXT
To select . . .	**You . . .**
any amount of text	click at the beginning or the end of the text and drag the mouse I-beam across it.
a single word	double-click anywhere on the word.
a paragraph	triple-click anywhere in the paragraph.
all the text in a frame	click anywhere in the frame, press and hold the Ctrl key [Ctrl] and press the A key.
a portion of the text	click at the beginning of the text you want to select, press and hold the Shift key [⇧ Shift], and then click at the end of the text you want to select.
text line by line	click at the beginning of the text you want to select, press and hold the Shift key [⇧ Shift], and then click the down arrow until each line of text is selected.
text character by character	click at the beginning of the text you want to select, press and hold the Shift key [⇧ Shift], and then click the right arrow until the desired characters are selected.

Note

In a template, clicking anywhere in a frame will cause all of the default text in that frame to be selected. As soon as you begin typing in the frame, the default text disappears. After the default text has been replaced by "real" text, the text can be selected using the methods described in Table 2.1.

You will also need to **select objects** in publications. You select an object by clicking on it. Selecting an object causes eight small boxes, called **handles,** to appear at the corners and sides of the frame around the object as shown in Figure 2.1. These handles not only indicate that the object is selected, but they are also used to resize or move the object and its frame. If you wish to *move* an object, select it and then move the mouse over the frame until you see the MOVE mouse pointer (a moving van) 🚚. You can then drag the object to a new location. To *resize* an object and its frame, move the mouse pointer over a handle until you see the RESIZE pointer 🔧. Drag the handle toward the center of the frame to make it smaller or away from the center to make it larger. You will practice moving and resizing objects and frames later in this lesson.

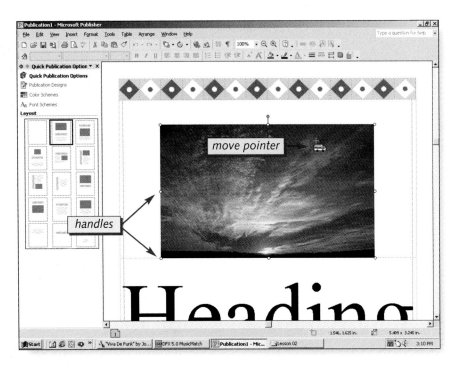

Figure 2.1
Handles on selected frame

You may also wish to select **more than one object** in a publication in order to change or delete them at the same time. To select more than one object in a publication:

1. Click the first object, press and hold the Shift key `⇧ Shift`, and then click the other objects.

or

2. Click Select All on the Edit menu to select all objects on a page.

After selecting text or objects, you may realize that you have selected the wrong item or you may decide that you do not need to select the item after all. To **deselect** text or a single object, click the mouse anywhere on the page outside the selected text or object or press the ESC key `Esc`. To deselect a single object when more than one object is selected, press and hold the Shift key `⇧ Shift` and then click the object that you want to deselect.

THE TRI-FOLD BROCHURE

A tri-fold brochure uses standard 8½ x 11" paper and is folded twice to create three panels on the front and three panels on the back as shown in Figure 2.2. The front of a tri-fold brochure contains the outside panels. The back of a tri-fold brochure contains the inside panels.

As you look at Figure 2.2, notice that the right outside panel is the front of the brochure. Use the front of the brochure to attract the reader's attention. As you can see, the company's name, motto, and telephone number appear. Readers often decide whether or not to open a brochure based on the visual appearance of this panel.

The center outside panel serves as the back panel of the brochure when it is folded. This panel usually contains basic information such as the contact information for your business. Some readers will never turn the brochure over to see the back. As a result, you should avoid placing essential information on this panel.

When the brochure is folded, the left outside panel is folded into the brochure. It actually functions like an inside panel. When the brochure is first opened, this panel appears alongside the left inside panel. Use this panel to summarize the contents of the brochure or to list products and services that your company offers.

The inside panels provide the space for the important information you need to share with the reader. Since the reader often opens the brochure fully, the three panels should work together to convey your message.

Look at Figure 2.2 once more. Notice that the business' name, Anderson Pet Mall, and basic contact information is given several times. When planning a brochure, be careful to include this contact information. Never underestimate the importance of letting your reader know how to get in touch with you.

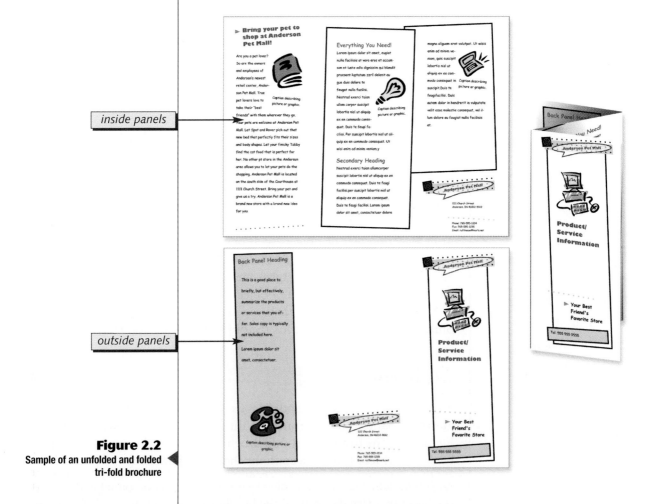

inside panels

outside panels

Figure 2.2
Sample of an unfolded and folded tri-fold brochure

People often plan and write the copy that will go in a brochure before they actually work with the brochure's design.

Using a Design Template to Create a Tri-Fold Brochure

In this activity, you will create a tri-fold brochure using one of Publisher's design templates. You will practice selecting and deselecting text and objects, and you will insert text from a word processing file.

 During this activity, you will be inserting text from the Publisher Data CD. Before beginning this activity, insert the Publisher Data CD into your CD-ROM drive, if it is not already there.

Publisher BASICS

Creating a Brochure from a Design Template

1. Select By Publication Type in the New Publication task pane.

2. Select Brochures from the list of publication types.

3. Select one of the types of brochures.

4. Click one of the designs shown in the Publication Gallery.

5. Enter the information to customize the brochure to your needs.

1. Under **By Publication Type** in the **New Publication task pane, click Brochures.**

2. **Click Informational.**

3. **Scroll down in the Publication Gallery until the Bubbles Informational Brochure template appears as shown in Figure 2.3.**

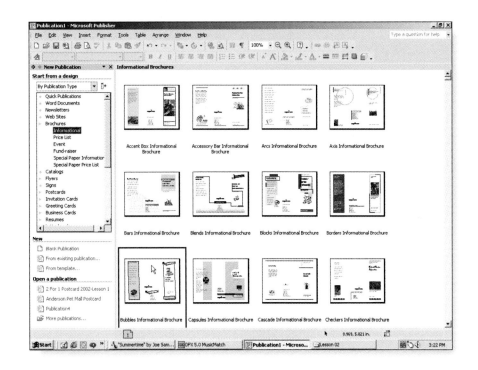

Figure 2.3
Select the Bubbles Informational Brochure template

4. **Click the picture for the Bubbles Informational Brochure.**

Page 1 of the template for the Bubbles Informational Brochure appears as shown in Figure 2.4. Page 1 contains the outside panels of the brochure. Notice in the task pane that the page size is set to 3-panel. This means that the brochure will be folded twice to create three panels on the front and three panels on the back.

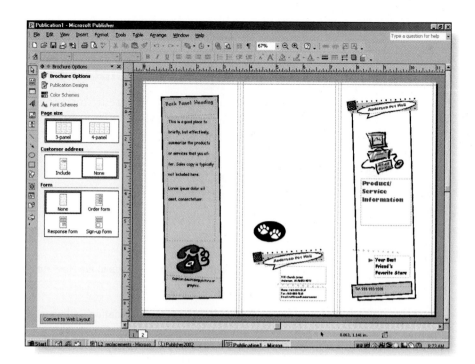

Figure 2.4 ◀
Page 1 of the Bubbles Informational
Brochure template

Note ➤ *The personal information for Anderson Pet Mall should be automatically inserted into the brochure if the Primary Business set has not been changed since it was created in Lesson 1. If the personal information for Anderson Pet Mall is not inserted, edit the Primary Business set, following the steps under Creating a Personal Information Set in Lesson 1. Press Update to save this information and insert it into your publication.*

5. Click page 2 .

Page 2 contains the inside panels for the brochure.

6. Click the down arrow next to the Zoom box in the Standard toolbar and select 100%.

This will allow you to read the text and captions in the panels more easily.

7. Scroll to the upper left corner of the publication as shown in Figure 2.5.

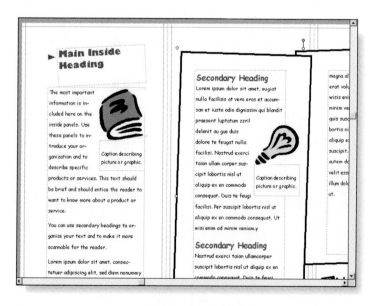

Figure 2.5 ◀
Upper left corner of page 2

Inserting text from a word processing file

1. Select the text to be replaced.

2. Click the right mouse button.

3. Select Text File... from the Change Text menu option.

4. Navigate to the location of the file and select the file.

5. Click OK.

8. **Click on** Main Inside Heading.

9. **Type** Bring your pet to shop at Anderson Pet Mall!

10. **Save the brochure using the file name** Anderson Information Brochure

11. **Select (highlight) the default text under the Main Inside Heading by clicking on it. (The default text begins: The most important information . . . .)**

The Style box on the Formatting toolbar changes to Body Text 3. This is the text style supplied by the template. Make a note of this style so that you can use it again later.

12. **Click the right mouse button.**

A menu that contains commands for changing and formatting text appears.

13. **Point to** Change Text.

A submenu appears.

14. **Click** Text File...

The Insert Text dialog box appears as shown in Figure 2.6.

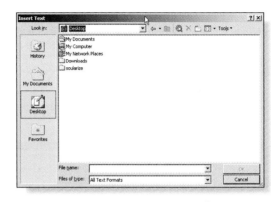

Figure 2.6
Insert Text dialog box

15. **Locate the drive in the** Look in: **box that contains the Publisher Data CD and click on it.**

16. **Click on the file named** Text for Panel One in Lesson 2 **and then click** OK.

Text from the Publisher Data CD is inserted in the first panel of page 2 as shown in Figure 2.7.

Figure 2.7
Text imported into first panel of page 2

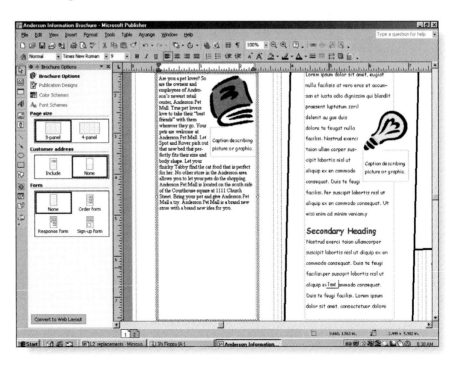

Ignore any misspellings or grammatical errors that you may see in the inserted text. They will be corrected later in this lesson.

You will notice that the Style and Font boxes on the Formatting toolbar have changed to Normal and Times New Roman. These are the style and the font that were used when the text was created in Microsoft Word.

17. Click 🖫 to save the file using the existing file name.

18. To change the style and font to the original style and font for the template, select (highlight) the text and then click the down arrow next to the Style box.

19. Scroll up in the drop-down list until Body Text 3 appears and click on it.

The text changes to the Body Text 3 style as shown in Figure 2.8. Notice that the change in font and size for Body Text 3 also appears on the Formatting toolbar.

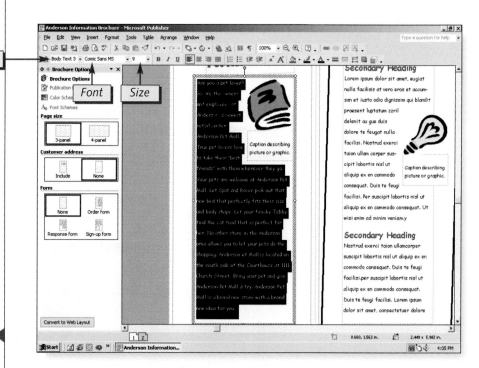

Figure 2.8
Text changed to Body Text 3

20. Scroll to the right until you can see the second panel of page 2 and click on the first Secondary Heading.

21. Type Everything you need!

22. Click on the text beginning Lorem ipsum dolor sit amet . . . and right-click.

Make sure you select only the first paragraph of text. Do not select the next reference to a Secondary Heading or the text below it.

23. Point to Change Text and then click Text File... .

24. Locate the drive in the Look in: box that contains the Publisher Data CD and click on it.

25. Click on the file named Text for Panel Two in Lesson 2 and then click OK.

Text from the Publisher Data CD is inserted in the second panel of page 2 as shown in Figure 2.9.

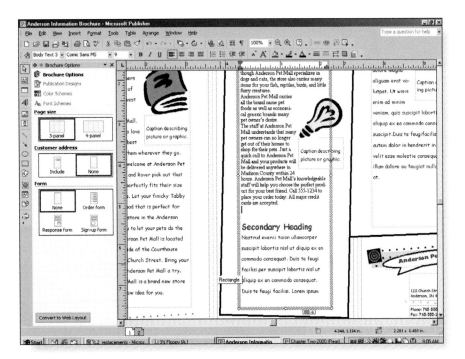

Figure 2.9
Text inserted in second panel

You will notice that there is still default text, including a secondary heading, below the inserted text. To remove this default text:

26. Make sure that the insertion point is below the last word of the inserted text ("accepted"). Then click the left mouse button and drag until all of the default text (including the text in the next panel) is highlighted. Press [Delete].

27. Change the style of the inserted text in this panel to Body Text 3, following the instructions in steps 18 and 19.

28. Click [icon] to save the file using the existing file name.

29. Scroll to the top of the third panel on this page.

In Figure 2.10, you will notice a button with a left arrow at the top of this frame. This is the Go to Previous Frame button [icon], and it indicates that the text in this frame is a continuation of the text in the previous frame. The two frames are called **connected** frames. When frames are connected, any text that will not fit in the first frame flows automatically into the next frame.

The text in this panel describes the delivery services offered by Anderson Pet Mall. To draw attention to these services, you will add a heading to this panel.

30. Click at the beginning of the text (before The staff at Anderson Pet Mall . . .), type We deliver, too! and press [Enter←].

As you can see, the new text does not look like a heading because it has the same text style as the rest of the text in the frame.

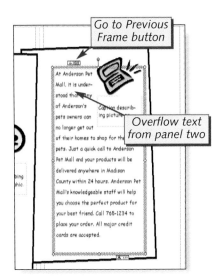

Figure 2.10
Text inserted in second panel

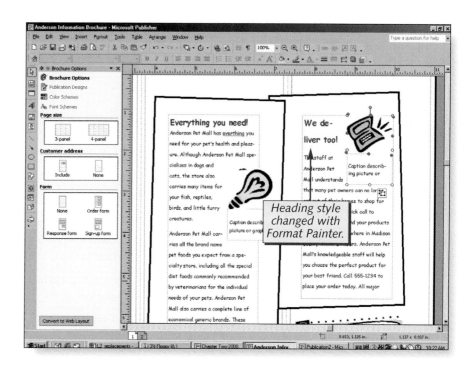

Publisher BASICS

Using the Format Painter

1. Select the text that has the formatting you want to copy.

2. Click the Format Painter button.

3. Select the text that you want to change.

31. To change the text style of this new heading to match the heading in the previous panel, select the heading in the previous panel.

32. Click the Format Painter button 🖌 on the Standard toolbar.

The **Format Painter** allows you to copy the formatting of text, including headings, to other text in the same publication. When you move the mouse, the pointer changes to a paintbrush 🖌 to show that the Format Painter is active.

33. With the Format Painter active, select the heading We deliver, too!

The formatting changes to match the heading style in the previous panel as shown in Figure 2.11.

Figure 2.11
Heading font changed on panel 3

Because the heading style is larger than the body text, the heading will no longer fit on one line. Publisher splits the heading onto two lines so that it wraps around the picture of the computer. When both objects and text appear on the same page, Publisher automatically **wraps** text around the objects. While this wrapping feature creates interest for the reader, you do not want to make the text difficult to read.

In this case, Publisher hyphenated the word *deliver* when it wrapped the text. However, as a general rule, headings should *not* be hyphenated. To give the heading additional space so that it can fit on one line, you will need to move the picture of the computer.

34. Click the picture of the computer and hold down the mouse button.

Handles appear around the picture and its caption as shown in Figure 2.12, and the mouse pointer changes to the Move pointer.

Publisher BASICS

Moving objects

1. Click on the object to be moved and hold down the mouse button.

2. Drag the object to a new location.

Figure 2.12
Computer clip art and caption selected

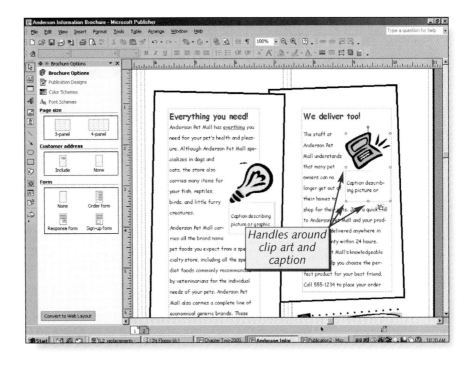

35. Drag the picture down so that the top of its frame is just below the heading **We deliver, too!** Release the mouse button.

The heading is now on one line, above the picture. You have now entered all of the text for page 2.

36. Click ▣ to save the file.

37. Close the publication.

CUSTOMIZING DESIGN TEMPLATES

Microsoft has created many design templates to help you create attractive publications. The frames that contain text and graphics are included with the template. As you entered text, you learned that the template included text styles for headings and the body text. You saw that text frames can be linked to allow text to flow from one frame to another.

As you have worked on the inside panels for the Anderson Pet Mall brochure, did you notice that the graphics do not fit with subject of your brochure? When you select a design template, you choose the one that is closest to the look and feel that you want to convey to your readers. Don't worry if the graphics used do not match your subject; you can change the graphics. Consider the graphics as placeholders. You can use the template's graphics, change them, move them, or delete them.

Changing Pictures and Captions to Customize the Brochure

As you plan brochures, you will want to make the text and the graphics work together to convey your message. Generally, you will enter the text first and then fit the graphics around the text. In this activity, you will now change the template's pictures and captions to make the graphics work with the text for Anderson Pet Mall.

1. Open the publication Anderson Information Brochure.

2. Move to the second page and click on the picture of the orange book.

A frame with eight handles appears around the picture and caption.

3. Click on the picture of the orange book again.

In addition to the frame around the picture and caption, a second frame appears around the picture as shown in Figure 2.13.

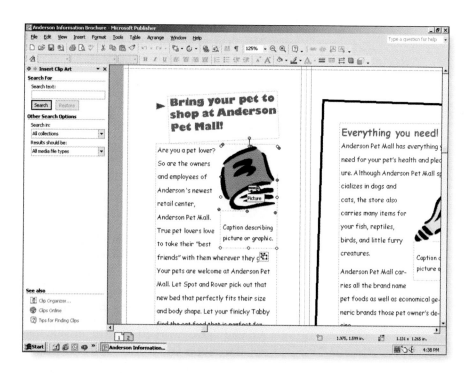

Publisher
BASICS

Changing pictures in a template

1. Click twice on the picture you want to change and then right-click.

2. Point to Change Picture and then click From File….

3. Locate the file name for the desired picture in the Insert Picture dialog box.

4. Click the file name and then click the Insert button.

Figure 2.13
Orange book clip art selected

4. With the picture of the orange book selected, right-click.

A menu appears that contains commands for changing and formatting pictures.

5. Point to Change Picture.

A submenu appears.

6. Click From File…

The Insert Picture dialog box appears as shown in Figure 2.14.

7. Locate the drive that contains the Publisher Data CD in the **Look in:** box and click on it.

8. Click on the file **Man and dog,** then click the **Insert** button.

A picture of a man walking a dog is inserted in your publication in place of the orange book.

9. Click on the caption underneath the new picture and **type** Your pet is welcome every day.

Notice that the frame around the caption is now made up of a series of diagonal lines.

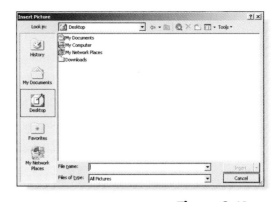

Figure 2.14
Insert Picture dialog box

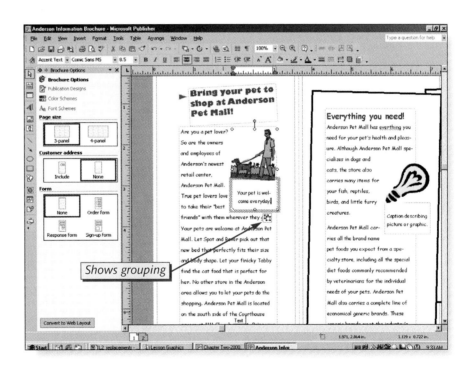

Figure 2.15
Clip art and new caption inserted

Shows grouping

To make the words fit in the caption frame, Publisher hyphenates the word *welcome* as shown in Figure 2.15. You can prevent this word from being hyphenated by increasing the size of the caption frame and picture.

To resize the caption frame and picture:

10. Click on the caption frame, then move the mouse pointer to the lower left handle of the frame until it changes to the Resize pointer . Click and drag the mouse pointer slightly down and to the left.

Note

The mouse pointer only needs to be dragged slightly. If you drag it too far, the caption frame and picture will take up valuable text space.

When you release the mouse button, the frame will be resized slightly so that the word *welcome* is no longer hyphenated.

11. Click 🖫 to save the file with its existing name.

12. Scroll to the right until the picture of the yellow light bulb appears.

13. Click twice on the yellow light bulb and right-click.

14. Repeat steps 5–7 above.

15. Click on the file Cat and dish, then click the Insert button.

16. Click on the caption under the new picture, press ⌨Enter← and type An extensive line of pet foods!

17. Click on the picture frame, then move to the upper left handle of the frame until it changes to the Resize pointer 🔲. Click and drag the mouse pointer slightly up and to the left until the We deliver too heading moves back to panel 3.

A picture of a cat with a dish is inserted in your publication in place of the yellow light bulb, and a new caption has been inserted, as shown in Figure 2.16.

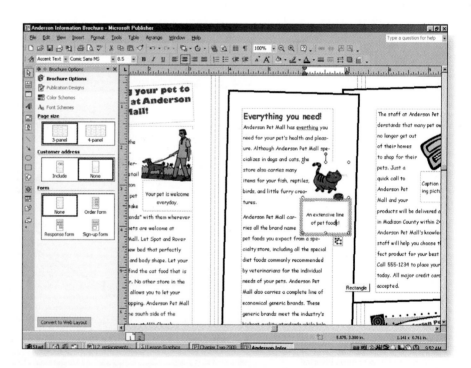

Figure 2.16
Cat and dish clip art and new caption in panel two

18. Scroll to the right until the picture of the computer appears.

19. Click twice on the picture of the computer and right-click.

20. Repeat steps 5–7 above.

21. Click on the file Delivery person, then click the Insert button.

22. Click on the caption under the new picture and type Free delivery in Madison County!

A picture of a delivery person is inserted in your publication in place of the computer, and a new caption appears, as shown in Figure 2.17.

23. Click 🖫 to save the file with its existing name.

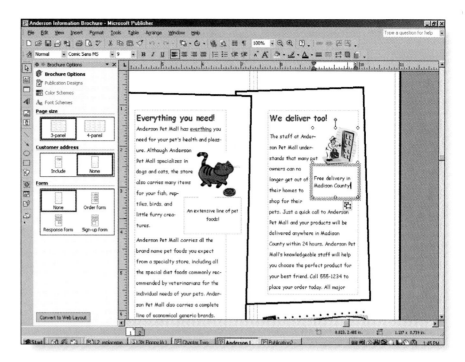

Figure 2.17
Delivery person clip art and caption in panel three

HOW PERSONAL INFORMATION SETS ARE USED BY THE TEMPLATE

When you open a design template, information from the Primary Business personal information set is automatically entered. In Lesson 1, you entered the information for Anderson Pet Mall in the Primary Business information set. Each time you select a template, Publisher enters the Anderson Pet Mall information into the publication. In a later lesson, you will learn how to select another personal information set for a different business.

The template that you are using for the Anderson Pet Mall brochure has frames set up to include the name of the business and the business's motto on the front panel of the brochure. The business's logo and contact information are also automatically entered on the back panel of the brochure. As soon as you open the template, this information is inserted in the proper frames on the brochure.

**HANDS
On**

Editing the Front (Outside Panels) of a Tri-fold Brochure

The text, clip art, and captions for page 2 are now complete. In this activity, you will enter text, clip art, and captions for page 1.

1. Click page 1 ⌐1⌐.

The outside panels of the brochure appear as shown in Figure 2.18.

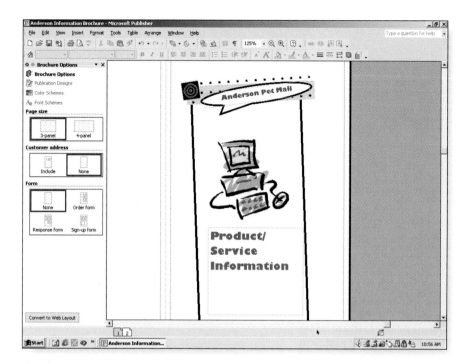

Figure 2.18
Page 1 of brochure

You will notice that the name of the store, Anderson Pet Mall, and the motto, Your Best Friend's Favorite Store, have already been inserted in the first panel. This panel will be the front of the brochure when it is folded. It should, therefore, have an eye-catching heading or slogan and an appropriate graphic, rather than a lot of text.

2. **To change the picture, click twice on the computer and right-click.**

3. **Navigate to the Smiling cat file on the Publisher Data CD.**

 *If you need help navigating to the files on the Publisher Data CD, review steps 5–7 under Changing Pictures and Captions to Customize the Brochure on pages 62–63.*

4. **Click Insert.**

A picture of a cat is inserted in place of the computer.

5. **Click on Product/Service Information and type A brand new store with a brand new idea for Anderson!**

6. **Scroll to the bottom of the page and click on the telephone number.**

7. **Type Tel: 765-555-1234.**

The front panel is now complete as shown in Figure 2.19 on the next page.

8. **Click [icon] to save the file under its existing name.**

9. **Scroll to the upper left corner of the page and click on Back Panel Heading.**

10. **Type Anderson Pet Mall.**

This panel will be the second one that readers will see when they open the brochure. This panel should continue to hold the readers' attention so that they continue to open and read the brochure. This panel should contain more information than the front panel, but less information than the inside panels. It is a good place for a bulleted list. A **_bullet_** is a character,

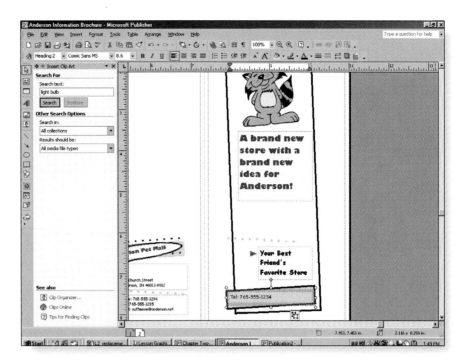

Figure 2.19
Completed front panel

typographical symbol, or graphic used as a special effect to highlight an item of text. Bullets are used to distinguish items in a list when the order of items is not critical. In the next few steps, you will create a bulleted list for the Anderson Pet Mall brochure as shown in Figure 2.20.

Publisher **BASICS**

Adding a bulleted list

1. Type the list and then select it.

2. Click the Bullets button.

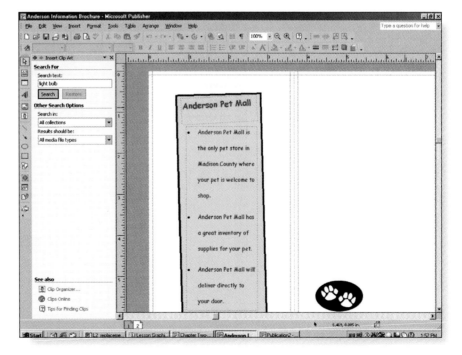

Figure 2.20
Bulleted list on back panel

11. Click on the text beginning This is a good place to . . . **and type** Anderson Pet Mall is the only pet store in Madison County where your pet is welcome to shop. `Enter⏎` Anderson Pet Mall has a great inventory of supplies for your pet. `Enter⏎` Anderson Pet Mall will deliver directly to your door.

12. Select the text that you have just typed.

13. Click the Bullets button  on the Formatting toolbar, or click Indents and Lists on the Format menu and select Bulleted list.

The three sentences that you have just typed become a bulleted list.

14. Click on the picture of the telephone under the text frame.

15. Navigate to the Pet store file on the Publisher Data CD.

> *Note* — *If you need help navigating to the files on the Publisher Data CD, review steps 5–7 under Changing Pictures and Captions to Customize the Brochure on pages 62–63.*

16. Click Insert.

The Pet Shop picture is inserted in place of the telephone.

17. Click on the caption underneath the new picture and type Anderson Pet Mall is located just south of the Courthouse square at 1111 Church Street.

18. Click 🖫 to save the file under its existing name.

19. Scroll to the right to view the middle panel.

As you can see in Figure 2.21, the Anderson Pet Mall logo and other information from the personal information set, such as the street address and phone numbers, have already been inserted in this panel. Because this is the back panel of the brochure, you do not need to add any further information to this panel.

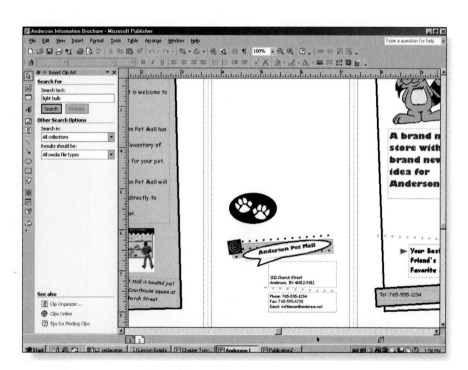

Figure 2.21
Middle panel of page one

20. Click 🖫 to save the file under its existing name.

Both sides of the tri-fold brochure are now complete. The brochure should now be proofread for typographical and other errors.

THE IMPORTANCE OF GOOD PROOFREADING SKILLS

All writers make errors—in spelling, punctuation, subject-verb agreement, word choice, typing, verb tense and many other things. Good writers correct their mistakes, declaring a publication final only when it is free of errors. Editing and proofreading are important for two reasons: communication and image. Errors in publications may cause readers to misunderstand your message, wasting your time and theirs. Besides, the publications you prepare—whether for yourself, an employer, or a customer—represent you. Their quality and appearance convey a message about your attitude and competence. Many readers will take you and your ideas less seriously if you misspell or mistype words or otherwise violate basic conventions of written English.

No software can edit and proofread for you. Publisher has features to help you, however. The Spelling feature, for example, flags potential errors. Then you can decide if a correction is needed. The wavy, red lines in your publications mark words not in the Spelling dictionary. When you right-click one of these words, a **shortcut menu** appears. If the menu lists the correct spelling, click the correct word. If the correct spelling is not on the menu, you may correct the spelling manually or click Ignore All. Clicking Ignore All tells Publisher to disregard all instances of the underlined word in the current publication. (Clicking Add would put the underlined word in the Spelling dictionary. You must **not** choose the Add option unless the computer belongs to you.) The wavy, red line disappears when you click one of these options.

HANDS On

Checking Spelling using Publisher

In this activity, you will check the spelling of words in your brochure that are underlined with wavy, red lines.

Note

If wavy, red lines do not show on your screen, the Spelling feature has been turned off. To activate this tool, click Spelling on the Tools menu, and then click Spelling Options…. When the Spelling Options dialog box appears, make sure these check boxes are marked: Check spelling as you type and Flag repeated words.

Publisher **BASICS**

Checking spelling

1. Point to a word that is underlined with wavy, red lines.

2. Right-click on the word.

3. Click the correct spelling on the shortcut menu or correct the spelling manually.

1. Point to the underlined word *stor* in the first panel on page 2.

2. Right-click on the word.

A shortcut menu with suggested spellings appears as shown in Figure 2.22 on the next page.

3. Click store from the list of words.

The spelling of the word is changed to store.

4. Point to the underlined word *everthing* in the second panel of page 2.

5. Right-click on the word.

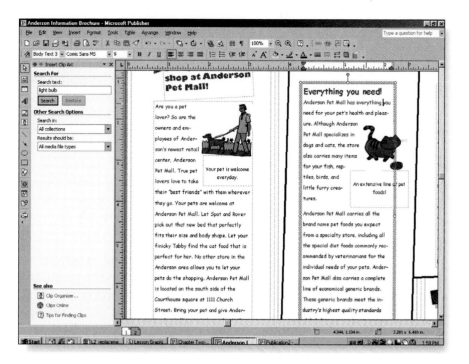

Figure 2.22 ◀
Shortcut menu with suggested
correct spellings

6. Click **everything** from the list of words.

7. Click 🖫 to save the file under its existing name.

Check all panels of the brochure for any other spelling errors.

Good editing and proofreading involve more than just checking spelling, of course. To proofread a publication properly, you should print a copy of the publication. Many errors are easier to spot on a printed copy than they are on a screen. Table 2.2 lists common proofreading marks that you can use as you proofread your publication.

TABLE 2.2	PROOFREADING MARKS	
PROOFREADERS' MARK		**DRAFT**
◡	Delete space	to‿gether
⋕	Insert space	It⌃may be
⌒	Move as shown	it is ⌒not⌒ true
∽	Transpose	believable
		is/it so
◯	Spell out	②years ago
		16 Elm ⟨St⟩
∧ or ⋏	Insert	How much ⌃is⌃ it?
⸹ or —	Delete a word or a punctuation mark	it may ~~not~~ be true. ⸹
⸹ or ℐ	Delete a letter and close up	commitᵗment to busy
	(continues)	

TABLE 2.2	PROOFREADING MARKS	*(continued)*

PROOFREADERS' MARK		DRAFT
⌒	Add on to a word	a real good day
⅃ or /	Change a letter	this supercedes
⅄ or —	Change a word	and if you won't
....	Stet (don't delete)	I was ~~very~~ glad
/	Lowercase a letter (make it a small letter)	Federal Government
≡	Capitalize	Janet L. greyston
⊙	Insert a period	Mr Henry Grenada
⋏	Insert a comma	a large old house
∨	Insert an apostrophe	my childrens car
∨∨	Insert quotation marks	he wants a loan
=	Insert a hyphen	a first=rate job
		ask the coowner
¦M	Insert a one-em dash or change a hyphen to a one-em dash	Success at last!
		Here it is cash!
——	Insert italics	Do it <u>now</u>, Bill!
~~	Change to boldface	<u>CONFIDENTIAL</u>
( )	Insert parentheses	left today (May 3)
¶	Start a new paragraph	¶If that is so
⌐	Move to the right	$38,367,000▭
⌐	Move to the left	⌐Anyone can win!

HANDS On

Using AutoCorrect

Another Publisher feature, AutoCorrect, helps prevent some common spelling errors by correcting them automatically. For example, if you type *teh*, Publisher automatically changes it to *the*. AutoCorrect can also be customized. Do you find yourself making the same typo over and over? AutoCorrect can be customized to correct your most common typing errors. AutoCorrect can also be used to convert abbreviations to complete words or phrases. Are you getting tired of typing Anderson Pet Mall? You can use AutoCorrect to insert the words Anderson Pet Mall every time that the letters APM are typed. In the following activity you will set up APM as the AutoCorrect abbreviation for Anderson Pet Mall.

**Customizing
AutoCorrect**

1. Click AutoCorrect Option…
   on the Tools menu.

2. In the Replace: box, type
   the word or abbreviation
   you wish to have changed
   automatically.

3. In the With: box, type the
   word or phrase you wish to
   have inserted in place of
   the word or abbreviation in
   the Replace: box.

4. Click Add and then click
   OK.

1. **Click the Tools menu, and then click
   AutoCorrect Options….**

The AutoCorrect dialog box appears as
shown in Figure 2.23.

2. **In the Replace: box, type** APM.

3. **In the With: box, type** Anderson Pet Mall.

4. **Click Add.**

APM is added to the AutoCorrect list.

5. **Click OK to save this change and close the
   dialog box.**

Each time you type APM, Publisher will
automatically substitute the words Anderson Pet Mall.

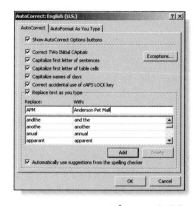

Figure 2.23
AutoCorrect dialog box

ENHANCING THE APPEARANCE OF PUBLICATIONS

After your brochure has been proofread, it could be printed and used without any further changes. However, some of the design elements in the
brochure can be improved or enhanced. In the next activity, you will modify
some of these design elements. Before making these changes, though, you
may need to understand more about the basics of design. This section sum-
marizes some basic design terms and principles.

Changing Font Design and Size

A *font* is a set of characters of one design. Publisher offers dozens of fonts,
as you will soon discover. The fonts available to you, though, depend upon
the printer you are using. A printer may convert a fancy Publisher font to
less desirable characters—or not print the font at all. Some fonts are ideal
for ordinary text, while others are best suited for headings. A few are spe-
cial-purpose fonts, designed for Web pages, posters, and so on. For larger
amounts of text, *serif* fonts are best. In serif fonts, the characters have *feet*
that form a straight line, guiding readers' eyes from left to right. Times New
Roman and Georgia are examples of this kind of font. A font without feet,
such as Arial or Century Gothic, is best for headings. These fonts are called
sans serif. Examples of serif and sans serif fonts are shown in Figure 2.24.

Figure 2.24
**Examples of serif and
sans serif fonts**

Serif Fonts	Sans Serif Fonts
Times New Roman	Arial
Georgia	Century Gothic

As you look at the fonts in Figure 2.24, notice the differences in the shapes
of letters and in the thickness of the lines that make up the letters. As you
work with publications, you will learn to choose fonts that work well
together and that enhance your message.

Font size is also important. A contrast in font size is useful to distinguish between ordinary text and special text, such as headings. Main headings in a publication use larger font sizes (18 and larger). Subheadings often use font sizes of 12 or 14. The most common font sizes for ordinary text are 10, 11, and 12. Figure 2.25 shows Times New Roman and Arial in sizes of 10, 11, 12, 14, 16, and 18.

10	Times New Roman	Arial
11	Times New Roman	Arial
12	Times New Roman	Arial
14	Times New Roman	Arial
16	Times New Roman	Arial
18	Times New Roman	Arial

Figure 2.25
Font sizes

Another way to enhance or emphasize text is to add one or more special effects or attributes (also called *font styles*). You can use **bold** to make words stand out from surrounding text. Bold helps readers see important points or terms at a glance. Another common font style is *italic*. Italic text has thin, delicate characters that slant slightly to the right. A large block of italic is hard to read, but italic is an attention-getter when used sparingly. Underlined text may also be used for emphasis. However, modern design makes sparing use of underlined text. UPPERCASE characters can also be used for emphasis. Headings often use bold and uppercase characters. Two basic rules apply to using font styles such as bold, italic, underlining, and uppercase:

1. Use styles to consistently mean the same thing. For example, if you decide to use bold for key words in one part of your publication, do not use italic for key words in another part of the same publication. If you decide to use uppercase for one main heading, use it for all main headings.

2. Use styles sparingly. When they are overused, readers ignore them and they lose their effectiveness.

Although variety is necessary to provide emphasis and contrast in a publication, consistency is also important. No more than two or three fonts should be used in the same publication. Font size should also be consistent, especially for the main text of a publication. Too much variety in fonts, font sizes, or font styles makes a publication look unprofessional.

Changing Colors

The default color in Publisher is black on a white background. As a Publisher user, though, you are certainly not limited to black-and-white text. Many font colors are provided, as well as background colors. You will, of course, need a color printer to print color publications. If you use color in a publication and then print it on a black-and-white printer, the colors will appear as shades of gray.

Effective use of colors is one of the best ways to draw attention to the information in a publication. However, colors should be changed carefully. For example, light font colors on light backgrounds can make a publication difficult, if not impossible, to read. As with font styles, color should be used consistently to help guide the reader through the publication. For example, headings are often placed in color to attract the reader's attention.

Publisher has many pre-designed color schemes from which you can choose. If you do not have a background in art or design, it is best to stick with Publisher's color schemes.

Proper Use of Hyphenation

Publisher automatically hyphenates text in a text frame. There are advantages and disadvantages to automatic hyphenation. Hyphenation allows more text to be included on each line and creates a more even right margin. However, having too many hyphens in a text frame makes the text look less attractive and can make it more difficult to read. Hyphens should also be avoided in headings.

It is possible to turn off the automatic hyphenation in Publisher. When hyphenation is turned off, Publisher removes all of the hyphens from the selected text.

Using the Style Feature

The Publisher feature called Style is a quick way to format and enhance text at the same time. A Publisher style combines format properties (alignment, indentations, and line spacing) and appearance properties (font, font size, and font styles). Thus, when you choose a style, one click takes care of all of these factors at once.

You should consider creating styles for any element in a publication that appears regularly. Examples include body text, primary headings, secondary headings, numbered lists, bulleted lists, and captions. If you later decide to change a style, the change affects all of the text in the publication that uses that style.

Changing Fonts and Using the Style Feature

In this activity, you will make changes to some of the design elements in the tri-fold brochure that you created in the previous activity. You will also change the hyphenation and modify styles.

1. Select the text in the first panel of page 2.
2. Click the down arrow next to the Font box on the Formatting toolbar.
3. Select Times New Roman as shown in Figure 2.26.

You will notice that changing the font has reduced the size of the text so that it no longer fills the frame. You could experiment with increasing and decreasing the font size until the text fits the frame, but you can save time by having Publisher find the *best fit* for you.

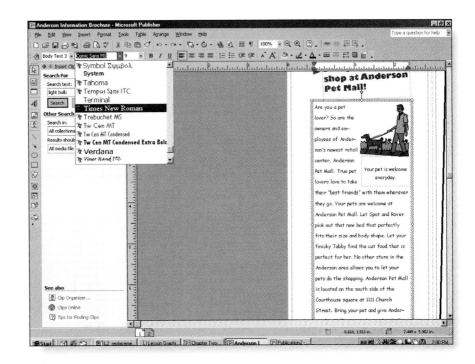

Changing fonts

1. Select the text you wish to change.

2. Click the down arrow next to the Font box on the Formatting toolbar.

3. Locate the desired font and click on it.

Figure 2.26
Changing text to
Times New Roman font

Using Best Fit to adjust text size in a frame

1. Select all of the text in a frame and right-click.

2. Point to Change Text and then AutoFit Text.

3. Click Best Fit.

4. While the text is still selected and your cursor is somewhere inside the text box, right-click.

5. In the shortcut menu, point to Change Text, and then AutoFit Text.

6. Click Best Fit as shown in Figure 2.27.

Notice that the text increases to fill the frame.

7. Click 💾 to save the file under its existing name.

As you have already learned, the font and font size of your main text should be consistent. To change the font and font size in the other panels to match the first panel, you could select the text in each panel and then change the font and font size boxes on the Formatting toolbar to match those in the first panel. Publisher also allows you to change the style (Body Text 3) so that the new font (Times New Roman) and the new font size are part of the definition for that style. Once the style has been redefined, all text with that style will be changed automatically.

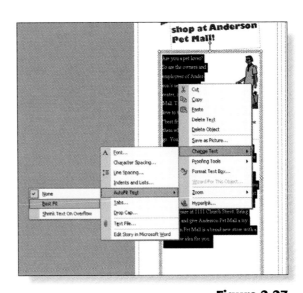

Figure 2.27
Using Best Fit to change text size

Redefining a Publisher Style to match selected text

1. Select the text with the original Publisher style.

2. Modify the style by changing the font or other characteristics.

3. Click Styles and Formatting on the Format menu.

4. Locate the name of the current style in the Styles and Formatting task pane and click the down arrow next to it.

5. Click Update to match selection in the drop-down menu.

Figure 2.28 ◀
Redefining Body Text 3

Turning off automatic hyphenation

1. Select the text from which the hyphens are to be removed.

2. Click Language on the Tools menu, and then click Hyphenation.

3. Remove the check mark in front of Automatically hyphenate this story.

4. Click OK.

8. While the text in the first panel is still selected, click Styles and Formatting on the Format menu.

The task pane changes to the Styles and Formatting task pane.

9. Scroll down to Body Text 3.

10. Right click on Body Text 3.

11. Click Update to match selection in the drop-down menu as shown in Figure 2.28.

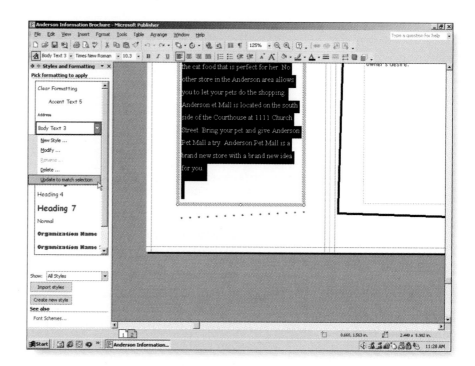

12. Click 💾 to save the file under its existing name.

The definition of Body Text 3 is changed to match the selected text, and all of the text with that style in the other panels is changed to match the first panel.

You may have noticed that Publisher has hyphenated several words in these panels, sometimes breaking the words in awkward places. To remove the hyphens, follow the next few steps.

13. Select the text in the first panel.

14. Click Language on the Tools menu, and then click Hyphenation.

15. In the Hyphenation dialog box, remove the check mark in front of Automatically hyphenate this story (by clicking on it), and then click OK.

All hyphens are removed from the text in the first panel.

16. Select the text in the second and third panels and repeat steps 14 and 15 above.

17. If the heading We Deliver too! flows back to the second panel, position the cursor in front of the word "We," press Ctrl + Enter⏎ to insert a box break.

18. Click 💾 to save the file under its existing name.

Adding Background Colors

In this activity, you will make changes to page 2 of the tri-fold brochure to draw more attention to the captions on this page. You will *fill* the caption boxes with background colors.

1. Click on the caption in the first panel (Your pet is welcome at everyday) and then right-click.

2. Click Format Text Box... in the short-cut menu.

The Format Text dialog box appears as shown in Figure 2.29.

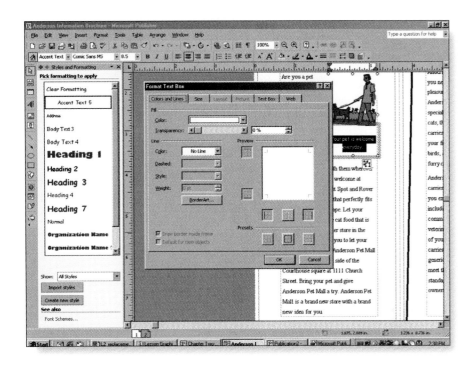

Figure 2.29
Format text box

3. Under Fill on the Colors and Lines tab, click the down arrow next to the Color box.

4. When the small dialog box appears, click on the third color choice (yellow-orange).

5. When the color appears in the Color box and the preview area, click OK.

6. Repeat steps 1–5 for each caption box on page 2. You may choose different colors for each caption.

7. Click 💾 to save the file under its existing name.

Changing Bullets

In this activity, you will make the final change to the tri-fold brochure. The bullets will be changed from ordinary dots to symbols that are appropriate to the text.

Changing bullets

1. Select a bulleted list.

2. Click Indents and Lists... on the Format menu.

3. Click the New Bullet... button on the Indents and Lists dialog box.

4. Click the down arrow next to the Font box.

5. Locate the preferred font and symbol and click on the symbol.

6. Click OK to return to the Indents and Lists dialog box and then click OK again.

1. Select the bulleted list on the left panel on page 1.

2. Click Indents and Lists... on the Format menu.

The Indents and Lists dialog box appears as shown in Figure 2.30.

3. Click the New Bullet... button New Bullet....

The New Bullet dialog box appears.

4. Click the down arrow next to the Font: box, and scroll down until Webdings appears.

5. Click Webdings.

The Webding symbols are displayed. These are a special set of characters that act like a font.

6. Scroll to the bottom row of the Webdings, click on the cat symbol, and click OK.

The Indents and Lists dialog box reappears with the cat symbol as the highlighted Bullet type.

7. Click OK.

The dots in the bulleted list have been changed to the cat symbol.

8. Click to save the file under its existing name.

9. Print your finished brochure by clicking.

Figure 2.30
Indents and Lists dialog box

Self CHECK

Test your knowledge by answering the following questions. See Appendix C to check your answers.

T F 1. A contrast in font size is useful to distinguish between ordinary text and special text, such as headings.

T F 2. A large block of italic is easy to read.

T F 3. Bold helps readers see important points or terms at a glance.

T F 4. Wavy, red lines in a publication mark words not in the Spelling dictionary.

T F 5. When you are checking spelling, clicking Add tells Publisher to change the spelling of the word in your publication.

SEARCHING THE WEB

Sometimes when you want to find information about a topic, you may not know a specific Web site address or find a hyperlink that leads to the topic. In these cases, you can use the Search Page on your Web browser. A ***Search Page*** allows you to type keywords that describe your topic and then uses one or more search engines (such as Alta Vista or Yahoo) to search the Web for documents that contain those keywords. A ***search engine*** is an Internet tool that allows you to search for information on a particular topic. Some search engines search every word of every document they find on the Internet; others search only portions of documents they find.

In this activity, you will use the Search button on the Internet Explorer toolbar to navigate to the Search Page. Then you will search for Web sites about companies that sell chocolates by mail order.

1. Open a new, blank publication. Click the Web Page Preview button.

Publisher opens the Internet Explorer window.

2. Click the Search button on the Internet Explorer toolbar.

Internet Explorer connects you to the Internet, if you are not already connected, and the designated Search Page appears.

3. If necessary, click a search engine option. (You may use the default search engine if one is already selected, or if you do not have a choice of search engines.)

4. Type chocolate in the Search text box. Click the button to process your search request. (This button may be labeled *Search, Submit search, Find, Find It,* or *Go.*)

 A Security Alert dialog box may appear, warning you of security issues and asking if you want to continue. Click Yes *to continue.*

5. When the results of your search appear, scroll to see the numerous sites to which you can connect.

The results of your search appear in the form of links that you can click to navigate to the page described. (Most search engines display the results that contain more occurrences of your keywords at the top of the list.) The results that you will get from typing the keyword *chocolate* will vary depending on the search engine you use. They will lead you to a variety of topics, including chocolate recipes, companies that sell various types of chocolate, restaurants that serve chocolate dishes, and more.

Your search probably resulted in many pages of results, containing thousands of links. Instead of sifting through thousands of results—some of which don't pertain to your situation—you can type additional keywords to narrow your search. Many search engines allow you to use special symbols to narrow your results even further. For instance, a search engine called Alta Vista allows you to use quotation marks around words that should always be found together, a plus symbol to specify that the keyword must be found in the result, and a minus sign to indicate that the word should not be found in the resulting pages. For instance, the keywords +*chocolate company "mail order" -coffee* will result in pages that all contain the word *chocolate,* may contain the word *company,* and may contain the words *mail order* together, but will exclude those pages that contain the word *coffee.* To find out if your search engine allows the use of special symbols, look for a Help or an Advanced Search button that describes them.

6. In the **Search text** box, **type the keywords** chocolate company mail order. **(If you are using Alta Vista, type** +chocolate company "mail order".**)**

7. **Click the appropriate button to process your request. If a Security Alert dialog box appears, click Yes if you wish to continue.**

When the results appear, scroll down to see them. As you can see, the results using several keywords usually suggest sites that are more targeted to the information you are seeking.

8. **From your results, click and explore on of the links that you think will lead to a Web page published by a company that sells chocolate items by mail. If time permits, explore other related sites.**

9. **Close Internet Explorer and disconnect from the Internet (unless your instructor tells you to remain connected.)**

10. **Exit Publisher.**

Lesson Summary & Exercises

SUMMARY

Although Publisher offers a variety of pre-designed templates that you can use to create publications, the templates are only a starting point. Not only can the text and graphics in the templates be changed, but the text styles, colors, and other design elements can be modified to enhance the appearance of your publication. The handles around text frames and objects also allow you to move and resize the frames to fit your publication better. In addition, Publisher provides features, such as Spell checking and AutoCorrect, that help prevent or correct typographical errors and other mistakes in your publications.

Now that you have completed this lesson, you should be able to do the following:

- Select text and objects in a publication.
- Move and resize frames around text and objects.
- Define and create a tri-fold brochure.
- Insert text from other files into a publication.
- Change pictures in a publication.
- Apply and change Publisher styles.
- Use the Format Painter.
- Create and change bulleted lists.
- Use AutoCorrect both to correct typos and to insert frequently used text.
- Spot and correct typos and other misspellings using the Spelling feature.
- Choose appropriate fonts and styles for each part of your publication.
- Change fonts, font sizes, and font styles.
- Use or turn off automatic hyphenation.
- Apply fill colors to captions and other text boxes.

CONCEPTS REVIEW

1 TRUE/FALSE

Circle T if the statement is true or F if the statement is false.

T F **1.** The front panel of a tri-fold brochure should have as much text as possible.

T F **2.** Publisher can edit and proofread for you.

T F **3.** When there is a wavy, red line under a word, a correction is always needed.

T F **4.** You should not click on Add in a Spelling menu if the computer does not belong to you.

T F **5.** To proofread a publication properly, you should print a copy of the publication.

T F **6.** Bold and italic characters should be used frequently in a publication to add variety.

T F **7.** Effective use of color is one of the best ways to draw attention to specific information in a publication.

T F **8.** Too much variety in fonts or font size makes a publication look unprofessional.

T F **9.** Light font colors on light backgrounds are easy to read.

T F **10.** Hyphens allow more text to be included on each line, so they should be used frequently.

2 MATCHING

Match each of the terms on the left with the definitions on the right.

TERMS

1. AutoCorrect
2. bold
3. bullets
4. font styles
5. fonts
6. Format Painter
7. handles
8. italic
9. panels
10. serif

DEFINITIONS

a. eight small boxes at the corners and sides of a frame

b. sections of a brochure

c. allows you to copy the formatting of text to other text

d. characters used to highlight items in a list

e. thick, dark characters

f. sets of characters of one design

g. characters that have feet

h. special effects, such as bold and italic

i. can be used to convert abbreviations to complete words and phrases.

j. delicate characters that slant slightly to the right

3 COMPLETION

Fill in the missing word or phrase for each of the following statements.

1. Selecting text causes it to be _____.

2. To select a single word, _____ it.

3. The MOVE mouse pointer looks like a _____.

4. A tri-fold brochure is folded _____ to create three panels on the front and three panels on the back.

5. When you move the mouse after clicking the Format Painter button, the pointer changes to a _____.

6. When there are both objects and text on the same page, Publisher automatically _____ text around the objects.

7. When you _____ on a word that has wavy, red lines under it, a shortcut menu appears.

8. When you are checking spelling, clicking _____ tells Publisher to disregard all instances of an underlined word in a publication.

9. _____ fonts are best for headings.

10. The Publisher _____ feature is a quick way to format and enhance text at the same time.

4 SHORT ANSWER

1. How do you increase the size of a frame in a publication?

2. What does the Go to Previous Frame button indicate?

3. How do you move an object in a publication?

4. How do you change a picture in a template?

5. Why would you add bullets to a list? How do you do it?

6. How do you change the bullets to other symbols?

7. Why are editing and proofreading important?

8. What are the advantages and disadvantages to automatic hyphenation? How do you turn if off?

9. What are three ways you can select a paragraph of text? Which is the fastest way?

10. Why are consistency and variety both important in a publication?

5 IDENTIFICATION

Label each of the elements of the Publisher window in Figure 2.31.

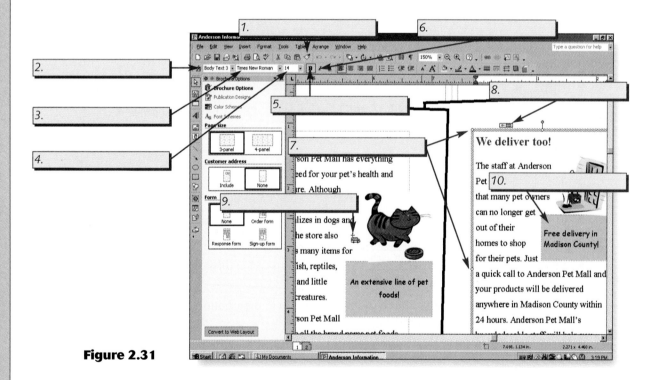

Figure 2.31

SKILLS REVIEW

Complete each of the Skills Review activities in sequential order to review the skills you learned in this lesson. In the process of creating a price list brochure, you will review your skills to insert text files and pictures; make formatting changes; create bulleted lists; move and resize frames; and check spelling.

1 Open a template, insert a text file, and make formatting changes

1. Under **By Publication Type** in the New Publication task pane, click **Brochures** and then click **Price List.**

2. Locate the **Bubbles Price List Brochure** template in the Publication Gallery and open it.

3. Switch from page 1 to **page 2.**

4. Change the Zoom to **100%.**

5. Scroll to the upper left corner of the page and change **Main Inside Heading** to read Everything You Need!

6. Use the **Best Fit** command to make the text fit the frame.

7. Delete the default text under the Main Inside Heading and insert the text file **Promotional Panel for Lesson 2** on the Publisher Data CD.

 Note   *This is the same promotional text that you inserted in the second panel of the brochure that you created earlier in this lesson.*

8. Change the Publisher style of this panel to **Body Text 3.**

9. Turn off automatic hyphenation.

10. Name and save the file as **Promo Price List.**

2 Edit default text in a template, change font sizes, and use the Format Painter to copy changes

1. Open the **Promo Price List** brochure if necessary. Scroll to the second panel on page 2. As you can see, the second and third panels contain a price list table.

2. Edit the default text in the table so that the table lists the following products and prices. Delete the phrase **"Include description if necessary"** from each box in the table.

Dog shampoo	$9.99
Puppy treats	4.99
Dog sweater	29.99
Leather collar	6.99
Pet bowl	8.99
Cat toy	4.99
Cat litter	5.99
Litter pan	4.99
Hamster wheel	3.99

Turtle food	1.99
Bird treats	4.99
Bird vitamins	8.99

3. Change the font size of the first product (Dog shampoo) in the table to **14.**

4. Copy this change to all of the products in the table using the **Format Painter.**

5. Change the font size of the first price ($9.99) in the table to **10.**

6. Copy this change to all of the prices in the table using the **Format Painter.**

7. Save the file under its existing name.

3 Change pictures and captions

1. Open the **Promo Price List** brochure if necessary. Change the picture of the orange book in the first panel of page 2 to the **Cat and Dish** picture on the Publisher Data CD.

2. Change the caption under the picture to read An extensive line of pet foods!

3. Fill the caption box with one of the colors in the **Format Text Box.**

4. Switch from page 2 to **page 1.**

5. Change the picture of the computer to the **Smiling Cat** picture on the Publisher Data CD.

6. Scroll to the far left panel and change the picture of the telephone to the **Pet Store** picture on the Publisher Data CD.

7. Change the caption to read Anderson Pet Mall is located just south of the Courthouse square at 1111 Church Street.

8. Fill the caption box with one of the fill colors in the **Format Text Box.**

9. Save the file under its existing name.

4 Create and change a bulleted list and use the AutoCorrect feature

1. Open the **Promo Price List** brochure if necessary. Change the Back Panel Heading on page 1 to read Your best friend's favorite store.

2. Type the following three sentences in place of the default text under the Back Panel Heading. Be sure to press the [Enter⏎] between each sentence.

APM is the only pet store in Madison County where your pet is welcome to shop.

APM has a great inventory of supplies for your pet.

APM will deliver directly to your door.

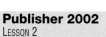

Lesson Summary & Exercises

 "APM" should automatically change to Anderson Pet Mall if you created the AutoCorrect shortcut earlier in this lesson. If it does not, repeat the steps under Using AutoCorrect on pages 71–72. Then delete and retype "APM" in each of the three sentences to activate this feature.

3. Convert the three sentences to a bulleted list.

4. Change the bullets to the cat symbol in the Webdings font.

5. Save the file under its existing name.

5 Move and resize frames

1. Open the **Promo Price List** brochure if necessary. Scroll to the far right of page 1.

2. Delete the yellow dotted line below the Smiling Cat picture. (This dotted line is in its own frame, so it can be deleted by selecting the frame and pressing Delete.)

3. Move the **Smiling Cat picture** so that it is above the text box (Price List) and just below the words Anderson Pet Mall. You will also need to move the text box (Price List) frame so that it is lower on the panel.

4. Change the text in the **Price List frame** to read Price List (good through 2/28/02). Publisher "shrinks" the text as you type so that it will fit the current frame.

5. Select the text you just typed and change the size to **22.**

6. Resize the frame around the text so that all of the text is able to be displayed.

7. Save the file under its existing name.

6 Proofread and check spelling

1. Open the **Promo Price List** brochure if necessary. Check both sides of the brochure for the wavy, red lines that indicate a potential spelling error.

2. Correct any typos or misspellings that Publisher has identified.

3. Print a proof copy of the brochure and proofread for other errors that Publisher has not identified. Correct any errors that you find.

4. Save the file under its existing name.

LESSON APPLICATIONS

1 Change the Font Style on a Postcard

You will open a publication that you created in Lesson 1 and enhance the text.

1. Locate and open the **Anderson Pet Mall Invitation Postcard** that you created and saved in Lesson 1.

2. Select the paragraph in the center of the postcard (Come join us . . .)

3. Change the font style to **Bold.**

4. Use the **Best Fit** command to reduce the font size so that all of the text fits in the frame.

5. Save the updated postcard.

Lesson Summary & Exercises

2 Change Bullets on a Postcard

You will add bullet symbols to the postcard you created in Lesson 1.

1. Open the **Anderson Pet Mall Invitation Postcard,** if necessary. Click on **page 2** to view the back of the postcard.

2. Select the list of items on the back of the postcard.

3. Change the list to a bulleted list.

4. Change the bullets to **cat symbols,** using the steps you learned in this lesson.

5. Save your changes.

3 Add Color to a Postcard

You will make an additional enhancement to the invitation postcard.

1. Open the **Anderson Pet Mall Invitation Postcard,** if necessary. Select the frame containing the bulleted list and right-click.

2. In the **Format Text** Box, change the fill color from No Fill to one of the options in the drop-down box. (Keep in mind that the color should not be so dark or so bright that you are not able to read the text.)

3. Click **OK** to make the change and return to the postcard.

4. If the color is too dark or too bright for the text, repeat the previous steps, choosing a different color.

5. Save the updated postcard and close the file.

4 Correct Spelling as You Type

You will open a new, blank publication and type as fast as you can. Then you will spell check what you have typed.

1. Open a new, blank publication by clicking the **New button** ☐ on the **Standard toolbar.**

2. Increase the Zoom to **100%.**

Publisher will not let you type in a blank publication until you insert a text frame. To insert a text frame:

3. Click the **Text Box** button 🔲 on the **Objects toolbar.** The mouse pointer changes to the crosshair pointer ⊞.

4. Click anywhere in the blank publication and use the crosshair pointer to draw a box that is large enough that you can type several sentences in it.

5. Type The quick, brown fox jumps over the lazy dog. six times as fast as you can (so that you are likely to make mistakes).

6. Watch the text as you type. Some of your mistakes will probably be corrected automatically by the AutoCorrect feature.

7. Correct the spelling of underlined words.

8. Close the publication without saving your changes.

Lesson Summary & Exercises

PROJECTS

1 Exploring Fonts

Scroll through the fonts in the **Font** box on the **Formatting toolbar.** Find five serif fonts, five sans serif fonts, and two fonts that could be used for bullets.

Open a blank publication and insert a text frame so that you can type. (Follow the instructions under Lesson Application 4 on the previous page if you are not certain how to do this.)

Type the names of the twelve fonts that you have chosen. For the serif and sans serif fonts, apply the corresponding font to each of the font names you have typed. For example, if you have typed the word Arial, apply the **Arial** font to that word. For the two bullet fonts, type the letters XYZ after each font name, and then apply the font to those three letters. The three letters will change to show three of the symbols in that font.

2 Pool Rules

On your Publisher Data CD, locate and open the file **Pool Rules.** Increase the Zoom so that the text is large enough to read. You will convert the list of rules into an eye-catching sign.

Select all of the text (including the heading) and change it to the **Arial** font. With all of the text still selected, use the **Best Fit** command to enlarge the text so that it fills the page. Make a note of the font size.

Select all of the lines of text except the heading *(Pool Rules)* and change the lines to a bulleted list. Change the bullets to the first symbol (**beach umbrella and water**) in the **Vacation MT** font or another appropriate symbol. Also change the size of the bullets to match the size of the text, by changing the **Size** box on the **Indents and Lists** dialog box to match the font size you noted earlier.

Turn off the Best Fit setting by clicking **None** under **AutoFit Text** on the **Format** menu. This will allow you to modify the heading to a different font size from the rest of the text.

Select the heading and change it to font size **48, bold.**

Print the sign and save it under the name **Pool Rules Revised.**

3 This flyer needs help!

Locate and open the file **Garage Sale Flyer** on your Publisher Data CD. Increase the Zoom so that the text is large enough to read. As you can see, the words *Garage Sale* take up nearly half of the flyer, and the items for sale are almost too small to read. To correct this problem, you will need to change font sizes and move and resize frames.

Resize the frame around the words *Garage Sale* so that the frame is about half as long as it was originally. This will also put the words *Garage* and *Sale* on the same line.

Move the other frames up so that the date frame is just under the Garage Sale frame. The top of each frame should be even with the bottom of the frame above.

Change the font size of the date, time and location (Our house is . . .) to **20.** Resize the frame around the location slightly, so that all of the text is able to fit in the frame.

Change the font size of the items for sale (the bulleted list) to **26.** Resize the frame around the items so that all of the text will fit in the frame.

Change the bullets to a symbol that would be more attention-getting, and increase the size of the bullets to match the font size (26).

Note — *If you are not certain how to do this, read the instructions under Pool Rules above.*

Save and print the flyer.

4 This report needs even more help!

Locate and open the file **Earth** on your Publisher Data CD. Increase the Zoom so that the text is large enough to read. This is the first page of a term paper that needs to be formatted and proofread.

Apply the **Heading 3** style to the heading *Earth.* Increase the font size to **20** and center this heading using the **Center** button ≡ on the **Formatting** toolbar.

Apply the **Heading 7** style to the subheading *Geology* and underline this subheading using the **Underline** button [U] on the **Formatting** toolbar. Copy the formatting of this subheading to the subheading *Atmosphere* using the **Format Painter.**

Apply the **Body Text 2** style to the paragraphs.

Check the text for spelling errors. Keep in mind that some technical terms may be correctly spelled, but Publisher may identify them as possible misspellings because the terms are not in Publisher's dictionary.

Save the report as **Earth Report-Revised.**

5 Come one, come all!

Create a tri-fold brochure advertising a seminar or special meeting that is being sponsored by a club at your school. Use one of the Event brochures, such as the Blackboard Event or the Floating Oval Event brochure.

After you have selected and opened the brochure, change the personal Information Set to the Other Organization information set. Edit the information in this set to include your name, the address of your school, an appropriate contact phone number and e-mail address, and the organization name (the name of the club). If your club has a motto, add that information also. Click **Update** to insert this information into the brochure.

 *Because you did not insert a logo into the information set, the logo for Anderson Pet Mall will continue to show on the brochure. Delete this logo by clicking it and pressing the Delete key.*

Edit the default text in the brochure to give the title of the seminar or meeting, as well as the date, time, and location. Also give the names of the speakers and some information about each one. (If there will be fewer than three speakers, you can delete the extra text boxes and graphics by clicking on them and pressing the **Delete** key.) Finally, edit the Back Panel Heading and the text directly under it to provide additional information about the seminar/meeting, including any registration requirements.

Save and print the brochure.

6 Exploring Venus

Your term paper about Venus is still in progress. Today you've set aside some time to search the Web for more information about the planet. Open a blank publication and then click the **Web Page Preview** button. Click the **Search** button on the **Internet Explorer** toolbar. On the Search page, use *Venus* and *planet* as keywords, and indicate that *Venus de Milo, Venus flytrap,* and *Venus Williams* should be excluded from the search results. Visit several of the resulting sites. make a list of the four sites that you found most informative.

Project in Progress

7 Project in Progress

As the newly-elected secretary of your local Friends of the Library organization, you are concerned that too few people in your community are aware of the work of the Friends of the Library and the purpose of its fundraising events. You feel that a tri-fold brochure, which could be distributed at the library's circulation desk and elsewhere, would help publicize the work of your group and increase its membership.

Using the **Floating Oval Informational Brochure,** or another appropriate template, create a tri-fold brochure to publicize the purpose and work of your group. (Hint: To get ideas about the kinds of information to include, search the Web using *"Friends of the Library"* as your key term. Read the Web sites of various Friends of the Library groups around the country.) Be sure to include information about the group's annual book sale. If necessary, edit the Other Organization personal information set, following the instructions in Lesson 1 (page 24). If the logo for Anderson Pet Mall (or another logo) is inserted on your brochure, delete it.

Save the brochure as **Friends Brochure.**

Working with Longer Publications

CONTENTS

OBJECTIVES

After you complete this lesson, you will be able to do the following:

- Create a newsletter using a Publisher template.
- Identify the parts of a newsletter and explain the purpose of each part.
- Define the four horizontal alignment options and understand how they are used.
- Explain the importance of white space in a publication.
- Edit articles to fit text boxes.
- Understand the sources of clip art and other graphics, including the Microsoft Clip Organizer and Design Gallery Live.
- Identify the buttons on the Picture toolbar.
- Crop and enlarge graphics using the tools on the Picture toolbar.

Although postcards and brochures, like the ones you created in Lessons 1 and 2, are ideal for many purposes, their very size limits the amount of information they can provide. When you need to include more information than you can fit on a postcard or brochure, a **newsletter** is often the answer. Newsletters are normally at least two pages long, but the final size will vary depending on the amount of information you need to provide. Business newsletters are frequently created to circulate announcements and other information to a company's own employees, but they may also be designed for distribution to customers, shareholders, and other people outside the company.

PARTS OF A NEWSLETTER

The title of a newsletter is called a *masthead.* The masthead is normally located at the top of the front page of the newsletter and often has a different font from the rest of the newsletter. Most newsletters also have a *dateline,* which is a line of text that gives the date and/or the volume and issue number of the newsletter. The dateline may also include the company's slogan.

When a newsletter is four pages or longer, a *table of contents,* or **TOC,** is often inserted on the front page. The table of contents lists the titles of the articles on the other pages of the newsletter, and thus provides an outline of the newsletter. The table of contents includes the page numbers on which the articles are located and serves as an index to help locate the articles on the other pages. Although it appears on the first page of the newsletter, it is often the last element to be completed.

In a longer newsletter, special *points of interest* may also be highlighted on the front page of the newsletter. These points of interest are normally arranged as a bulleted list and summarize key points or information not apparent from the table of contents.

To draw attention to a particular article in a newsletter, special text boxes, called *pull quotes* or *callouts,* are sometimes inserted within the text of the article or next to it. Pull quote boxes contain phrases taken directly from the text of the article. The phrases that are selected for pull quotes should give your readers a better idea about the information contained in the article and should make them want to read further. Pull quotes usually have a larger font size than the text of the articles and may also be bold or italic. Borders or fill colors can also be used to add emphasis to pull quote boxes.

Part of the back page of a newsletter is often reserved as a *mailing panel.* The return address of the business or organization is normally included on this panel, along with sufficient space for mailing labels. Other contact information, such as phone numbers and e-mail addresses, may also be included on this panel. If the business or organization has a bulk-mailing permit, the permit information must be included in a box in the upper right corner of this panel. Such permits allow businesses and organizations to send large mailings at a reduced rate. The U.S. Postal Service has specific requirements for the placement of information and labels on mailing panels when bulk mailing permits are used. If you are planning to use a bulk-mailing permit, contact your local post office to find out about the current requirements before designing a mailing panel.

Of course, most of the text in a newsletter consists of *articles* or stories. Although these articles can be typed directly into Publisher frames, it is often easier to create articles and any other long blocks of text in Microsoft Word. The Word files can then be imported into Publisher, using the steps you learned in Lesson 2. Creating articles in Microsoft Word has several advantages. Working in Word allows you to concentrate on the content of the articles, without being distracted by formatting and layout issues. Once the articles are imported into Publisher, layout and formatting can then be addressed. Microsoft Word also provides grammar checking, in addition to spell checking, which aids in proofreading your articles.

ARRANGEMENT OF TEXT IN A NEWSLETTER

The text in a newsletter is usually arranged in *columns* like a newspaper. Columns help you to arrange text easily, and they are often easier to read than long lines of text. The columns in a newsletter can be separated by vertical lines or by white space.

Horizontal Alignment

The *horizontal alignment* of the text—how the text lines up with the left and right margins—is an important consideration. When text is arranged in columns, as it is in most newsletters, the alignment is normally either *left aligned* or *justified*. **Left aligned** text means that every line begins at the same horizontal position on the left, making the left margin perfectly even. Text may also be aligned so that *both* margins are perfectly even. This alignment is called *justified.* Although justified text creates a neater right margin than left aligned text, it must be used carefully. In order to *justify* the text (make both margins even), Publisher must increase the spacing between the letters and words within a column, which could make the text less attractive and more difficult to read. Justified text also has a more formal look than left aligned text.

The other kinds of alignment are rarely used for column-formatted text because they are more difficult for the eye to read. Text that is *right aligned* contains lines that end at the same position on the right. The left margin appears jagged. You may see captions in a publication that are right aligned with the photo. Text may also be *center aligned,* or centered. With this alignment, short lines of text are placed an equal distance from the left and right margins. Although center alignment is not used for text in columns, it may be used for pull quotes. The Formatting toolbar provides all of these alignment options.

Line and Paragraph Spacing

Line spacing—the amount of white space between text lines—is another formatting consideration. Newsletters frequently use single spacing, which means that no extra white space appears between the lines of text. To provide a more open feel, some newsletters use 1.5 line spacing, which places one-half a blank line between each line of text. Line spacing can be changed on the Format menu. You may also add additional space above and below paragraphs. This is called *paragraph spacing.*

Increasing line spacing and adding paragraph spacing increases the amount of *white space* on a page. Having sufficient white space in a publication is important because it provides contrast and makes a publication easier to read. In addition to changing line spacing and paragraph spacing, you can also increase white space by enlarging margins and using left aligned text rather than justified text. In order to have enough white space on a page, it may even be necessary to delete text or move it to another page. Readers often ignore or skim over pages that are too crowded.

Using a Template to Create a Newsletter

In this activity you will begin to create a newsletter for Anderson Pet Mall. You will select the template that is closest to the final look that you want for the newsletter.

 During this activity, you will be inserting text from the Publisher Data CD. Before beginning this activity, insert the Publisher Data CD into your CD-ROM drive, if it is not already there.

1. Under By Publication Type in the New Publication task pane, click **Newsletters.**

2. In the Publication Gallery, click the picture for the **Axis Newsletter.** (See Figure 3.1.)

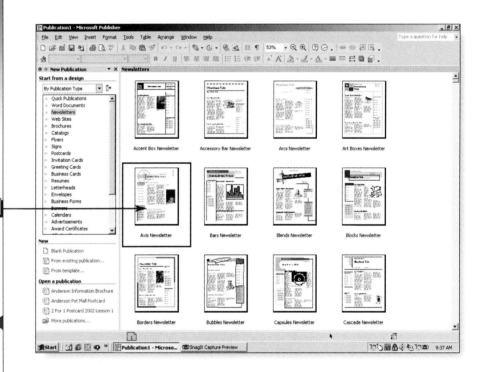

Axis Newsletter

Figure 3.1
Publication Gallery with
Axis Newsletter selected

Page 1 of the template for the Axis Newsletter appears, and the task pane changes to the Newsletter Options task pane, as shown in Figure 3.2.

 *When selecting a template, focus on the design of the elements rather than the colors of the elements. You can easily change a newsletter's color scheme.*

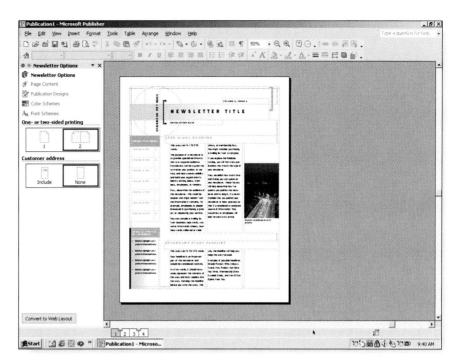

Figure 3.2
Newsletter Options pane and
Axis Newsletter template

The personal information for Anderson Pet Mall should be automatically inserted into the newsletter if the Primary Business set has not been changed since it was created in Lesson 1. If the personal information for Anderson Pet Mall is not inserted, edit the Primary Business set, following the steps under Creating a Personal Information Set in Lesson 1. Press Update to save this information and insert it into your publication.

3. Click the down arrow next to the Zoom box in the Standard toolbar and select 100%.

4. Scroll to the top of page 1 until the masthead (NEWSLETTER TITLE) appears.

5. Click on NEWSLETTER TITLE and type PET PERIODICAL.

You will notice that the dateline on this template is split into two parts, with the volume and issue number above the masthead and the date of the issue below the masthead. Because this is the first issue of Pet Periodical, and because the default text is VOLUME 1, ISSUE 1, the portion of the dateline above the masthead does not need to be changed. However, the portion of the dateline below the masthead (NEWSLETTER DATE) should be changed.

6. Click on NEWSLETTER DATE and type JANUARY 20, 2002.

7. Save your newsletter using the file name Pet Periodical 1-1.

The masthead and dateline should now resemble Figure 3.3. You will now insert articles that were created in Microsoft Word into your newsletter.

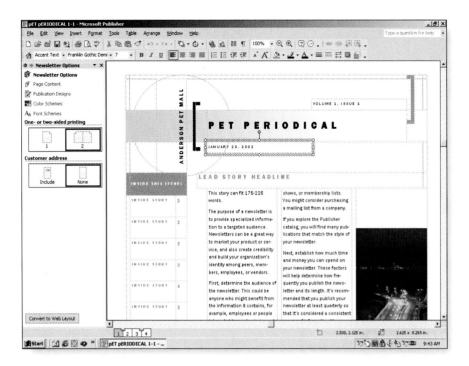

Figure 3.3
Revised masthead and dateline
for PET PERIODICAL

Inserting Word Files into a Newsletter

In this activity you will review the steps for importing text files that you learned in Lesson 2, as you build the main text of your newsletter.

1. Click on the first story box (beginning **This story can fit 175–225 words**.)

2. Right-click, point to Change Text and then click Text File….

3. In the Insert Text dialog box, locate the drive that contains the Publisher Data CD and click on it.

4. Click on the Lesson 03 folder and click on the file named First issue of Pet Periodical and click OK.

Text from the Publisher Data CD is inserted in place of the default text as shown in Figure 3.4.

Often several people contribute articles to a newsletter. Since most people are familiar with word processing programs such as Microsoft Word, you can easily gather files from various writers to incorporate into the newsletter. You may want to give the article writers target word counts for their articles.

Figure 3.4
Inserting text for lead article

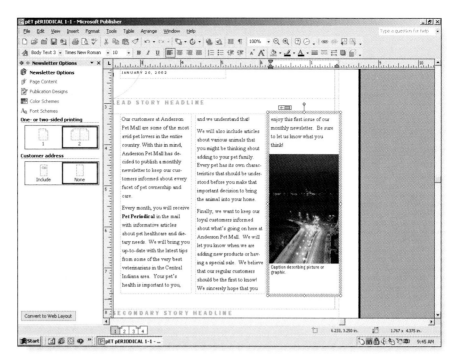

Figure 3.4
Inserting text for lead article

5. Scroll to the next story box on this page and click on the text beginning: **This story can fit 75–125 words.**

6. Repeat steps 2 and 3 above.

7. Click on the file named CanineChow and click OK. The results are shown in Figure 3.5.

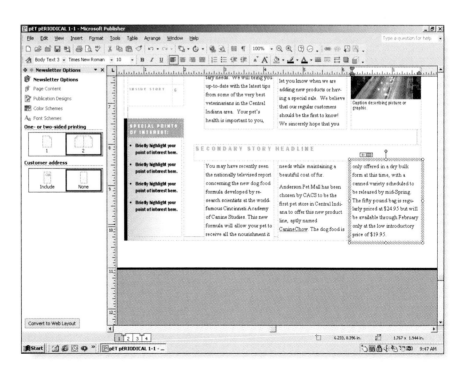

Figure 3.5
Inserting text for
Canine Chow article

8. Save your newsletter and click page 2 .

The icons for page 2 and page 3 are both highlighted, as shown in Figure 3.6, because this is a *two-page spread*. A two-page spread allows you to work with two facing pages at the same time. This can be useful if you wish to place a graphic across the inside margins of a publication, so that part of the graphic is on the left page and part is on the right page. (You will learn how to do this in Lesson 4.) If you do not need to work with both pages at the same time, however, it can be easier to navigate within each page if the two pages are displayed separately.

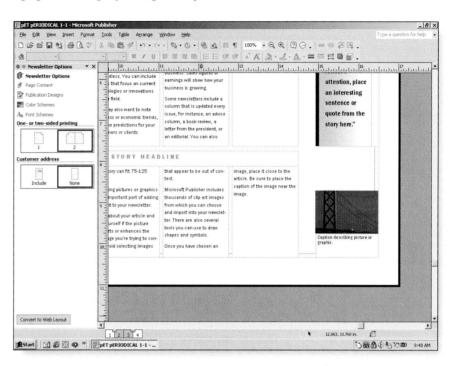

9. To work with one page at a time, click Two-Page Spread on the View menu. Because Two-Page Spread was already selected (has a check mark) as shown in Figure 3.7, clicking it will deselect it.

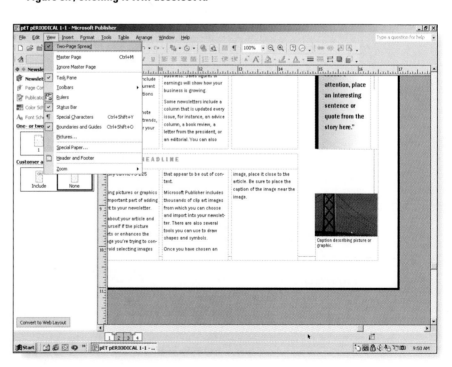

10. Scroll to the top of page 2.

As you can see in Figure 3.8, the title of the newsletter, PET PERIODICAL, and the page number have been inserted automatically.

Figure 3.8
Page 2 of newsletter with
masthead and page number
automatically included

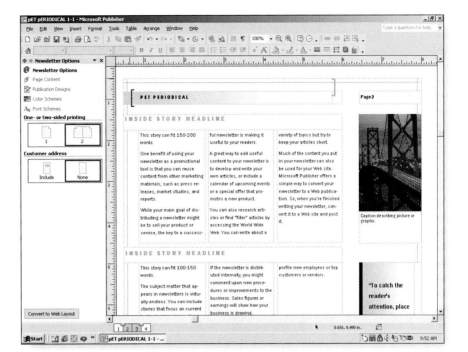

11. Using the steps for importing text files that you have just reviewed, replace the default text in each of the story boxes on page 2 with the following Word files on the Publisher Data CD:

Replace the first story box on page 2 (beginning This story can fit 150–200 words) with the Word file named Indiana state bird.

Replace the second story box on page 2 (beginning This story can fit 100–150 words) with the Word file named Employee of the month.

Replace the last story box on page 2 (beginning This story can fit 75–125 words) with the Word file named Bichon Frise.

Page 2 should now look like Figure 3.9.

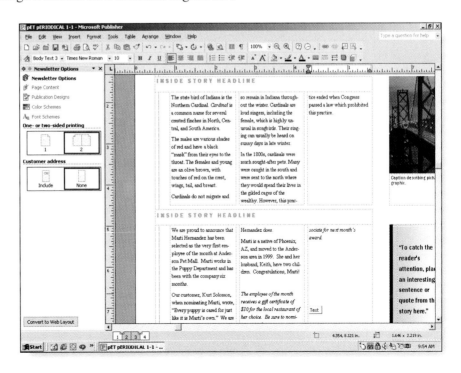

Figure 3.9
Completed page 2

12. Save your newsletter and click **page 3** 📄.

13. Replace the default text in each of the story boxes on this page with the following Word files on the Publisher Data CD:

Replace the first story box on page 3 (beginning This story can fit 150–200 words) with the Word file named Piranha.

Replace the second story box on page 3 (beginning This story can fit 100–150 words) with the Word file named Free Delivery in Madison County.

Replace the last story box on page 3 (beginning This story can fit 75–125 words) with the Word file named Cats are pets.

Page 3 should now look like Figure 3.10.

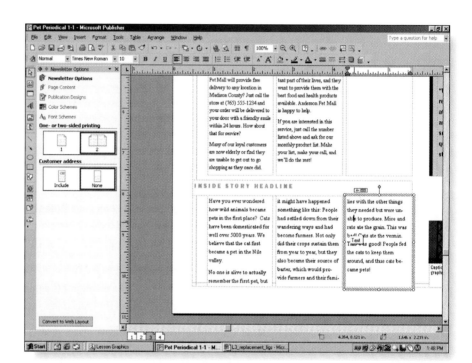

Figure 3.10
Completed page 3

14. Save your newsletter and click **page 4** 📄.

The top half of this page is designed to be the mailing panel. Anderson Pet Mall's name, address, logo, and contact information have been inserted automatically from the Personal Information Set as shown in Figure 3.11. You will make some changes to this part of the newsletter later in this lesson.

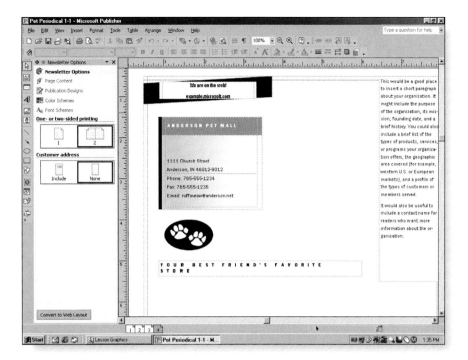

Figure 3.11
Anderson Pet Mall information
automatically entered on
page 4 of newsletter

15. Scroll to the story box at the bottom of this page (beginning This story can fit 175–225 words) and replace the default text with the Word file named Overweight pets on the Publisher Data CD.

Page 4 should now look like Figure 3.12.

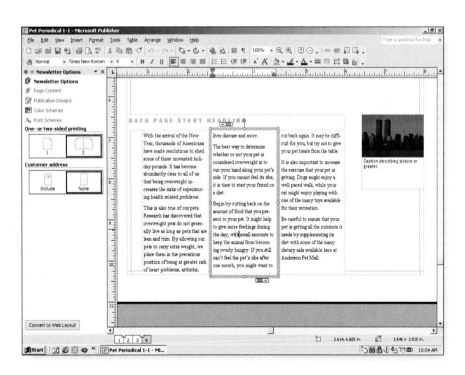

Figure 3.12
Page 4 with Overweight Pets article

16. Save your newsletter.

All of the articles for your newsletter have now been inserted.

Editing Text to Fit Text Boxes

Although all of the articles that you just inserted were created in Microsoft Word using font size 10, the Publisher template has reduced the font size for some of the articles to font size 9. As you will recall from Lesson 2, the font size of the main text (also called *body text*) should be consistent throughout a publication. In the next few steps, you will change the font size of the text in some of the story boxes so that all of the body text is in the same font size (10).

1. Click page 2.

2. Scroll to the first story box (beginning The state bird of Indiana . . .) and click on it.

3. Press Ctrl + A to select the entire story box.

4. Click the down arrow next to the font size box on the Formatting toolbar and select 10. (See Figure 3.13.)

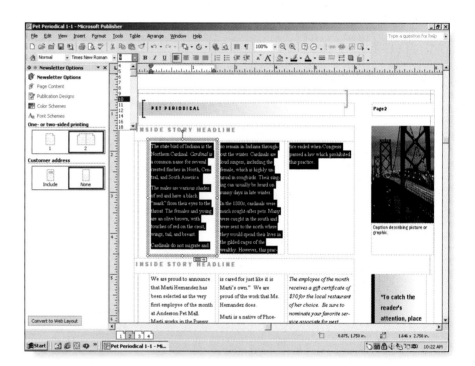

Figure 3.13
Changing the size of the text

5. Scroll to the second story box on page 2 (beginning We are proud to announce . . .) and click on it.

6. Repeat steps 3 and 4 to change the font size to 10.

 Because the third story box on this page is already in font size 10, it does not need to be changed.

7. Click page 3.

8. Scroll to the first story box on this page (beginning Piranha!) and click on it.

9. Repeat steps 3 and 4 to change the font size to 10.

10. Scroll to the second story box on this page (beginning Did you know . . .) and click on it.

11. Repeat steps 3 and 4 to change the font size to 10.

12. Scroll to the third story box on this page (beginning Have you ever wondered . . .) and click on it.

13. Repeat steps 3 and 4 to change the font size to 10.

14. Click page 4 [4].

15. Scroll to the story box at the bottom of this page (beginning With the arrival of the New Year . . .) and click on it.

16. Repeat steps 3 and 4 to change the font size to 10.

17. Save your newsletter.

As you will notice, increasing the font size to 10 has caused the text to exceed the limits of the story box. Although it might be tempting to decrease the font size to make the text fit, consistency requires that the font size stay at 10. A better option is to edit (reduce) the text to fit the story box.

18. With the text for the Overweight pets article highlighted, click Edit Story in Microsoft Word on the Edit menu. (See Figure 3.14.)

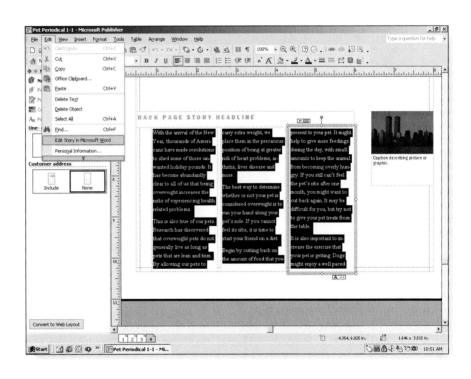

This launches Microsoft Word, as shown in Figure 3.15. You can then edit the text as a Word document.

Publisher BASICS

Editing Stories in Microsoft Word

1. Click on the story box.

2. On the Edit menu, click Edit Story in Microsoft Word.

3. Edit the text within Microsoft Word.

4. On the File menu, click Close & Return to [publication name].

Figure 3.14
Selecting Edit Story in Microsoft Word from the Edit menu

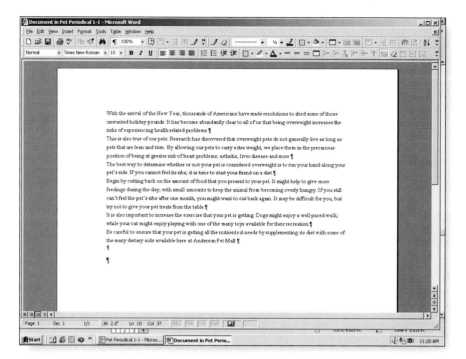

Figure 3.15
Overweight pets article
in Microsoft Word

19. Edit the article to fit the story box by deleting the sentence beginning: Research has discovered . . . and the paragraph beginning: It is also important to increase the exercise that your pet is getting . . . (Be sure to delete any blank lines between paragraphs.)

20. Click **Close & Return to Pet Periodical 1-1** on the File menu. (See Figure 3.16.)

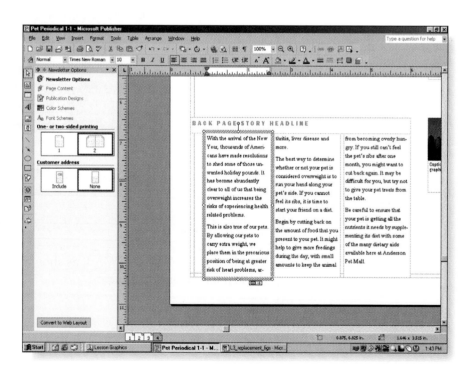

Figure 3.16
Closing the Word document and
returning to Publisher

The text should now fit the story box. If it does not, you will need to do some additional editing.

21. Save your newsletter.

You may have noticed that the second article on page 3 does not fill its story box, leaving excess white space at the end of the article. Although sufficient white space is important in a newsletter, large blocks of white space can make a newsletter look unfinished. You can view these types of spaces as opportunities to add graphics, pull quotes, or even more text to an article. In the next few steps, you will add extra text to an article that does not fill its story box.

22. **Click on page 3** ⬚.

23. **Click on the second story box on this page (beginning Did you know that Anderson Pet Mall . . .), and then click Edit Story in Microsoft Word on the Edit menu.**

Within Microsoft Word, make the following edits to the text:

24. **At the end of the first sentence, press** `Enter⏎` **to split the paragraph into two paragraphs. (Be sure to delete any extra spaces at the end of the sentence.)**

25. **At the end of the sentence Anderson Pet Mall is happy to help press** `Enter⏎` **to create a new paragraph, and type the following sentences:**

Others find that transporting heavy bags of feed to and from their vehicles is more than they can handle. Our delivery staff of young people is ready and willing to carry your load.

26. **Click Close & Return to Pet Periodical 1-1 on the File menu.**

The text should now fill most of the story box.

27. **Save your newsletter.**

Creating Headlines and Tables of Contents

Each article in a newsletter needs a *headline.* A well-written headline should get your readers' attention and also give them a good idea about the subject of the article. Publisher's templates provide default headlines that need to be changed to reflect the contents of each article. These headlines, or parts of them, can then be used to create a table of contents on the front page of the newsletter. In the following steps, you will change the default headlines in your newsletter to more accurately represent the subject of each article. You will then create a table of contents based on these headings.

1. **Click on page 1** ⬚.

2. **Scroll to the first headline (LEAD STORY HEADLINE) and click on it.**

3. **Type** WELCOME TO THE FIRST ISSUE OF PET PERIODICAL. **(See Figure 3.17.)**

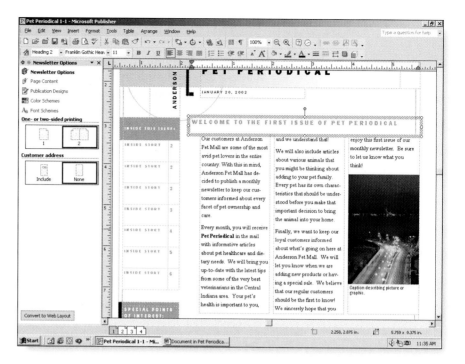

4. Scroll to the second headline (**SECONDARY STORY HEADLINE**) and click on it.

5. Type ANDERSON PET MALL NOW CARRIES CANINECHOW. **(See Figure 3.18.)**

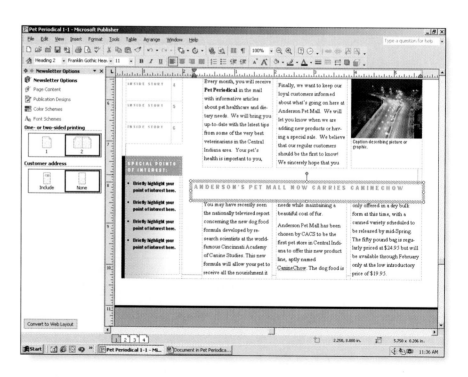

6. Click on **page 2** ⬚.

7. Scroll to the top of this page and click on the first **INSIDE STORY HEADLINE**.

8. Type INDIANA STATE BIRD: THE CARDINAL.

9. Scroll to the second **INSIDE STORY HEADLINE** on this page and click on it.

10. Type MARTI HERNANDEZ IS OUR EMPLOYEE OF THE MONTH.

11. Scroll to the third **INSIDE STORY HEADLINE** on this page and click on it.

12. Type DOG OF THE MONTH: BICHON FRISE.

13. Click on page 3 .

14. Scroll to the top of this page and click on the first **INSIDE STORY HEADLINE**.

15. Type PIRANHA!

Note   *Be sure to include the exclamation point with the piranha headline.*

16. Scroll to the second **INSIDE STORY HEADLINE** on this page and click on it.

17. Type FREE DELIVERY AVAILABLE IN MADISON COUNTY!

18. Scroll to the third **INSIDE STORY HEADLINE** on this page and click on it.

19. Type THE HISTORY OF CATS: CATS BECOME PETS.

20. Click on page 4 .

21. Scroll to **BACK PAGE STORY HEADLINE** and click on it.

22. Type OVERWEIGHT PETS—TIME FOR A NEW YEAR'S DIET?

23. Save your newsletter.

All of the articles in your newsletter now have appropriate headings. In the next few steps, you will use these headings to create a table of contents.

24. Click on page 1 and scroll to the left side of this page.

Under the heading INSIDE THIS ISSUE, you will see seven default text lines that all begin INSIDE STORY, as shown in Figure 3.19.

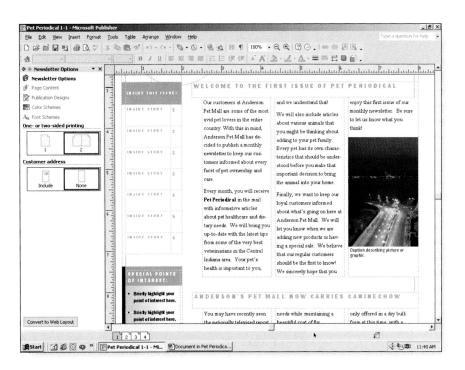

Figure 3.19
Default text in table of contents

25. Click on each of these default text lines and change them to read:

INDIANA STATE BIRD: THE CARDINAL
EMPLOYEE OF THE MONTH
DOG OF THE MONTH: BICHON FRISE
PIRANHA!
FREE DELIVERY IN MADISON COUNTY!
THE HISTORY OF CATS: CATS BECOME PETS
OVERWEIGHT PETS

26. Change the page numbers after these headlines to correspond to the correct page for the articles. For example, change the page number after OVERWEIGHT PETS to 4, as this article is on the fourth page. (See Figure 3.20.)

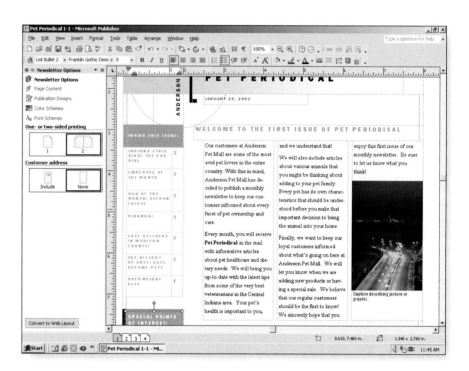

Figure 3.20
Inserting page numbers in
table of contents

27. Save your newsletter.

This template also contains a special points of interest box under the table of contents. This area of the newsletter can be used to draw attention to, or emphasize, key pieces of information. In the next few steps, you will change the default text in this box to emphasize information in the newsletter that specifically promotes Anderson Pet Mall.

28. Click on the text under SPECIAL POINTS OF INTEREST and change the default items to read:

Anderson Pet Mall begins a monthly newsletter.
CanineChow is now available.
We have Bichon Frise puppies just for you!
Free delivery is available in Madison County!

(**Be sure to press** Enter ← **between each item.**)

The special points of interest on the first page of your newsletter should now resemble Figure 3.21.

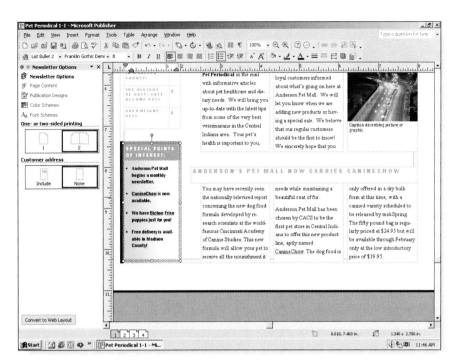

Figure 3.21
Special Points of Interest section

29. Save your newsletter.

ENHANCING A PUBLICATION USING GRAPHICS

You have now entered all of the main text for your newsletter, and you have added headlines, a table of contents, and special points of interest to draw your readers' attention to the articles in the newsletter. However, you may have a hard time getting your readers' attention with text alone. In such cases, you can add a *graphic* (also called an *object* or *image*) to a publication. A graphic is any element in a publication that is not text. Examples include pictures (clip art or a photograph) and objects made with lines, curves, or decorative text (called *WordArt*). There are many sources for pictures and other graphics. As you learned in Lesson 2, pictures can be inserted from CDs and disks. Publisher also allows you to access the *Microsoft Clip Organizer,* which includes professionally designed objects (pictures, photographs, sound, and video clips) from which you can choose. The pictures in the Clip Organizer are called *clip art,* or clips.

There are three different ways to access the Clip Organizer—through the Insert menu, through the Objects toolbar, or through the Change Picture submenu. To access the Clip Organizer through the Insert menu, point to Picture on this menu and then click Clip Art.... The task pane changes to the Insert Clip Art task pane, as shown in Figure 3.22. Clicking the Clip Organizer Frame button 🖾 on the Objects toolbar also opens this task pane, as does clicking Clip Art... on the Change Picture submenu. (This submenu, as you may recall from Lesson 2, is accessed by right-clicking on an existing picture in a publication.)

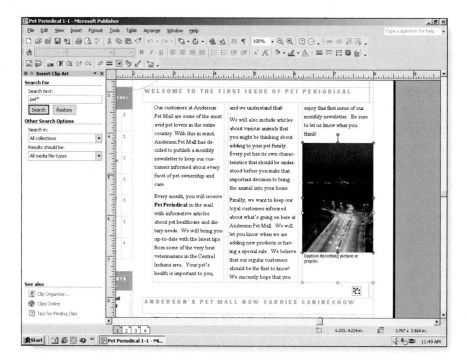

Figure 3.22 ◄

Insert Clip Art task pane

Once the Insert Clip Art task pane is displayed, you can search for clips by typing keywords in the Search text: box, or you can browse the Clip Organizer by clicking Clip Organizer . . . near the bottom of the task pane. Clips in the Clip Organizer are divided into three collections—My Collections, where you can create your own collection of clip art; Office Collections, which contains clips that are accessible to all of the Microsoft Office products; and Web Collections. Within Office Collections, clips are organized by subject categories such as Animals, Buildings, and Food as shown in Figure 3.23. The Media Gallery allows you to preview each clip before inserting it into your publication.

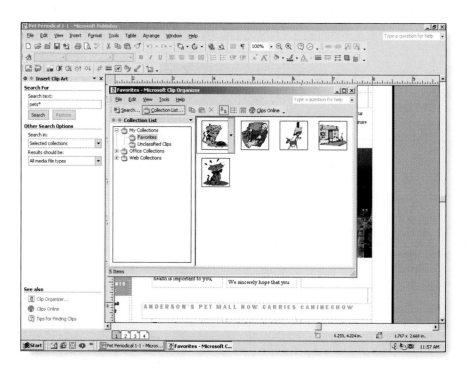

Figure 3.23 ◄

Office Collections clips organized by subject

You can use any Clip Organizer image in the publications you create, as long as you are not selling the publications that contain the image. Before you add any graphic to a publication, be sure to verify the legal restrictions for using it. If you are working in a computer lab, always secure permission from your instructor before you add a graphic to the Clip Organizer.

Publisher also gives you access to Microsoft's collection of clip art on the Web, called Design Gallery Live. You will learn more about importing graphics from the Web in the On the Web section at the end of this lesson.

Importing Graphics from the Clip Organizer

In this activity, you will learn how to search for, and then import, a picture from the Clip Organizer into your newsletter.

Another Way

- Press Ctrl + C to copy the picture from the Clip Organizer.

1. Go to page 1 and click twice on the graphic (a highway scene).

2. Right-click, point to Change Picture, and then click Clip Art....

3. Click Clip Organizer at the bottom of the Insert Clip Art task pane.

4. Scroll to find the magnifying glass over the paper as shown in Figure 3.24.

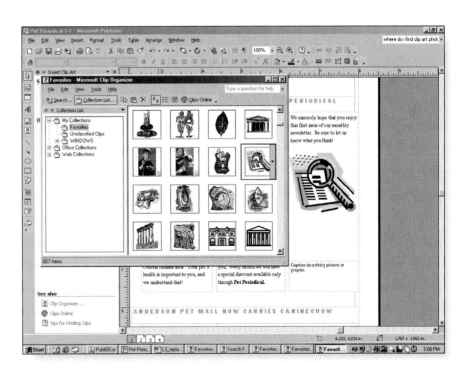

Figure 3.24
Magnifying glass clipart

If you cannot locate the picture that is in Figure 3.24, select a suitable substitute.

5. Right click on the picture and click Copy.

Ungrouping Objects

1. Click one of the objects that you wish to ungroup.

2. Click the Ungroup Objects icon.

3. Click the other object that you wish to ungroup.

6. **Close the Clip Organizer.**

7. **Press** `Ctrl` **+ V to Paste the magnifying glass clipart.**

8. **Click** Ungroup Objects 🖵.

This icon indicates that the caption and picture are grouped—connected as one object. When items are grouped, any actions that you make will affect both objects.

9. **Double-click on the text box containing the caption.**

10. **Press** `Delete`.

The picture is inserted in place of the default graphic and the caption is removed, as shown in Figure 3.25.

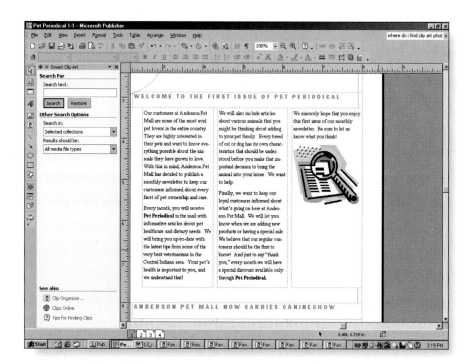

Figure 3.25
Default graphic replaced with new photograph

11. **Save the newsletter.**

12. **Click on the magnifying glass clipart.**

13. **Move the clipart to align with the bottom of the text frame.**

14. **Resize the clipart by dragging the upper left resize handle up and to the left to eliminate the extra white space.**

The text in the second column will wrap around the graphic.

15. **Save the newsletter.**

Publisher Basics

1. Click twice on the graphic to be changed.

2. Right-click.

3. Point to Change Picture and then click From File....

4. Locate the file that contains the desired graphic and click on it.

5. Click the Insert button.

Importing Graphics from a CD

In this activity, you will review the steps for importing graphics into a template that you learned in Lesson 2.

1. Go to page 2 and click twice on the graphic (a bridge scene).

2. Right-click, point to Change Picture, and then click From File....

3. In the Insert Picture dialog box, locate the drive that contains the Publisher Data CD and click on it.

4. Click on the file Cardinal and then click the Insert button.

A photograph of a cardinal is inserted in place of the bridge scene.

5. Repeat the steps above to replace each of the default graphics on pages 2 and 3, using the following information:

   Replace the skyline scene on page 2 with the graphic file named Bichon.

   Replace the highway scene on page 3 with the graphic file named Piranha.

   Replace the bridge scene on page 3 with the graphic file named Curious Cat.

6. Save your newsletter.

HANDS

Importing Graphics from the Web

The On the Web section at the end of this lesson (p. 126–127) provides an introduction to getting graphics from the Web, using Microsoft's Web site, Design Gallery Live. Read the information in that section and then complete the following steps to insert a clip from the Web in place of the default graphic on page 4.

1. Go to page 4 and click twice on the graphic (a skyline scene).

2. Right-click, point to Change Picture, and then click Clip Art....

3. On the Insert Clip Art task pane, click Clips Online.

The Internet Explorer window appears. If you are not already connected to the Web, Publisher connects you and then locates the Design Gallery Live Web site.

4. In the Search for: box, type fat cats.

The results of your search should include the cat shown in Figure 3.26.

Figure 3.26

Note

If you cannot locate this particular image, type cats *in the Search for: box and browse through the results until you locate any clip of an overweight cat.)*

5. Click the Download arrow under the selected clip.

When the downloading is completed, the Clip Organizer appears, with the downloaded clip in the preview window.

6. **Click the down arrow next to the downloaded clip.**

7. **On the drop-down menu, click** Copy.

8. **Click the** Close button ☒ **to close the Clip Organizer.**

9. **When Publisher asks if you would like your clips to remain on the clipboard after Clip Organizer shuts down, click** Yes.

10. **Close the Design Gallery Live window and disconnect from the Internet.**

Page 4 of Pet Periodical reappears.

11. **Click the** Paste button 📋.

The downloaded clip is inserted in place of the default graphic.

12. **Save the newsletter.**

USING GRAPHICS EFFECTIVELY

An inserted clip may be the wrong size or in the wrong place. Therefore, you must be able to resize, move, and align the image on the page. As you learned in Lesson 2, you can perform these tasks with move and resize handles. There are other tools in Publisher that allow you to manage images more precisely, however. These editing tools are found on the Picture toolbar. Using these tools you can, for example, change the *contrast* between light and dark, *crop* (cut off) unnecessary parts of the picture, and change the *text wrapping* (how text aligns and wraps in relation to the picture.)

To activate the Picture toolbar, point to Toolbars on the View menu and then click Picture. Once the toolbar is activated, clicking on a picture causes the toolbar to be displayed. If the toolbar is in your way, it can be dragged to a more convenient location.

Table 3.1 provides a summary of the tools on the Picture toolbar.

Another Way

- To activate the Picture toolbar, click on a picture, right-click and then click Show Picture Toolbar.

TABLE 3.1		THE PUBLISHER PICTURE TOOLBAR	
Button		**Name**	**Description**
	🖼	Insert Picture From File	Opens the Insert Picture dialog box, which allows you to insert a picture stored on a disk or drive.
	🖼	Insert Picture From Scanner or Camera	Allows you to insert a picture directly from a scanner or digital camera.
	🖼	Color	Displays a menu that allows you to change a picture to grayscale, black and white, or washout.
◑↑	◑↓	More/Less Contrast	Increases or Decreases the contrast between light and dark in a picture.
☼↑	☼↓	More/Less Brightness	Brightens or Darkens a picture.
	⌗	Crop	Changes the handles around a picture to crop handles so that you can crop (cut off) part of a picture.

Button	Name	Description
TABLE 3.1	THE PUBLISHER PICTURE TOOLBAR	*(continued)*

Button	Name	Description
	Line/Border Style	Gives you a choice of borders to put around a picture.
	Text Wrapping	Displays a menu that allows you to change the way text wraps around pictures.
	Format Picture	Opens the Format Picture dialog box, which allows you to make precise changes to a picture's size, color, and other characteristics.
	Set Transparent Color	Allows you to make a color transparent by clicking on the color in a picture.
	Reset Picture	Restores a picture to its original formatting.

For best results, use both methods to resize objects. If you want to change the size only slightly—an inch or less—drag the handles. If you need to make a bigger change, or need to be more precise, use the Format Picture dialog box.

You change the height or width of an object in the Format Picture dialog box. Format Picture is a button on the Picture toolbar. It is also an option on the Format menu. When you change the height and/or width of an object, you need to guard against distortion. If you make a clip wider, for example, without changing the height an equal amount, you change its height-width relationship, or *aspect.* Before you change either the height or width, select Lock the aspect ratio. With the lock on, Publisher will automatically respond to a change in one dimension by changing the other dimension proportionately. If you forget to lock the aspect ratio, or otherwise make a mistake in resizing, you can click the Reset Picture button on the Picture toolbar to restore the image to its original size.

You may want to add a *caption*—a short description, an explanation or a title—to a graphic. You can type a caption on a page just above, beside, or beneath a graphic or include it as part of the graphic. To add a caption to a graphic, you must create a text box (a special area reserved for typing) by clicking the Text Box button on the Objects toolbar. In templates, caption boxes are often provided along with the default pictures.

Editing and Formatting Graphics

In this activity you will make changes to some of the graphics that you have added to your newsletter.

1. Click page 2
2. Scroll to the bottom picture on the page (Bichon) and click on it.

The Ungroup Objects icon appears under the caption box as shown in Figure 3.27.

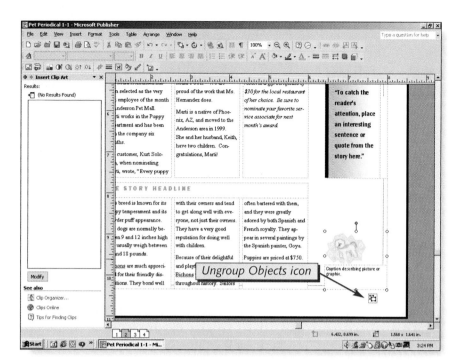

Figure 3.27
Ungroup Objects icon

3. **Click the** Ungroup Objects icon .

4. **Click the caption in the caption box attached to the picture.**

The Ungroup Objects icon disappears, indicating that the caption and picture are no longer grouped. The status bar shows that the width of the caption box is 1.568 inches. (See Figure 3.28.) Make a note of this width, because you will need to adjust the width of the picture to match the caption width.

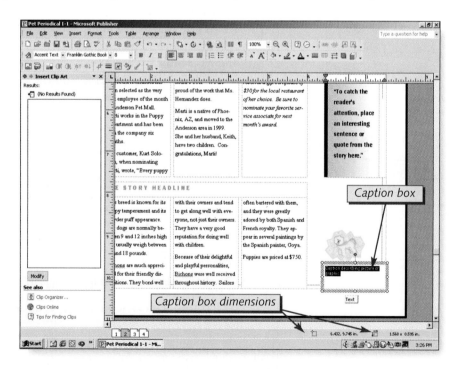

Figure 3.28
Width of caption box

5. **Click the picture of the Bichon. If the** Picture **toolbar does not appear, right-click, then click** Show Picture toolbar.

6. **Click the** Format Picture button **on the** Picture **toolbar.**

Publisher BASICS

Grouping Objects

1. Select (click) the first object to be grouped.

2. Press and hold the Shift key.

3. Click the second object to be grouped.

4. Click the Group Objects icon.

Changing the Width of a Picture

1. Select (click) the picture.

2. Click the Format Picture button on the Picture toolbar.

3. Click the Size tab.

4. Click the Lock aspect ratio box, if it is not already checked.

5. Click the Width box and type the desired width in inches.

6. Click OK.

The Format Picture dialog box appears as shown in Figure 3.29.

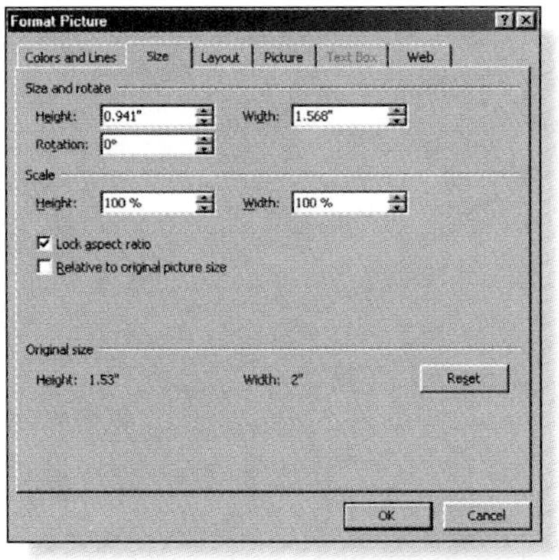

7. Click the Size tab. Make sure that Lock aspect ratio is checked.

8. Click the Width box, type 1.568, **and click OK.**

The picture is now the same width as the caption box, but increasing its size has caused it to overlap the caption box.

9. Move the picture of the Bichon so that it is just above the caption box, as shown in Figure 3.30.

10. With the picture still selected, press the Shift key ⬆ Shift and click the caption box.

The Group Objects icon appears as shown in Figure 3.30.

Figure 3.29
Format Picture dialog box

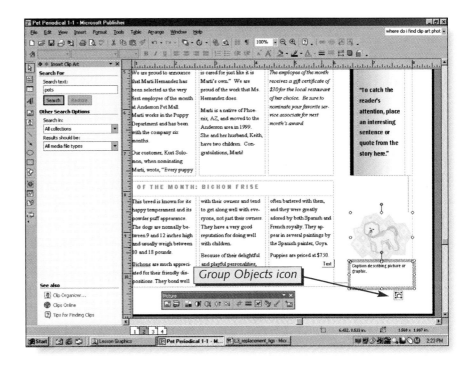

Figure 3.30
Group Objects icon

11. Click the Group Objects icon.

The picture and caption are now grouped again. Grouping captions and pictures allows them to be moved together as one object.

12. Click page 3 ⬛.

13. Scroll to the picture of the piranha and click on it.

You may notice that the picture does not fill the available space.

14. Click the Ungroup Objects icon and then click on the caption.

15. Click on the picture again and then the Format Picture button 🖼 on the Picture toolbar.

16. Click the Size tab. Make sure that Lock aspect ratio is checked.

17. Click the Height box, type 2.0", **and click OK.**

The picture is now 2" high, but it needs to be cropped to fit the available space.

18. **Click the Crop button** ⊞ **on the Picture toolbar.**

The handles around the picture change, as shown in Figure 3.31.

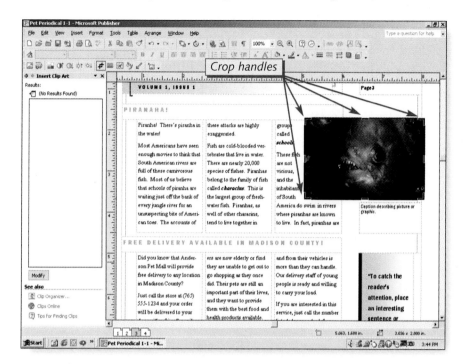

Figure 3.31
Crop piranha picture

19. **Click and hold the left crop handle and drag it to the edge of the piranha's mouth.**

20. **Move the picture so that its left edge is even with the left edge of the caption box. If there is any white space (gap) between the picture and caption box, move the picture down slightly to eliminate the gap.**

21. **Click and hold the right crop handle and drag it to make the picture the same width as the caption box, as shown in Figure 3.32.**

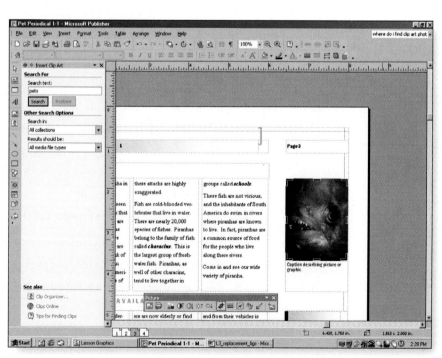

Figure 3.32
Resized and cropped piranha

22. Reconnect (group) the picture and caption frames following steps 9–11 above.

23. Enlarge and crop the picture of the cat on page 3 using the steps you just learned.

24. Save your newsletter.

Editing Captions and Adding Pull Quotes

As you are already aware, the caption boxes that are provided with templates contain default text that must be changed to correspond to the pictures. In the next activity, you will edit the text in the caption boxes and add pull quotes to some of the articles.

1. Click page 2 ⬚.

2. **Click on the caption under the cardinal and type** The state bird of Indiana is the Northern Cardinal. This beautiful bird does not migrate but remains in the area throughout the winter months.

3. **Click on the caption under the Bichon and type** The Bichon Frise is a friendly and well-mannered breed. They make adorable pets for children and seniors alike.

4. Click page 3 ⬚.

5. **Click on the caption under the piranha and type** Piranha are known as vicious meat-eating fish. This reputation is highly exaggerated. Anderson Pet Mall has a large selection of these fish.

6. **Click on the caption under the curious cat and type** Cats have been pets to human beings for over 5000 years. They were indispensable in keeping mice out of the grain!

7. Click page 4 ⬚.

8. **Click on the caption under the fat cat and type** Is your pet overweight? Now may be the time to enhance your animal's health with a timely diet.

You still need to add pull quotes to pages 2 and 3. These quotes will attract your readers' attention and encourage them to read more.

9. **Click on** page 2 ⬚.

10. **Click on the box to the right of the Employee of the Month article ("To catch the reader's attention . . .) and type** "Every puppy is cared for just like it is Marti's own."

11. **Press** ⬚Enter⬚, **type** Kurt Solomon, **press** ⬚Enter⬚ **again and type** Customer. **Select the words** Kurt Solomon **and** Customer, **and then click the** Align Right button ⬚ **on the Formatting toolbar.**

The words Kurt Solomon and Customer are now right-aligned, as shown in Figure 3.33.

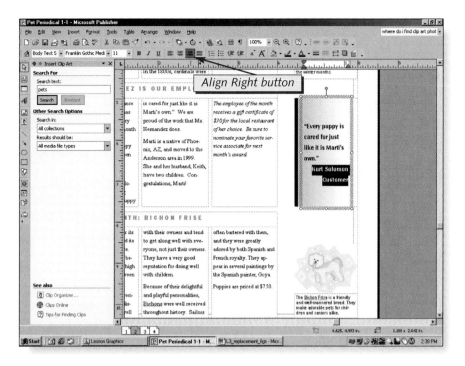

Figure 3.33
Right alignment of part of pull quote

14. **Click on** page 3 ⬚.

15. **Click on the box to the right of the Free Delivery in Madison County article ("To catch the reader's attention . . .) and type** Did you know that Anderson Pet Mall will provide free delivery to any location in Madison County?

16. **Save your newsletter.**

The captions and pull quotes now correspond to the pictures and articles in your newsletter.

Modifying the Mailing Panel

In this activity, you will make the final changes to your newsletter. You will modify the mailing panel and inspect this section of the newsletter to verify that it meets the United States Postal Service's requirements for bulk mailings.

1. **Click** page 4 ⬚.

Scroll to the top of the page until the mailing panel information appears.

2. **On the** Newsletter Options **task pane, click** Include **under** Customer Address.

A mailing address box appears, and the default text box that was on the right side disappears.

There are three different ways that the mailing address box on a newsletter can be used:

◼ The box can be used as a space holder for a mailing label, indicating where the mailing label is to be placed. When a newsletter is duplicated at a commercial print shop, this is normally how the address box would be used.

- A real name and address can be typed directly into this box. When the newsletter is printed, the name and address will print along with the rest of the text of the newsletter. Obviously, this would mean typing a new name and address for each copy of the newsletter, so this method would only be used if a few copies were being printed.

- Publisher allows you to merge names and addresses from a data file. As each copy is printed, Publisher inserts a different name and address. As more businesses and organizations acquire high-speed printers, more newsletters will be printed this way. You will learn more about merging names and addresses in Lesson 6.

3. **Click on the slogan Your Best Friend's Favorite Store and resize its frame so that the entire slogan fits within the frame as shown in Figure 3.34.**

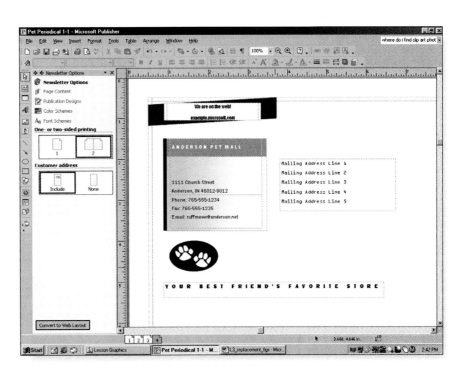

Figure 3.34
Mailing panel with resized slogan frame

The U.S. Postal Service's requirements for bulk mailings indicate that any printing or other markings that are not part of the delivery address should be positioned above the delivery address lines in order for the address to be OCR processed. (OCR stands for Optical Character Reader, which is an automated mail sorting machine that "reads" the address information on a mailpiece and sprays a barcode on the piece.) In the next few steps, you will modify the mailing panel so that it is OCR compatible.

4. **Delete the We are on the web! object at the top of the page.**

5. **Move the Anderson Pet Mall logo so that it is just above the words Anderson Pet Mall in the return address area.**

6. **Move the slogan (Your Best Friend's Favorite Store) so that it is to the right of the Anderson Pet Mall logo.**

7. **Move the mailing address block straight down until the top address line is lower than the bottom of the return address block, as shown in Figure 3.35.**

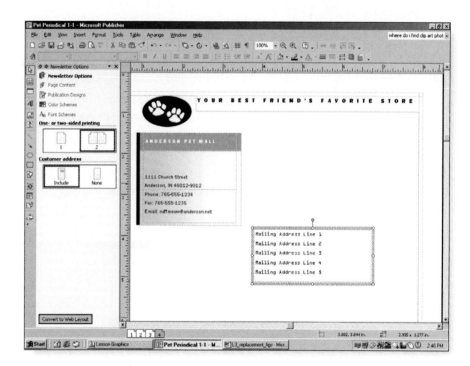

Figure 3.35
Modified mailing address block

> *Note*   The mailing address block should be only slightly lower than the return address block. When the newsletter is folded, there should be at least ⅝" of white space under the mailing address (so that there is sufficient space for a barcode to be sprayed).

8. Save the newsletter.

> *Note*   In Lesson 6, you will learn how to use mail merge to automatically insert customers' names and addresses into publications such as newsletters. Since Anderson Pet Mall is planning for Pet Periodical to be a monthly newsletter, mail merge will save significant time.

Test your knowledge by matching the terms on the left with the definitions on the right. See Appendix C to check your answers.

TERMS

_____ **1.** Horizontal alignment

_____ **2.** Line spacing

_____ **3.** Clip

_____ **4.** Aspect

_____ **5.** Caption

DEFINITIONS

a. the height-width relationship of an object

b. a picture in the Microsoft Clip Organizer

c. a short description or title of a graphic

d. the amount of white space between text lines

e. how text lines up with the left and right margins

GETTING GRAPHICS FROM THE WEB

As you learned earlier in this lesson, you can import graphics, not only from CDs and disks, but also from the Web. As a Publisher user, you have access to an extensive online collection of clip art, photographs, sound clips, and animation. This collection, called the Design Gallery Live, is a Web site that Microsoft provides for its users and updates regularly.

 *There are some restrictions on the use of the clips found on this site. Read the Terms of Use (a link at the bottom of the Design Gallery Live home page) to make sure that you understand and comply with these restrictions.*

In the following activity, you will search the Design Gallery Live for a piece of clip art and insert it into a blank publication.

1. On the New Publication task pane, click Blank Publication.

The task pane disappears, and a new, blank publication is displayed.

2. Click Clip Organizer Frame on the Objects toolbar.

The Insert Clip Art task pane appears.

3. Click Clips Online near the bottom of the task pane.

The Internet Explorer window appears. If you are not already connected to the Web, Publisher connects you and then locates the Design Gallery Live Web site.

 *If this is the first time you have accessed this Web site, an end-user license agreement appears, which you must read and accept before accessing the clip art.*

5. In the Search for: box on the left side of the Web site, type dogs and then click Go.

The results of your search appear. As you can see, there are many clips, including photos, clip art, sounds, and motion, that matched your search.

6. To narrow your search, so that only photos of dogs are included, click the down arrow next to the Results should be: box.

The four types of clips (clip art, photos, sounds, and motion) are displayed.

7. Select Photos and click Go.

Only photos of dogs are now included in your search results. You could also narrow your search by typing the name of a particular breed of dog, or by limiting the search to a certain collection. (The collections available on this Web site can be viewed by clicking the down arrow next to the Search in: box.)

8. Choose a clip that you wish to download. Below each clip is the size of the clip, a Download arrow, and a check box.

9. Click the **Download arrow** to download the clip.

A progress dialog box is displayed as the clip is downloaded.

Note *If you want to download more than one clip at a time, click the check box under each clip you wish to download. The clips are added to a "Selection Basket." After all of your selections are made, clicking the Selection Basket link allows you to download the selections as a group.*

When the downloading is completed, the Clip Organizer appears, with the downloaded clip in the preview window.

10. Click the down arrow next to the downloaded clip.

A drop-down menu appears.

11. Click **Copy.**

Clicking Copy places the clip on the Publisher clipboard. The Publisher clipboard works like the clipboard in all Windows-based software, allowing items to be copied and pasted from one location to another.

12. Close the Clip Organizer by clicking the **Close button** ☒.

Publisher responds: You currently have one or more clips on the clipboard. Would you like these to remain on the clipboard after Clip Organizer shuts down?

13. Click **Yes.**

14. Close the Design Gallery Live window and disconnect from the Internet, if necessary.

The blank publication reappears.

15. Click the **Paste button** 📋 on the **Standard toolbar.**

The downloaded clip is inserted in the blank publication window and can be moved and resized as needed.

It is also possible to get graphics from other sites on the Web. For example, Yahoo has a picture gallery that contains photos that can be downloaded. However, there are restrictions on the use of these photos. Always read the restrictions before using a graphic from the Web in one of your publications.

Lesson Summary & Exercises

SUMMARY

Newsletters allow you to provide more information than you can fit on smaller publications like post-cards and brochures. Because newsletters contain so much text, it is often preferable to create the articles for newsletters in a word processing program, such as Microsoft Word. The articles can then be imported into Publisher frames (text boxes), where formatting and layout issues can be addressed. When articles do not properly fit the text boxes, they can be edited in either Word or Publisher. Pull-quotes and graphics can be used to fill extra space in a newsletter and to draw attention to articles. Special tools in Publisher allow you to crop and enlarge graphics to fit the available space.

Now that you have completed this lesson, you should be able to do the following:

- Identify the parts of a newsletter and explain the purpose of each part.
- Understand the advantages of creating text in Microsoft Word.
- Import articles that were created in Microsoft Word and edit the articles to fit text boxes.
- Explain the importance of white space and consistency in font size in newsletters.
- Create headlines and tables of contents for newsletters.
- Use special points of interest boxes to emphasize key pieces of information in a newsletter.
- Import clip art and other graphics from various sources, including CDs, the Microsoft Clip Organizer, and the Design Gallery Live.
- Identify the buttons on the Picture toolbar.
- Use tools on the Picture toolbar to crop and enlarge graphics.

CONCEPTS REVIEW

1 TRUE/FALSE

Circle T if the statement is true or F if the statement is false.

T F **1.** The U.S. Postal Service has requirements for the placement of information on mailing panels when bulk mailing permits are used.

T F **2.** It is often easier to create articles and longer amounts of text in Microsoft Word.

T F **3.** Before you add any graphic to a publication, be sure to verify the legal restrictions for using it.

T F **4.** The alignment options are found on the Objects toolbar.

T F **5.** You should reduce the amount of white space in a publication to make room for as much text as possible.

T F **6.** The font size of body text should be consistent throughout a publication.

T F **7.** Grouping captions and pictures allows them to be moved together.

T F **8.** You can use any Clip Organizer image in your publications regardless of what you will be doing with the publications.

T F **9.** A well-written headline should get your readers' attention and give them a good idea about the subject of an article.

T F **10.** Always read the restrictions before using a graphic from the Web in one of your publications.

2 MATCHING

Match each of the terms on the left with the definitions on the right.

TERMS DEFINITIONS

1. centered   **a.** the title of a newsletter

2. crop   **b.** a line of text that gives the date and/or volume and issue number of a newsletter

3. dateline   **c.** a phrase taken directly from the text of an article

4. graphic   **d.** text with the left margin perfectly even

5. grouped   **e.** text with both margins perfectly even

6. justified   **f.** short lines of text placed an equal distance from the left and right margins

7. left aligned   **g.** additional space above and below paragraphs

8. masthead   **h.** any element in a publication that is not text

9. paragraph spacing   **i.** cut off unnecessary parts of a picture

10. pull quote   **j.** connected as one object

3 COMPLETION

Fill in the missing word or phrase for each of the following statements.

1. The _____ lists the titles of the articles on the other pages of a newsletter.

2. Part of the back page of a newsletter is often reserved as a _____.

3. The text is a newsletter is usually arranged in _____ like a newspaper.

4. The Microsoft _____ includes professionally designed objects from which you can choose.

5. When you click Clip Art... under Picture on the Insert menu, the _____ task pane appears.

6. When text is arranged in columns, the alignment is normally either _____ or _____ .

7. The cropping tool is located on the _____ toolbar.

8. You change the height or width of an object in the _____ dialog box.

9. If you make a mistake in resizing a picture, you restore the picture to its original size by clicking the _____ button.

10. To add a caption to a graphic, you must first create a _____ .

4 SHORT ANSWER

1. What are the advantages of creating text in Microsoft Word?
2. List five ways to increase white space in a publication.
3. How do you insert a Word file into a template?
4. What happens when you click Edit Story in Microsoft Word on the Edit menu?
5. List three different ways to access the Clip Organizer.
6. What are the two different ways to resize objects?
7. What are the three collections in the Clip Organizer and what do they contain?
8. How are clips organized under Office Collections in the Clip Organizer?
9. What does the Ungroup Objects icon indicate?
10. How do you download a clip from the Design Gallery Live? How do you download more than one clip at a time?

5 IDENTIFICATION

Identify the masthead, dateline, table of contents, left aligned button, centered button, justified button, headline of an article.

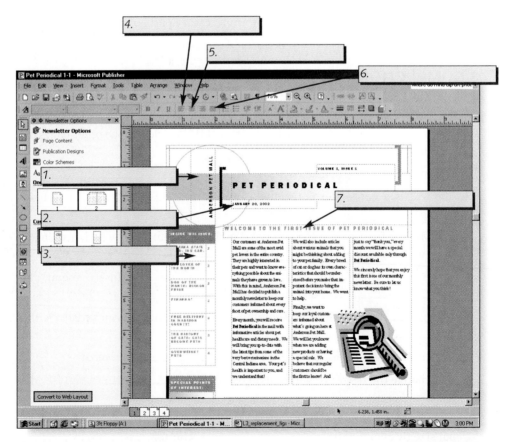

Figure 3.36

Lesson Summary & Exercises

SKILLS REVIEW

Complete each of the Skills Review activities in sequential order to review your skills as you create a two-page newsletter.

1 Open a newsletter template, change the personal information set, and create a masthead and dateline

1. Open the **Cascade newsletter template** from the Publication Gallery.
2. Click on **page 2** ▢.
3. On the Edit menu, click **Delete Page.** The Delete Page dialog box appears, with Both pages selected.
4. Click **OK.** Publisher asks: Delete this page?
5. Click **OK** again. The newsletter is reduced from four to two pages.
6. Go to **page 1** ▢.

As you can see, Anderson Pet Mall has been inserted automatically. Since this newsletter is not for Anderson Pet Mall, you will need to change the personal information set.

7. On the Edit menu, click **Personal Information,** and then click **Other Organization.**
8. Edit the Other Organization information set, using the following information:

Address:	Administration Building
	Room 354
	Anderson, IN 46012
Phone:	765-555-PLAY
Organization Name:	University Intramural Sports Program
Tag line:	Building Life Skills Through Competition

9. Click **Update** to insert this information into your newsletter.
10. Change the Newsletter Title to Inside the Walls.
11. Change Newsletter Date to January 20, 2002.
12. Save the file as *Intramural Newsletter.*

2 Insert Word files and edit text to fit text boxes

1. Open the Intramural Newsletter if necessary. Change the text in the first story box (beginning This story can fit 175-225 words . . .) by inserting the text file *Basketball Finals* on the Publisher Data CD.

Publisher asks: Do you want to use autoflow?

2. Click **No** and edit the text to fit the story box by deleting the last paragraph, most of which is in Overflow, as it is not essential to the rest of the article.
3. Change the text in the second story box (beginning This story can fit 75-125 words . . .) by inserting the text file *Bowling* on the Publisher Data CD.

4. Go to **page 2**  and scroll to the top of the page. As you can see, the personal information that has been inserted is the information that you entered in the Other Organization information set.

5. Change the text in the story box beginning: This would be good place to insert a short paragraph . . . by inserting the text file **Intramural Sports** on the Publisher Data CD.

> *Note* — *You will not be using the back page of this newsletter as a mailing panel.*

6. Scroll to the story box at the bottom of the page (beginning This story can fit 175–225 words . . .) and change the text by inserting the text file ***Intramural Golf*** on the Publisher Data CD.

7. Save the newsletter.

3 Create headlines, a table of contents, and special points of interest

1. Open the Intramural Newsletter if necessary. Change the Back Page Story Headline to Sign Up for Spring Golf on the University North Course!

2. Go to **page 1** .

3. Change the Lead Story Headline to Off Campus "Over the Hill" Gang Wins Basketball Finals.

4. Change the Secondary Story Headline to Mixed Bowling League at Halfway Point!

5. Change the table of contents (Inside this issue) box so that it contains the following (partial) headlines:

Off Campus team wins

Mixed bowling

Intramural sports

Spring golf to begin

6. Change the page numbers in the TOC box to the correct page numbers for each article, and delete the unused headlines (Inside story) and their page numbers.

7. Change the Special points of interest to:

Ron Lehmann scores 32 points as the off-campus "Over-the-Hill" Gang wins its first ever intramural basketball championship.

The mixed bowling league is having a highly successful opening season.

Spring golf begins soon.

8. Save the newsletter.

4 Add and edit graphics and change captions

1. Open the Intramural Newsletter if necessary. Change the graphic in the lower right corner of page 1 to the graphic named **_Bowler_** on the Publisher Data CD.

2. Ungroup the graphic and its caption and change the width of the graphic to match the width of the caption box.

3. Move the graphic so that the bottom of its frame is even with the top of the caption's frame.

4. Regroup the graphic and caption box.

5. Change the caption to read: The team of Wynn, Jessup, Overton, and Robinson are leading the mixed bowling league.

6. Go to **page 2** 2.

7. Delete the Anderson Pet Mall logo (which Publisher inserted from the Primary Business Personal Information Set when you opened the template).

8. Delete the object containing the words We're on the Web!

9. Scroll to the graphic at the bottom of page 2.

10. Change this graphic to the graphic named **_Golfer_** on the Publisher Data CD.

11. Ungroup the graphic and its caption and change the width of the graphic to match the width of the caption box.

12. Move the graphic so that it does not overlap the caption box.

13. Regroup the graphic and caption box and move them so that the top of the graphic is even with the headline for this story (Sign Up for Spring Golf . . .)

14. Change the caption to read: Sign up now to be included in the Spring golf league. Teams will be playing on the new University North course. Call 555-PLAY for more details.

15. Save the newsletter.

LESSON APPLICATIONS

1 Create a flyer and insert a text file

You will open a flyer template, insert a text file, and change the personal information set.

1. Locate and open the Cascade Informational Flyer in the Publication Gallery.

2. Change the personal information set to the Other Organization information set that you created for the University Intramural Sports Program in the Skills Review section of this lesson. If you did not create this information set, or if it has been deleted from your computer, create the University Intramural Sports Program information set again, following the steps under Skills Review on page 131. Click Update to insert this information into your flyer.

3. Delete the Anderson Pet Mall logo if it has been inserted in the upper right corner of your flyer.

4. Scroll to the text box beginning Place text here . . . and change the text by inserting the text file **Intramural Golf** on the Publisher Data CD.

Publisher tells you that the inserted text doesn't fit in this box and asks if you want to use autoflow.

5. Click No and save your publication as Intramural Golf Flyer. You will take care of the overflow problem in the next section.

2 Move and resize text frames on a flyer and format text

1. Open the Intramural Golf Flyer, if necessary. Change the default text Product/Service Information to Spring Golf Registration.

2. Resize the frame around Spring Golf Registration by dragging the bottom resize handle up until the frame no longer contains excess space. (Tip: This will put the bottom of the frame at approximately 6 ½ inches on the left ruler.)

3. Resize the frame with the text beginning Spring golf leagues . . . by dragging the top resize handle up until the top of the frame is even with the bottom of the frame above.

4. Click the text in this frame and then press `Ctrl` + A to select all of the text.

5. Right-click, point to Change Text, and then point to AutoFit Text.

6. Click Best Fit.

7. Add paragraph spacing to the text in this frame. This will increase the amount of white space and make the text easier to read. (Hint: You can insert blank lines by pressing `Enter←` at the end of each paragraph, or you can change spacing before and after paragraphs through Line Spacing on the Format menu.)

8. Save the flyer.

3 Change, move, and resize a graphic on a flyer

1. Open the Intramural Golf Flyer, if necessary. Change the default graphic to the graphic named **Horizontal Golf** on the Publisher Data CD.

2. Resize the graphic by dragging the right resize handle until the right side of the graphic is even with the right side of the text frame below it.

3. Move the graphic slightly to the left, so that it is even with the text boxes below it.

4. Save the flyer and close the file.

PROJECTS

1 Exploring the Picture Toolbar

Select any publication in the Publication Gallery that contains a picture and open it. Click the picture so that the Picture toolbar appears.

Click each of the toolbar buttons. Write the name of the button (check its ScreenTip if you're not sure) and indicate whether the button opens a dialog box, provides a drop-down menu, or changes the picture directly.

If the button provides a drop-down menu, also indicate how many choices are available on the menu. Which button provides the greatest number of options for changing the look and formatting of a picture?

2 Exploring the Microsoft Clip Organizer

Open the Insert Clip Art task pane by clicking the Clip Organizer Frame button on the Objects toolbar or by clicking Clip Art… under Picture on the Insert menu. Click Clip Organizer… near the bottom of the task pane.

Open the My Collections folder by double-clicking it, if it is not already open. Make a list of the folders contained within this folder. Click on each of the folders to view their contents in the gallery to the right. As you can see, some of these folders are linked to the Windows software. Describe, in general terms, the contents of each folder.

Open the Office Collections folders and click on each of the categories (folders) to view their contents. Make a list of the categories that have subcategories. Pick the two categories that you think contain the most useful or interesting graphics and explain your choice.

Click the Search… button above the Collection list. In the Search text: box, type a word or words to search by. (Hint: Choose a common term, such as dog or tree that you might expect to find a picture of.) Note that you can also specify which collection(s) to search and which media type (clip art, photographs, movies, or sounds) you are looking for, by changing the selections under Other Search Options. Click the Search button and describe the results of your search. If you have difficulty locating a picture, click Tips for Finding Clips at the bottom of the task pane.

3 Exploring the Design Gallery Live

Open a new, blank publication and click Clip Organizer Frame on the Objects toolbar. On the Insert Clip Art task pane, click Clips Online. When the Design Gallery Live Web site appears, scroll through the home page (the first screen that appears). Microsoft highlights different clips and collections each month. Describe the items that are highlighted this month.

Click Browse at the top of the Search box. When the Browse box appears, click the down arrow next to the Browse for: box and scroll through the drop-down list. Choose a category that interests you and click on it. (Make a note of the category.) Then click Go.

The results of your choice will appear in the area to the right of the Browse box. Scroll through the pages by clicking the double-arrows in the upper right corner. How many pages of results are there?

Limit your search to Sounds only by clicking Sounds in the Results should be: box. Click Go again. How did limiting your search affect the number of pages of results?

4 CATS!

The owner of Anderson Pet Mall loves cats and would like to create a booklet describing various cat breeds, as well as proper care and nutrition for cats. She already has a picture of one of her own cats that she wishes to use for the cover. A former employee, who had done some work on this project, has scanned the picture and added the title CATS as part of the picture. The owner likes what has been done so far, but she would like for you to make some changes to the picture and then enlarge it so that it fills an entire sheet.

Open a new, blank publication.

On the Insert menu, point to Picture and then click From File.... Locate the picture Cat with title on the Publisher Data CD and click on it. Increase the Zoom so that you can see the picture better.

Crop the picture so that only the head of the cat is left. Be careful not to crop any of the cat's ears or nose. If you crop too much, press the Reset Picture button and start again.

Enlarge the picture so that it fills all of the printable area (the area within the blue lines) of the page. Make sure that Lock aspect ratio is selected, so that the picture will not be distorted as it is enlarged.

Save the picture and print it.

5 Earth to Venus

Locate and open the file named Venus on your Publisher Data CD. Increase the Zoom so that you can read the text more easily. This is a one-page report that needs to be formatted before it can be submitted for an astronomy class. The formatting changes will include changes to the line and paragraph spacing and the horizontal alignment of the text. The professor also requires that certain information be added at the end of each report.

Before you make changes to the formatting of the report, click at the end of the last paragraph, press Enter two times, and type the following text that is required by the professor:

Your Name
Submitted to Professor Myers
AST 100
Current Date

Select the heading of the report (Venus), increase the font size to 20, and change the font to Arial, bold. Center the heading.

Select the first paragraph and increase the font size to 12. Click Line Spacing . . . on the Format menu and change the spacing between lines to 1.5 and the spacing before and after paragraphs to 6 pt. Apply this formatting to the other two paragraphs using the Format Painter.

Select the subheading Geology, increase the font size to 14, and change the font to Arial, italic, underlined. Apply this formatting to the other subheading (Atmosphere) using the Format Painter.

Select the four lines of text that you typed and change the alignment to right-aligned. Select the paragraphs and change the alignment to justified.

Add additional space between the heading (Venus) and the first paragraph by pressing Enter after the heading or by increasing the line spacing.

Save the report and proofread it, checking for any possible misspellings that Publisher may have identified. Make any corrections that are needed, save it again, and print it. Check the printed copy for any additional corrections that may need to be made.

6 But What Does Venus Look Like?

Now that you have completed your report on Venus, you would like to make the report look more interesting by adding a picture of the planet. Open the Venus report that you formatted in Project 5. (If you have not completed that project, open a new, blank publication instead.) Click the Clip Organizer Frame button on the Objects toolbar, and then click Clips Online on the Insert Clip Art task pane. When the Design Gallery Live Web site appears, search for graphics of the planet Venus. Choose the one you like best, and download it. Insert it into your report and move it to the bottom of the page. Resize the graphic to fit the available space. (If you are using a blank publication, center the graphic on the page and enlarge it to fill most of the page.)

7 Project in Progress

In your on-going efforts to publicize the work of your Friends of the Library group, you have decided that a quarterly newsletter would be a good way to periodically remind people about the activities of your organization, as well as special events and needs at the library.

Using the Floating Oval newsletter, or another appropriate template, create a newsletter for your Friends of the Library group. If necessary, edit the Other Organization personal information set, following the instructions in Lesson 1 (page 25). If you wish to create a two-page, rather than a four-page, newsletter, click on pages 2–3 and delete them, using the Delete Page command on the Edit menu. Do NOT delete the logo on the last page of the newsletter, even if it is the Anderson Pet Mall logo. (You will create a logo for your Friends of the Library group in Lesson 4 and then you will update your newsletter to include the new logo.)

Starting with a Blank Publication

CONTENTS

OBJECTIVES

After you complete this lesson, you will be able to do the following:

- Plan and evaluate the design of a publication.
- Create a newsletter from a blank publication.
- Identify the buttons on the WordArt toolbar.
- Use WordArt to create a logo.
- Change the way objects are layered on top of each other.
- Create a masthead and dateline.
- Create text boxes and use layout guides and ruler guides to align text and graphics on a page.
- Change the way text wraps around graphics.
- Locate and insert objects from the Design Gallery.
- Use Design Checker to check for potential design problems.
- Prepare publications for outside printing using the Pack and Go feature.

In the first three lessons, you created publications using Publisher templates. Although you learned how to modify some of the design elements in the templates, the basic layout and formatting were already provided for you. In this lesson, you will learn how to create a publication without using a template. You will also learn what points to consider when planning a publication, and you will address some printing issues.

PLANNING A PUBLICATION

Before you begin to create a publication, you should *plan* the publication. Planning a publication involves asking yourself, or the person or persons for whom you are creating the publication, certain questions. Some of the questions you should consider are:

1. *What is the purpose or objective of the publication?* Is it intended to sell something? Is it primarily a notice or announcement of an event? Do you wish to give your readers information on certain topics? If so, how much information do you need to provide? What do you want them to remember after reading your publication? What do you want them to do with the information?

2. *Who are your intended readers (audience)?* Are they people within your own business or organization, such as employees, or are they people outside your organization, such as customers? Do you know the demographics of your audience? Are they young or old, men or women? Or are you creating a publication for personal friends or family members?

3. *How much can you afford to spend on the publication?* Can you afford color printing or will you need to stick with black and white? Can you afford special paper, or will you need to use standard sizes and common paper types? Will you be mailing the publication? If so, how will the weight of each piece affect the cost of the mailing? Can you afford to use envelopes or will you simply fold your publication and use a mailing panel instead of an envelope?

After you answer these questions, you can begin to plan the **content** and **format** of your publication. For example, if you simply need to announce an upcoming event, a postcard may be adequate. If you wish to provide information on various topics, however, a newsletter or a brochure would be a more logical format. Brochures are used to supply information one time. Newsletters are generally considered an ongoing form of communication. Some organizations have weekly newsletters, but monthly, quarterly, or yearly newsletters can effectively communicate your information.

Paper Size, Format, and Color

If you will be creating a newsletter, the amount of information will determine the **length** of the publication. If there will only be three or four articles, a two-page newsletter is probably sufficient. If there will be several articles, however, your newsletter may need to be four pages or longer. If cost is a concern, the length of the publication may affect your decisions about what **paper** to use and how you will mail the publication. Keep in mind that letter (8½" x 11") and legal (8½" x 14") size papers are the most common and least expensive sizes. Tabloid (11" x 17") size paper, which can be folded to produce two 8½" x 11" sheets, is also common, but some printers cannot handle paper this large. (However, if you will be taking your publication to a print shop or copy center to have copies made, you may be able to print onto 8½" x 11" paper and have two 8½" x 11" pages copied onto 11" x 17" paper.) Also keep in mind that if you will be printing a double-sided publication, you may need to use a heavier weight of paper so that the print and graphics do not "bleed" through from one side to the other.

You may consider using colored paper, especially if your budget only allows you to print in one color. The color of the paper will create more interest than standard white paper. However, the color should fit the nature of the publication. For example, you might use a bright, neon paper to announce a playground opening, but the same paper choice would not work as well for an investment counselor announcing a financial planning seminar. If you stick with standard sizes and paper types, using colored paper will not add significantly to the overall cost of the publication.

Number of Colors

If you plan to print the publication from a desktop printer, you can either print in one color or full color, depending on the printer's capabilities. If your printer only supports black printing, you may still include color graphics. The graphics will appear in shades of gray. Some color graphics will print satisfactorily in shades of gray, but many will not. If possible, use black and white graphics in one-color publications.

If you plan to have a printer or print shop produce your publication, you have more color choices. You may use one, two, or four colors. One color printing is the least expensive. The one color of ink may be black or some other color; black is most common. If your publication will include photographs, black ink is the best choice. The photographs will appear like black and white photos.

Two-color printing generally uses black and one additional color. Although it is more expensive than one-color printing, it falls into many budgets. If you use two-color printing, all graphics must be changed to use one or both of your colors. You cannot include a full color graphic in the file.

The most expensive type of printing is full-color printing, commonly called four-color, CMYK, or process-color printing. You may be familiar with the primary colors: red, blue, and yellow. You may have also heard of the three colors used to display the full range of colors on computer monitors: red, green, and blue (RGB). To get full-color printing, four colors of ink are used: cyan (C), magenta (M), yellow (Y), and black (K). By using these ink colors, printers can produce full-color output. If you look at a full-color publication with a magnifying glass, you will see lots of colored dots. The number and color of these dots produce the full range of colors. A comparison of the printing choices is shown in Figure 4.1.

Figure 4.1 ◄
One-, two-, and four-color samples

When creating a full-color publication, all graphics should be either black and white or in CMYK format. Some graphics that look fine on an RGB monitor do not print well. Before sending a full-color publication to the printer, review all graphics after conversion to CMYK.

After you have made the basic decisions about paper size, format, and color, and the number of ink colors, you should begin to plan the layout of your publication. Where will you place the graphics, and where will you place the text? Do you wish to use a *symmetrical* layout, where the text and graphics are equally balanced on each side of a page, or do you prefer an *asymmetrical* layout? If you are planning a newsletter, how many columns will you use? What space should be allowed for the masthead and for page numbers?

Here are some tips that may help you make layout decisions:

1. Your main objective is to get your intended readers to actually read your publication. Headlines, graphics and captions are crucial in achieving this objective. They get your readers' attention and, hopefully, convince them to read further.

2. Plenty of white space makes your publication look "friendly" (easy to read). Keep in mind that margins need to be wide enough that your readers' thumbs do not cover words when they hold your publication.

3. Symmetrical layouts are neat and consistent, but they are also formal and may seem boring. Asymmetrical layouts are less formal and may create a more interesting look. Once you have made your decision about whether to use a symmetrical or an asymmetrical layout, you should use this layout consistently throughout your publication.

4. When planning a newsletter, keep in mind that two-column layouts are formal and serious-looking. Three-column layouts are less formal and can give you more flexibility. It is also possible to use a single-column layout, especially for the front of a newsletter. Be careful that the single column does not exceed 5 inches, since many readers have difficulty reading longer lines of type. The front and back pages of a newsletter may use column layouts that are different from the inside of a newsletter, but the inside (facing) pages should have the same number of columns.

5. When creating facing pages, always consider the two pages together. Be consistent with your design elements. By considering the two pages as one, you may also be able to place graphics or other elements, such as headings, across both pages.

Creating a Newsletter from a Blank Publication

In this activity, you will open a blank publication and make setup changes that are necessary to create a four-page newsletter. The newsletter, called *The Traveler,* is the first issue of a newsletter from a travel agency. To save on printing costs, this newsletter will be printed in black and white. It will also be printed on legal size paper, which will be folded to create four 7" X 8½" pages. Check with your instructor about the availability of legal size paper in your computer lab.

1. Click on Blank Publication in the New [or New from Existing] Publication task pane. (See Figure 4.2.)

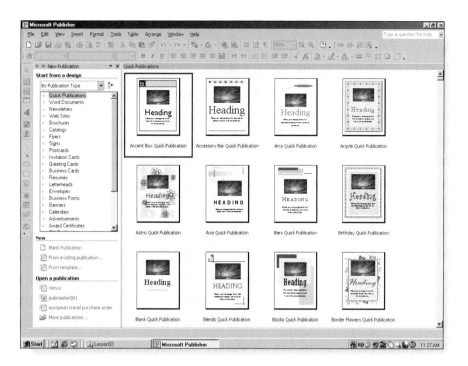

Figure 4.2
Blank publication

The task pane and Publication Gallery disappear, and a blank publication appears in the Publisher window, as shown in Figure 4.3.

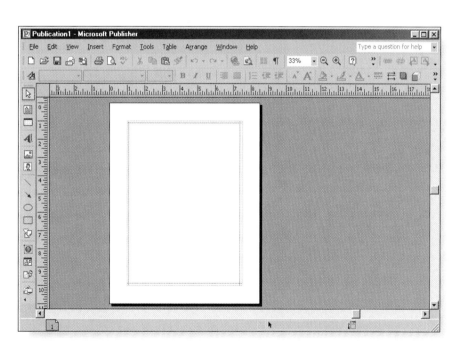

Figure 4.3
Blank page of newsletter publication

2. Click Page Setup on the File menu as shown in Figure 4.4.

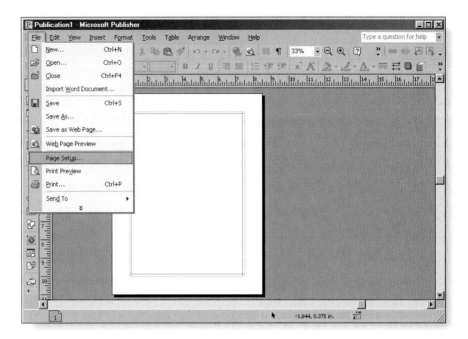

Figure 4.4
Page Setup selected from
File menu

3. **Click the Printer & Paper tab.**

4. **In the Size: box, click the down arrow and select Legal 8.5 x 14 in.**

You also need to change the *page orientation* from portrait to landscape. In *portrait* orientation, the top and bottom of the page are the shorter sides of the paper, and the page is taller than it is wide. In *landscape* orientation, the top and bottom of the page are the longer sides of the paper, and the page is wider than it is tall. Because portrait orientation is more common than landscape orientation, landscape orientation is sometimes referred to as printing *sideways*.

5. **Under Orientation, click Landscape, as shown in Figure 4.5.**

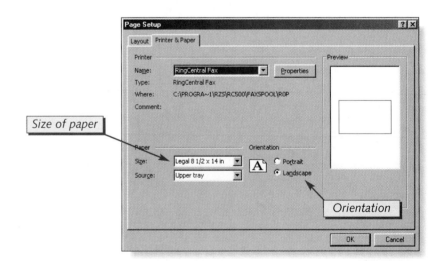

Size of paper

Orientation

Figure 4.5
Printer & Paper tab

6. Click the Layout tab and then click Booklet under Publication type. (See Figure 4.6.)

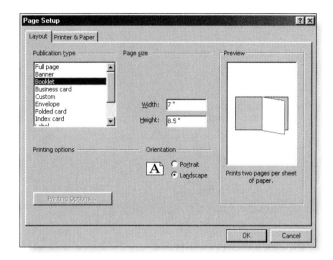

Figure 4.6
Booklet under publication type

The Preview box shows an example of this layout and indicates that it is designed to print two pages per sheet of paper.

7. Click OK.

Publisher asks: Automatically insert pages?

8. Click Yes.

The blank publication reappears, with four pages indicated in the status bar.

9. Click Layout Guides... on the Arrange menu.

The Layout Guides dialog box appears. Because you will be folding legal size paper to create four small (7" x 8½") pages, the margins need to be reduced so that they are better suited to the smaller page size.

10. Change Inside: to 0.5", Outside: to 0.5", Top: to 0.75", Bottom: to 0.5". Make sure that the box Create Two Master Pages with Mirrored Guides is checked. (See Figure 4.7.)

11. Click OK.

The blank publication reappears. The pink and blue dotted lines (called *lay-out guides*) indicate the margins that you just set. The pink lines mark the actual margin settings, and the blue lines indicate where frames should be aligned. The lines appear on the screen but do not print.

12. On the Edit menu, click Personal Information.

13. In the Personal Information dialog box, click Secondary Business.

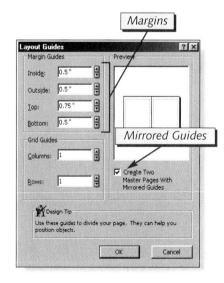

Figure 4.7
Layout Guides dialog box

14. Change the information as follows. When the information has been entered, the secondary business information will appear as shown in Figure 4.8.

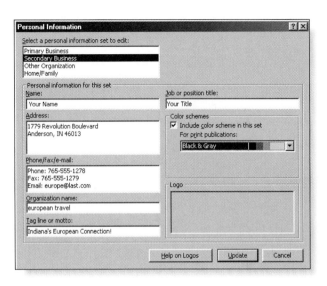

Figure 4.8
Personal Information Set for
Secondary Business

Name:	Your Name
Address:	1779 Revolution Boulevard, Anderson, IN 46013
Phone:	765-555-1278
Fax:	765-555-1279
E-mail:	europe@last.com
Organization Name:	european travel *(all lower case)*
Tag line:	Indiana's European Connection!

Also check Include color scheme in this set. **Select** Black & Gray **as the color set.**

15. Click Update.

The blank publication reappears.

16. Click page 4.

17. On the Insert menu, click Personal Information...

18. Click Logo. (See Figure 4.9.)

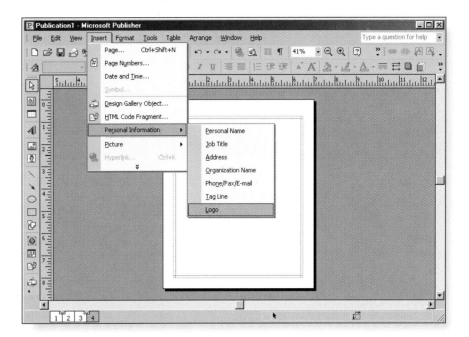

Figure 4.9
Logo selected from Personal
Information Drop-Down menu

A default logo is inserted into your publication.

19. Repeat step 17 and then click Organization Name.

A text box for the organization name is inserted into your publication.

20. Repeat step 17 and then click Address. Repeat step 17 again and click Phone/Fax/Email.

There are now three text boxes in your publication.

 If the three text boxes were inserted on top of each other, use the Move handles to pull them apart.

21. Select the text in each of the text boxes and change the font size to 10, if necessary.

22. Move the text boxes and logo to the upper left corner of the page so that they appear approximately as shown in Figure 4.10.

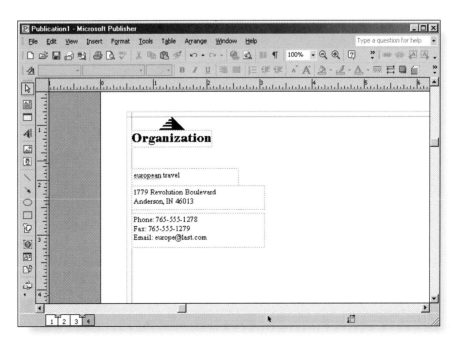

Figure 4.10
Text boxes below logo

Note You may need to zoom in to see the publication more clearly. You may also need to resize the address and phone boxes.

23. Save the newsletter under the name the traveler.

EXPLORING WORDART

If a business or organization does not already have a logo, a logo can be created within Publisher, using specially formatted text and/or graphics. Publisher allows you to use the **WordArt** feature to stretch, skew, or rotate text, or to fit text to a particular shape. The **Word Art Gallery** provides 30 preformatted designs of special text effects.

Creating a Logo Using WordArt

In this activity, you will use the WordArt feature to create a logo for **european travel**.

1. Open the newsletter (the traveler), if it is not already open, and go to page 4.

2. Click the Insert WordArt button 4 on the Objects toolbar.

The WordArt Gallery, appears as shown in Figure 4.11.

3. Click the second WordArt style in the first row and then click OK.

4. Select the default text (Your Text Here) and type european travel (all lower case, with one space at the end). Note: The extra space at the end will be necessary for proper formatting of the logo.

5. Change the font size to 18.

Your choices appear in the Edit WordArt Text dialog box as shown in Figure 4.12.

6. Click OK.

The words **european travel** are inserted into your publication, and the WordArt toolbar appears. Table 4.1 provides a summary of the tools on the WordArt toolbar.

Publisher BASICS

Inserting WordArt Text

1. Click the Insert WordArt button on the Objects toolbar.

2. Select a WordArt style and click OK.

3. Select the default text and type your own text in its place.

4. Change the font size if necessary.

5. Click OK.

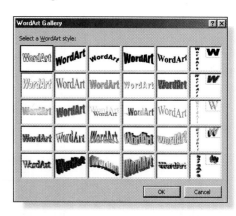

Figure 4.11
WordArt Gallery

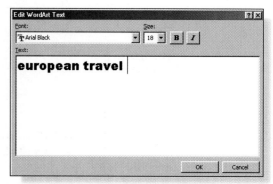

Figure 4.12
Edit WordArt Text dialog box

TABLE 4.1	WORDART TOOLBAR FUNCTIONS
Name	**Description**
Insert WordArt	Opens the WordArt Gallery to select and insert a WordArt style
Edit Text…	Opens the Edit WordArt Text dialog box, which allows you to edit the text and change fonts and font size
WordArt Gallery	Opens the WordArt Gallery to change the WordArt style
Format WordArt	Opens the Format WordArt dialog box to make changes to colors, size, layout and other features
WordArt Shape	Provides choices of WordArt shapes
Text Wrapping	Provides text wrapping choices
WordArt Same Letter Heights	Makes all of the WordArt letters the same height
WordArt Vertical Text	Changes horizontal text to vertical
WordArt Alignment	Provides alignment options, including stretching
WordArt Character Spacing	Allows you to change the character spacing within words

7. Click the WordArt Shape button 🔳 on the WordArt toolbar. (See Figure 4.13.)

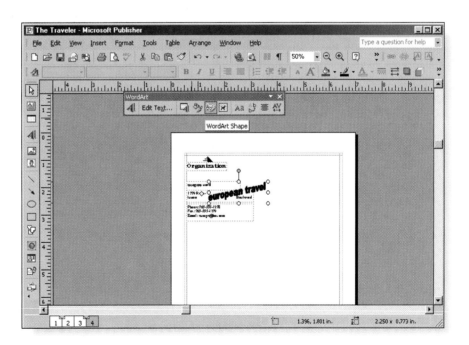

Figure 4.13
WordArt toolbar

A menu of shapes appears.

8. Click on the Circle (Curve) shape (the third shape in the second row), as shown in Figure 4.14.

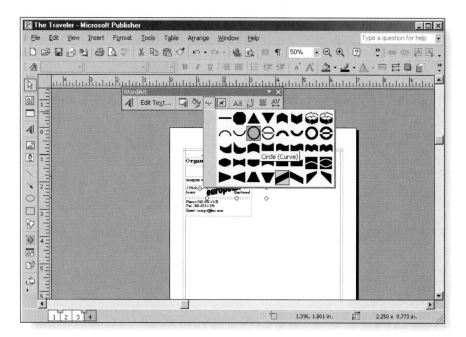

Figure 4.14
WordArt toolbar with circle shape
selected

The words **european travel** are shaped as an oval.

9. Increase the Zoom to 100%, if necessary.

10. Using the resize handle, drag the frame around the words european travel until a dotted circle appears, as shown in Figure 4.15.

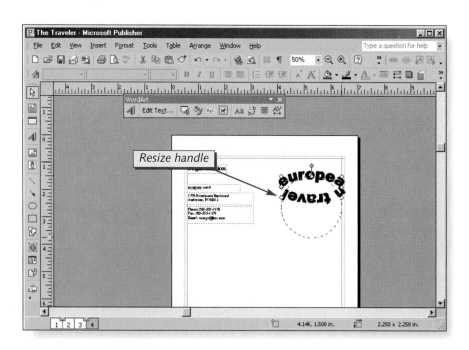

Figure 4.15
european travel selected

11. Release the resize handle.

The words **european travel** are shaped as a circle. (See Figure 4.16.)

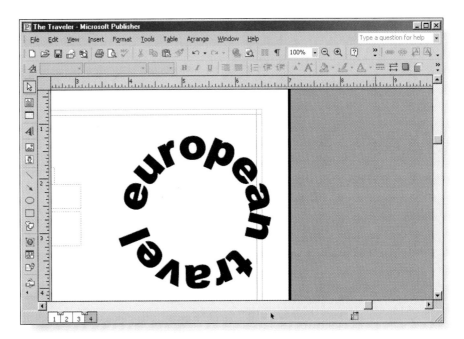

Figure 4.16
european travel shaped as circle

You will see a green dot near the top of the word **european.** When you point at the green dot, the rotation pointer appears.

12. Click and hold the rotation pointer and rotate the text counterclockwise until the word european forms a semi-circle at the top of the circle and the word travel is at the bottom of the circle, as shown in Figure 4.17.

 You may need to rotate the text more than once until the desired layout is achieved.

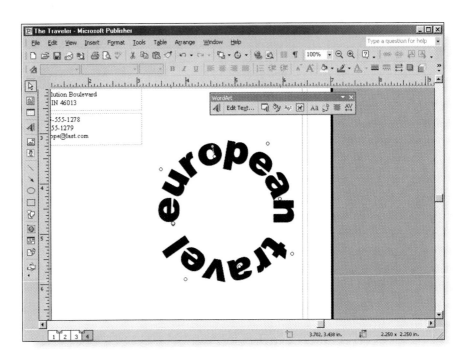

Figure 4.17
european travel text rotated

You will now insert a picture into your logo.

13. Save the file.

14. On the Insert menu, click Picture **and then** From File….

15. Locate the picture named Europe Circle with Plane **on the Publisher Data CD and insert it into your publication.**

As you are already aware, Publisher provides rulers to help you measure objects and text. Publisher also provides ***ruler guides,*** green lines that allow you to align objects on a page. The lines appear on the screen but do not print. In the next few steps, you will create ruler guides to help you complete your logo.

16. Point at the horizontal ruler and press and hold `⇧ Shift`.

The pointer changes to the Adjust pointer.

17. Click the Adjust pointer **and release** `⇧ Shift`. **As you move the Adjust pointer into the work area, a green line (the ruler guide) appears.**

18. Drag the green ruler guide to the 3½ inch mark on the vertical ruler, as shown in Figure 4.18, and release the Adjust pointer.

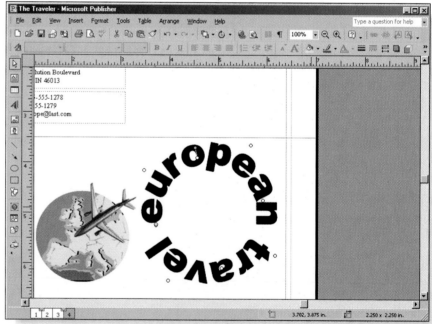

Figure 4.18 ◄
Vertical ruler guide

If you release the Adjust pointer too soon, or otherwise make a mistake in placing a ruler guide, you can adjust the guide. Press and hold the Shift key and move the pointer over the guide until the Adjust pointer appears. Then drag the guide to the desired place on the page. If you drag the guide off the page, the guide is deleted.

19. Move the Europe Circle **picture so that the top of the circle is even with the green ruler guide. (The top of the frame around the picture will extend beyond the green ruler guide.)**

As you move the mouse pointer, your place on the page is indicated by marks on the rulers. By placing the pointer at the top edge of the Europe Circle picture, you can check the picture's position on the page. If the top edge is not at the 3½ inch mark on the vertical ruler, continue to adjust the position of the picture.

20. Move the words european travel so that the top of that circle is also even with the green ruler guide, as shown in Figure 4.19.

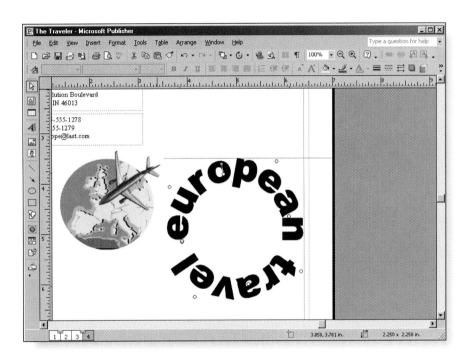

Figure 4.19
Repositioned european travel

21. Resize the Europe Circle picture until it is approximately the same size as the european travel circle.

22. Select the european travel circle and move it so that it is centered over the Europe Circle picture.

The words **european travel** disappear.

As you know, when you place a picture frame on top of a text frame, the text automatically wraps around the picture. When you place a picture frame on top of another picture frame, however, one frame covers the other. Placing frames on top of each other is called *layering* or *stacking.* Because WordArt frames are considered picture frames, moving the WordArt frame **european travel** over the Europe Circle picture causes the words **european travel** to disappear, because Publisher has *stacked* the Europe Circle picture on top. This problem can be corrected, however, by using commands on the Arrange menu.

23. On the Arrange menu, click Order and then click Bring to Front, as shown in Figure 4.20.

Publisher BASICS

Rearranging Stacked Objects

1. Select the stacked object that you wish to rearrange.

2. On the Arrange menu, click Order.

3. Click Bring to Front or Send to Back as needed to change the order of the stacked objects.

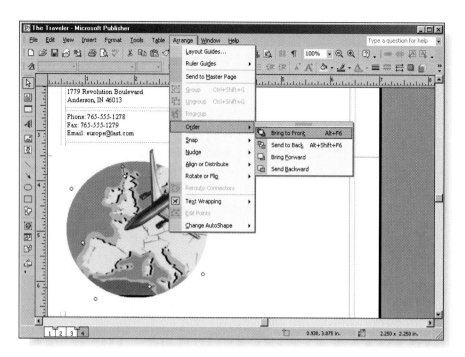

Figure 4.20
Bring to Front

The words **european travel** reappear, because Publisher has brought them to the front of the stack.

24. Save the file.

The outside edge of the **european travel** circle should be even with the outside edge of the Europe Circle picture. If it is not, complete the Steps 25 and 26.

25. Click on the tail of the plane, which causes handles to appear around the Europe Circle picture.

By clicking on the tail of the plane that extends beyond the words **european travel,** you can easily select the Europe Circle picture, rather than the **european travel** circle.

26. Resize the Europe Circle picture so that it looks like Figure 4.21. You may also need to move the picture slightly, so that it lines up properly with the words european travel.

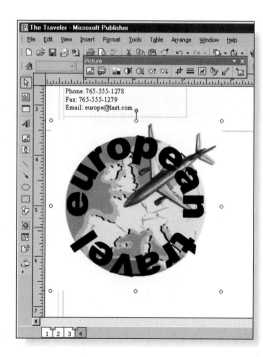

Figure 4.21
Completed logo for european travel

Converting WordArt Logo to a Picture Format and Using Picture Format in Publication

If you plan to use a logo in more than one publication, you should convert it to a picture format. The logo becomes a piece of art that can be easily placed in various publications. Once it is converted to a piece of art, however, it cannot be changed. In this activity, you will convert the european travel logo to a JPEG file, save it as part of the secondary business personal information set, and insert it into your publication.

1. With the traveler publication open and the european travel logo visible, click on the words european travel.

The WordArt toolbar will reappear.

2. While holding ⇧ Shift , click on the tail of the plane.

The Group Objects icon appears below the picture.

3. Click Group Objects 🔳.

The picture and words are now grouped as one logo.

4. Right-click the logo and click Save as Picture… (See Figure 4.22.)

Figure 4.22
Save as Picture

The Save As dialog box appears.

5. In the File name: box, type European Travel Logo. In the Save as type: box, select JPEG File Interchange Format. (See Figure 4.23.)

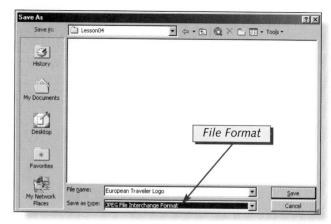

Figure 4.23
JPEG file format selected
for saving logo

6. Select your folder in the Save In: box and click the Save button.

Your logo is now saved as a picture, so that you can insert it in place of the default logo.

7. Right-click on the logo again and click Cut.

 Clicking Cut places the logo on the Publisher **clipboard.** *The Publisher clipboard works like the clipboard in all Windows-based software, allowing items to be cut and pasted from one location to another.*

8. Scroll to the upper left corner of the page and click on the default logo.

The Wizard icon appears, as shown in Figure 4.24.

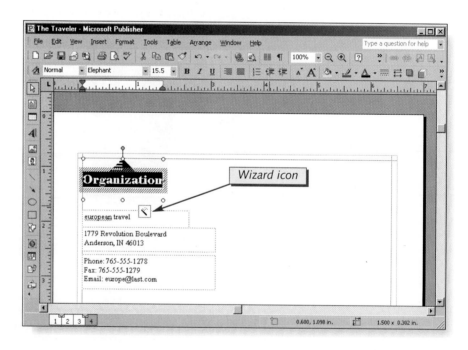

Figure 4.24
Logo wizard

9. Click the Wizard icon 🖉.

The Logo Design task pane appears.

10. Click Logo Options.

The Logo Options task pane appears.

11. Under **New or existing,** click **Inserted picture.**

12. Click the **Choose Picture...** button **Choose picture...** , as shown in Figure 4.25.

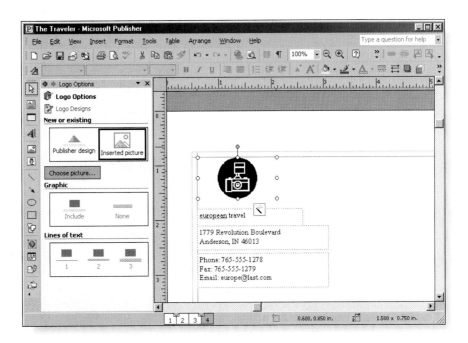

Figure 4.25
Choose Picture button

The Insert Picture dialog box appears.

13. Locate the **European Travel Logo** in your folder and insert it into your publication.

The European Travel Logo replaces the default logo in your publication, as shown in Figure 4.26.

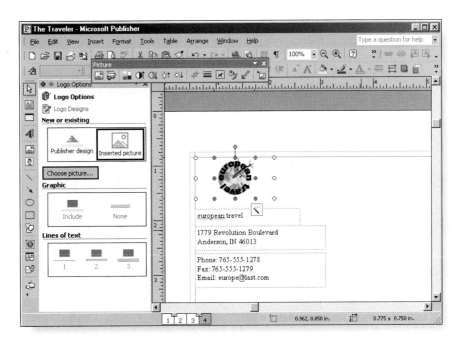

Figure 4.26
european travel logo inserted in
publication

14. Click the Save button 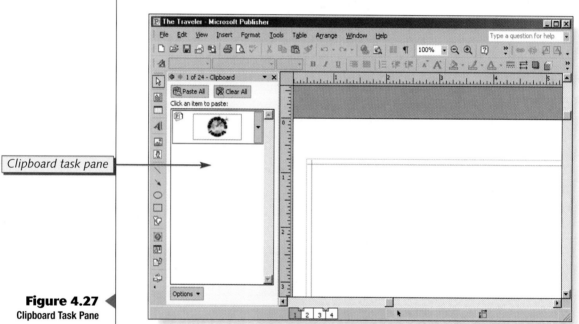 on the Standard toolbar.

As you are saving, Publisher asks: "You have modified the logo in this publication. Do you want to save the new logo to the Secondary Business Personal Information Set?"

15. Click Yes.

The logo is inserted into the Personal Information Set, and the updated newsletter is saved.

16. Right click on the logo and select Copy.

17. Go to page 1.

18. Click the Edit menu and select Office Clipboard....

The task pane changes to the Clipboard task pane, and the European Travel Logo appears in the Click an item to paste box, as shown in Figure 4.27. (You placed the logo on the clipboard in step 16.)

Clipboard task pane

Figure 4.27
Clipboard Task Pane

19. Click the European Travel Logo.

The european travel logo is inserted, or *pasted,* on page 1 of your newsletter.

20. Right-click on the logo and click Format Object.

The Format Object dialog box appears.

21. Click the Size tab, click Lock aspect ratio, change the height to 2.5 inches and click OK.

Once you have made these choices, the Format Object dialog box appears as shown in Figure 4.28. Notice that by changing the height and width of the logo, the scale percentages change accordingly.

With the Lock aspect ratio checked, Publisher will main-tain the relationship between the height and width of the object. When you enter 2.5 for the height, it will automatically calculate the proportional width.

22. Point to the horizontal ruler, press `⇧ Shift` and drag the Adjust pointer to the half-inch mark on the vertical ruler.

23. Point to the vertical ruler, press `⇧ Shift` and drag the Adjust pointer to the ⅜-inch mark on the horizontal ruler.

Two intersecting ruler guides are inserted in your newsletter.

24. Move the logo until the logo's frame fits within the border created by your ruler guides.

25. Right-click on the logo and then click Format Object....

The Format Object dialog box appears.

26. Click the Color and Lines tab, change the Fill color to No Fill and the Line Color to No Line, as shown in Figure 4.29, and click OK.

The border around your logo is removed.

27. Save the publication.

Figure 4.28
Resized logo

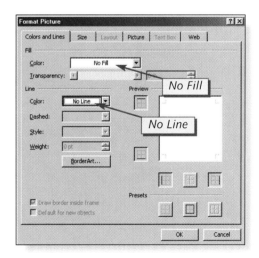

Figure 4.29
Format picture to remove lines around logo

DESIGNING MASTHEADS AND DATELINES

The area at the top of the first page of a newsletter is reserved for the masthead. The masthead is the distinctive element that clearly identifies the newsletter. The logo of the business, organization, or group may appear in the masthead, along with the title of the newsletter. All elements in the masthead—type and graphics—should work together to create a unique look and feel. Mastheads should be distinctive, but they do not need to be complex. The basic masthead design stays the same from newsletter to newsletter allowing the newsletter's readers to quickly identify the publication.

Datelines often appear directly above, below, or to the side of the masthead. Common elements of datelines include the date of publication and the number of the publication. Weekly newsletters would give a month, day, and year of publication. Newsletters that are published monthly or less often carry only the month and year of publication. Newsletters that are seasonal may carry the season of the year, rather than the month. For example, a newsletter about gardening that is published four times a year may use Spring, Summer, Autumn, and Winter along with the year in the dateline.

Numbering the publication can be useful in letting readers know how long the newsletter has been published. Two common forms of numbering are number only and volume and number. The table below describes these two systems using a monthly newsletter as an example.

TABLE 4.2	NUMBERING PUBLICATIONS	
	Numbers Only	Volume and Number
First year, first month	No. 1	Vol. I, No. 1
Third year, fourth month	No. 28	Vol. III, No. 4
Fifth year, first month	No. 49	Vol. V, No. 1

Datelines may contain other information such as the place of publication, but the critical information is the date and number of the publication.

HANDS On

Creating a Masthead and Dateline

In this activity, you will create a masthead and dateline from scratch.

1. Open the newsletter (the traveler), if it is not already open, and go to page 1.
2. Adjust the vertical ruler guide by aligning it with the 2½-inch mark on the horizontal ruler.
3. Adjust the horizontal ruler guide by aligning it with the ³⁄₁₆-inch mark on the vertical ruler.
4. Insert a second horizontal ruler guide at the 2⅝-inch mark on the vertical ruler. (See Figure 4.30.)

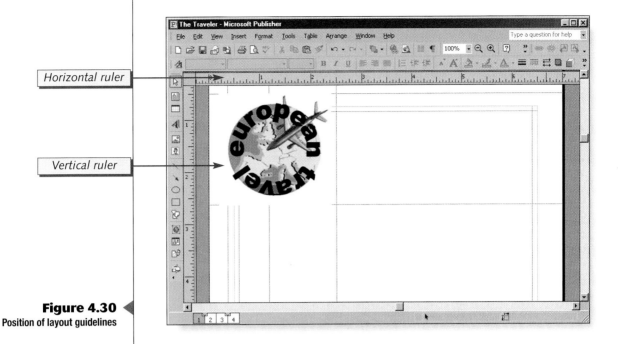

Figure 4.30
Position of layout guidelines

Horizontal ruler

Vertical ruler

5. Click the Text Box button 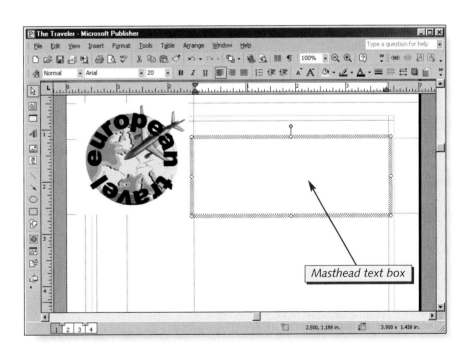 on the Objects toolbar.

6. Using the crosshair pointer, draw a text box to fit within the ruler guides you set in steps 1-3. The right side of your box will be even with the blue margin line on the right side of the page as shown in Figure 4.31.

Masthead text box

Figure 4.31
Masthead text box

7. Change the font size of the text box to Arial, 20, and type the traveler (all lower case).

Note that the *t* in *the* changes to a capital *T*.

8. Move the pointer over the T.

A small blue box appears. When you place the pointer on the blue box, the AutoCorrect Options box appears as shown in Figure 4.32.

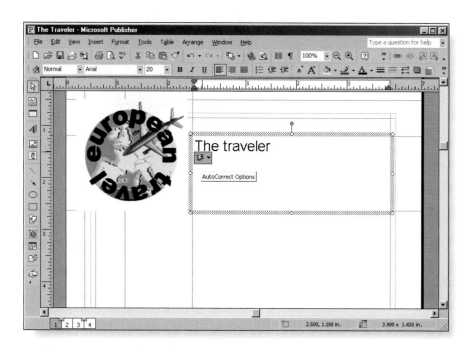

Figure 4.32
AutoCorrect Options box

9. Click the down arrow on the AutoCorrect Options box and then click Undo Automatic Capitalization.

The capital *T* changes to a lower case *t*.

10. Place the cursor at the end of the line. Move to the next line by pressing the Enter key, change the font to Baskerville Old Face, 48, and then type France.

 If you do not have the Baskerville Old Face font available, select another serif typeface.

11. Right-align the word France.

In order to highlight the masthead on your black and white newsletter, you will reverse the colors, so that the text is white and the background is black.

12. Click Ctrl + A to highlight all of the text in the box.

13. Click the down arrow next to the Font Color box on the Formatting toolbar and then click White as shown in Figure 4.33.

Publisher BASICS

Reversing Font and Fill Colors (to Create White Text on Black Background)

1. Select the text you wish to change.

2. Click the down arrow next to the Font Color box on the Formatting toolbar.

3. Click White.

4. Click the down arrow next to the Fill Color box on the Formatting toolbar.

5. Click Black.

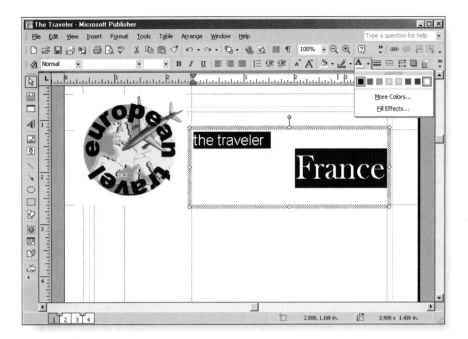

Figure 4.33
Format color options

The text "disappears", as it is now white on white.

14. In order to change the fill color of the text box and make the text reappear, click the down arrow next to the Fill Color box on the Formatting toolbar and click Black as shown in Figure 4.34.

15. Save the newsletter.

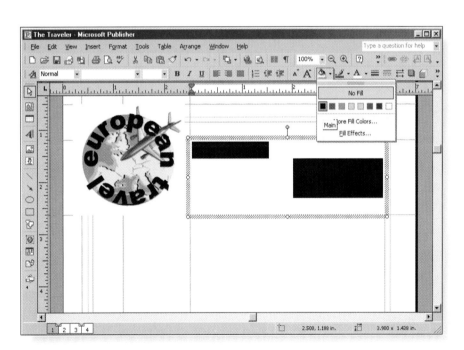

Figure 4.34
Fill color options

The text reappears as white on black, and the masthead is complete. You will now create a dateline, with part of the information above the masthead and part below the masthead.

16. Create a text box above the masthead, so that the top of the text box is even with the blue margin line at the top of the page, the right side is even with the right margin line, the left side is just above the *F* in *France,* and the bottom is even with the top of the masthead.

17. Change the font to Arial Black, 10, and click the Align Right button ▤ on the Formatting toolbar.

18. Type Volume 1, No. 1.

19. Create a text box below the masthead, by copying the text box above the masthead.

20. Move the text box immediately below the masthead.

21. Type February 1, 2002.

The masthead and dateline are now complete. Your newsletter should appear as shown in Figure 4.35.

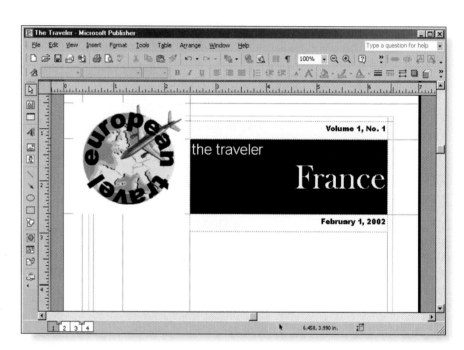

Figure 4.35
Completed masthead and dateline

22. Save the newsletter.

ADDING ARTICLES AND GRAPHICS TO NEWSLETTERS

In Lesson 3, you worked with a template that included text and graphics boxes. When you create a newsletter from a blank publication, you must insert these boxes. Use the planning guidelines discussed earlier in the lesson for deciding on the width and depth of the boxes. Also, plan the size and style of type for the newsletter articles and the placement of graphics. Remember that graphics should complement, not compete with, the text.

HANDS On

Creating Text Boxes and Inserting and Formatting Text

In this activity you will create text boxes and insert and format the text of the newsletter's articles.

1. **Open the newsletter (the traveler), if it is not already open, and go to page 1.**

2. **Insert a new horizontal ruler guide that is even with the bottom edge of the second dateline box.**

3. **Decrease the Zoom to 50% so that you can see the entire layout.**

4. **Click the Text Box button 🔲 on the Objects toolbar.**

5. **Using the crosshair pointer, create a text box that starts at the intersection of the green ruler guides under the dateline and ends at the lower right corner of the page where the two blue margin lines intersect as shown in Figure 4.36.**

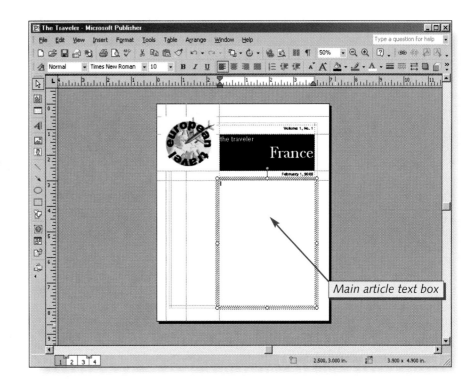

Main article text box

6. **With the pointer inside this text box, right-click, click Change Text and then click Text File.... Locate the Word document European Traveler on your Publisher Data CD and insert it.**

> *Note*
>
> *If the text runs longer than the box, Publisher asks if you want to use autoflow. Click No if this happens.*

7. **Click `Ctrl` + A to select all of the text, and change the font size to Times New Roman, 10.**

8. **Go to pages 2–3. (This is a two-page spread.)**

9. **Decrease the Zoom if needed so that you can view both pages at once.**

Publisher BASICS

Creating Text Boxes

1. Click the Text Box button on the Objects toolbar.

2. Use the crosshair pointer to draw a text box and at the desired place on the page.

3. With the pointer inside the text box, right-click, and then click Format Text Box....

4. Change the size, font, and horizontal alignment, as needed.

Figure 4.36
Text box on page 1 of newsletter

10. On the Insert menu, click Picture and then click From File…. Locate the graphic file Map of France on your Publisher Data CD and insert it.

A green map of France is inserted in your two-page spread as shown in Figure 4.37.

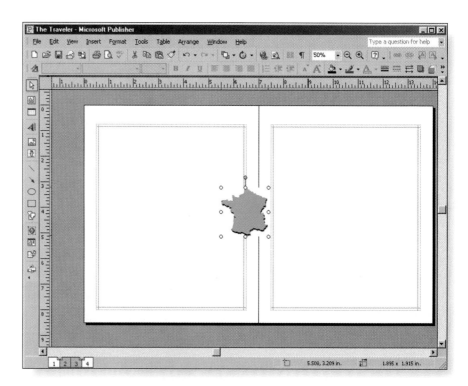

Figure 4.37
Map of France

11. Move the green map to the upper left corner of the two-page spread so that the top of the map is even with the top blue margin line.

12. Resize the map by dragging the lower right resize handle until the bottom of the map is even with the bottom blue margin line.

13. Move the map so that it is centered between the two pages as shown in Figure 4.38.

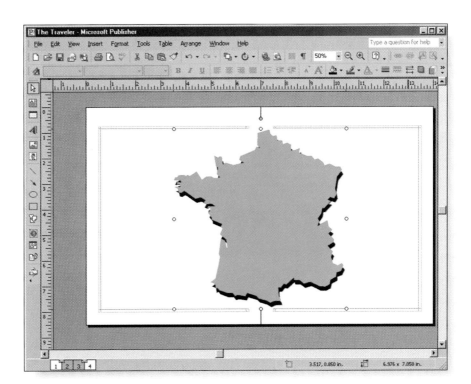

Figure 4.38
Map of France centered
across spread

14. Click the Color button 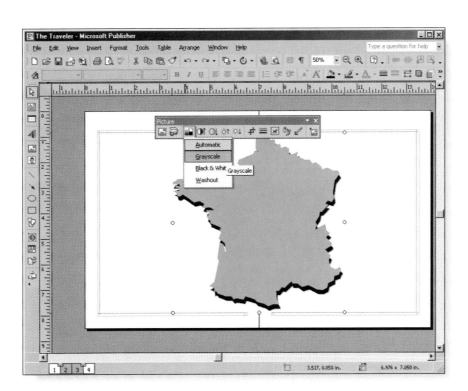 on the Picture toolbar and then click Grayscale. (See Figure 4.39.)

Figure 4.39
Grayscale selected

15. Click the More Brightness button  on the Picture toolbar four times to lighten the map.

16. Increase the Zoom to 100% and scroll to the top of page 2.

17. Save the newsletter.

18. Draw a text box at the top of page 2 starting at the 2⅞-inch mark on the horizontal ruler and ending at the intersection of the blue margin lines on the right side of the page. The top edge of the text box should be even with the top blue margin line, and the box should be ⅜-inch deep.

19. With the pointer inside the text box, right-click, and then click Format Text Box….

20. In the Format Text Box dialog box, click the Size tab and change the height to ½ inch and the width to 3½ inches. Then click OK.

21. Change the font of the text box to Baskerville Old Face, 22, and right-align.

Note *If you do not have the Baskerville Old Face font available, use the serif type face that you selected for France in the masthead.*

22. Type The Bullet Train: TGV.

23. Change the font and fill colors in the text box so that the text is white on black.

24. Insert a horizontal ruler guide at the 4¼-inch mark on the vertical ruler to divide the page in half.

25. Draw a text box starting at the point where the new ruler guide intersects the blue margin line on the left side of the page and ending at the bottom right corner of the Bullet Train heading. (See Figure 4.40.)

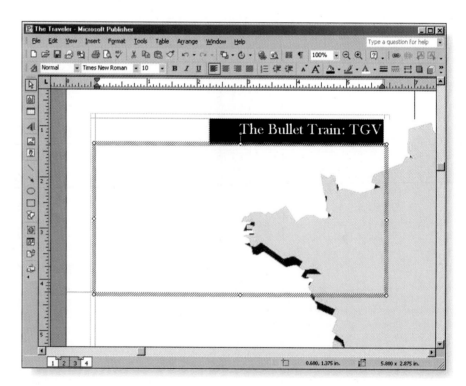

Figure 4.40
Text box inserted on page 2

26. With the pointer inside the new text box, right-click, click Change Text, and then click Text File....

27. Locate the Word document TGV trains on your Publisher Data CD and insert it.

28. Change the font and size to Times New Roman 10.

29. Scroll to the top of page 3.

30. Save the newsletter.

31. Create a text box the same size as the Bullet Train heading box on the previous page. Align the left side of this box with the left blue margin line on this page and the top of this box with the top blue margin line.

32. Change the font of this box to Baskerville Old Face, 22, and left-align.

 *If you do not have the Baskerville Old Face font available, use the serif type face that you selected for* France *in the masthead.*

33. **Type** The Arc de Triomphe.

34. Change font and fill colors in this box so that the text is white on black.

35. Draw a text box starting at the point where the horizontal ruler guide intersects the right blue margin line and ending at the lower left corner of the Arc de Triomphe heading.

36. Repeat step 26 and insert the Arc de Triomphe Word document.

37. Repeat step 28.

38. Scroll to page 2.

39. Save the newsletter.

Your newsletter should look similar to the one shown in Figure 4.41.

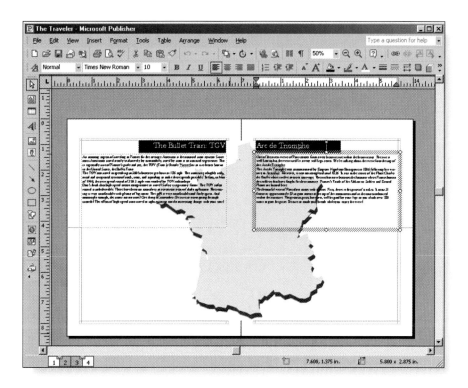

Figure 4.41
Pages 2 and 3 of newsletter with
two articles added

40. Select The Bullet Train: TGV headline text box. Then hold down ⌃Ctrl and click on the bullet train article text box. Click Group Objects 🖼.

41. Copy and paste the article. Move the pasted article to the bottom of page 2 so that the bottom of the text box lines up with the intersection of blue margin lines at the bottom of the page.

42. Click in the headline box, press ⌃Ctrl + A and type The Eiffel Tower.

43. Click in the article box, press ⌃Ctrl + A and press Delete.

44. Repeat step 26 to insert the Eiffel Tower Word document.

45. Change the text of the article to Times New Roman, 10.

The text for page 2 is now complete and should appear as shown in Figure 4.42.

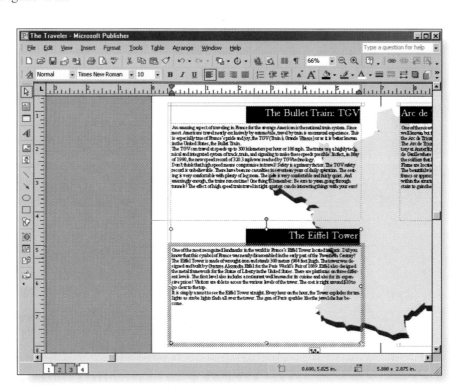

Figure 4.42
Page 2 with articles inserted

46. Scroll to page 3.

47. Select Arc de Triomphe headline text box. Then hold down ⌃Ctrl and click on the Arc de Triomphe article text box. Click Group Objects 🖼.

48. Copy and paste the article. Move the pasted article to the bottom of page 3 so that the bottom of the text box lines up with the intersection of blue margin lines at the bottom of the page.

49. Type French Food Delights.

50. Click in the article box, press ⌃Ctrl + A and press Delete.

51. Repeat step 26 to insert the French food Word document.

52. Change the text of the article to Times New Roman, 10.

All of the text boxes are now complete, as shown in Figure 4.43.

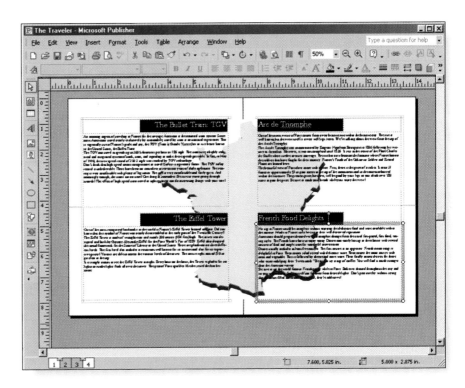

Figure 4.43
Pages 2 and 3 completed

53. Save the newsletter.

Inserting and Formatting Graphics

In this activity you will insert graphics appropriate to the newsletter articles and wrap the text around the graphics.

1. Open the newsletter (the traveler), if it is not already open, and go to pages 2-3.

2. On the Insert menu, click Picture and then click From File....

3. Locate the graphic file The train on your Publisher Data CD and insert it.

4. Move the train picture to the upper left corner of page 2 so that the right edge of the picture is at the 2¾-inch mark on the horizontal ruler and the bottom of the picture is just above the Bullet Train story box.

5. Resize the picture by dragging the bottom left resize handle down to the 1¾-inch mark on the vertical ruler as shown in Figure 4.44.

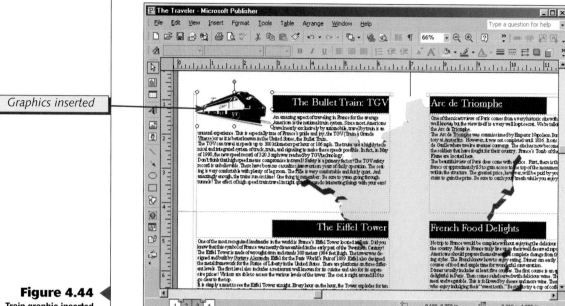

Figure 4.44
Train graphic inserted

Graphics inserted

6. Scroll to page 3.

7. Repeat step 2 and insert the graphic file Arc de Triomphe.

8. Move the Arc de Triomphe picture so that the upper right corner is even with the intersection of the blue margin lines in the upper right corner of the page.

9. Resize the picture by dragging the bottom left resize handle so that it is even with the 11¼-inch mark on the horizontal ruler as shown in Figure 4.45.

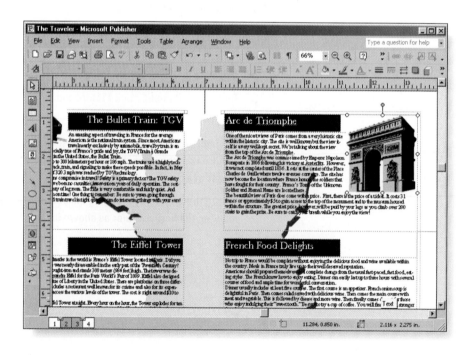

Figure 4.45
Arc de Triomphe graphic inserted

10. Scroll to the bottom of page 2.

11. Save the newsletter.

12. Repeat step 2 and insert the graphic file Eiffel Tower.

13. Move the Eiffel Tower picture so that the bottom left corner is even with the intersection of the blue margin lines in the bottom left corner of the page.

14. Resize the picture by dragging the top right resize handle so that it is even with the 3⅛-inch mark on the vertical ruler as shown in Figure 4.46.

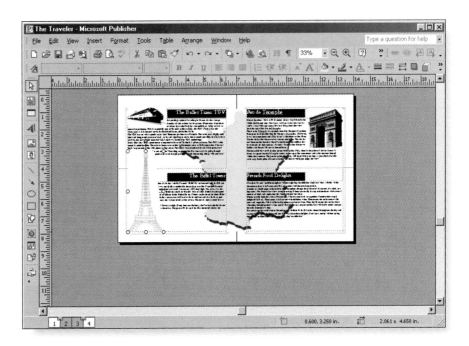

Figure 4.46 ◄
Eiffel Tower graphic inserted

Customizing Text Wrapping

1. Select the picture to be wrapped.

2. Click the Text Wrapping button on the Picture toolbar.

3. Select Edit Wrap Points.

4. Adjust the red wrapping lines by dragging the wrap points until the desired wrapping style is achieved.

5. Click the Text Wrapping button again.

6. Select Tight and then click No.

Wrap points

Figure 4.47 ◄
Edit wrap points around Eiffel Tower graphic

15. Decrease the Zoom to 33%.

16. While the Eiffel Tower picture is still selected, click the Text Wrapping button 🖼 on the Picture toolbar and select Edit Wrap Points.

Red lines with black corner points (called ***wrapping lines***) appear around your picture.

17. Drag the corner points so that the red lines appear as shown in Figure 4.47.

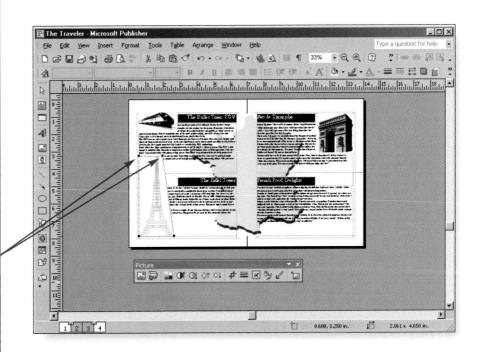

18. Click the Text Wrapping button on the Picture toolbar and select Tight.

Publisher asks: Do you want Publisher to create a new boundary?

19. Click No.

20. The text wraps to correspond to the wrapping lines that you drew around the picture.

 Since the exact location of the wrap points may vary, your text may wrap at different points. You can adjust the wrap points to achieve the desired goal.

21. Change the Zoom to 50% and scroll to the lower half of page 3.

22. Save the newsletter.

23. Repeat step 2 and insert the graphic file French food.

24. Move the French food picture to the lower right corner of the page so that the lower right corner of the picture is even with the intersection of the blue margin lines.

25. Resize the picture by dragging the top left resize handle so that it is even with the 6-inch mark on the vertical ruler.

The inside pages of your newsletter are now complete and should appear as shown in Figure 4.48.

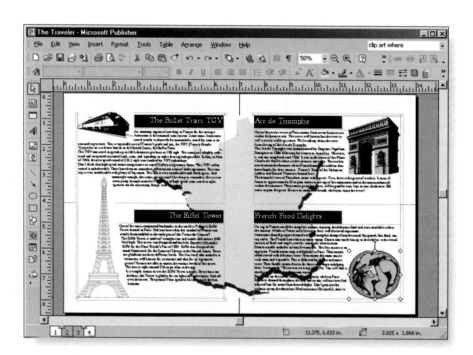

Figure 4.48
Completed pages 2 and 3 of newsletter

26. Save the newsletter.

USING THE DESIGN GALLERY

The Publisher **Design Gallery** contains predesigned objects that you can insert in your publication. The kinds of objects in the Design Gallery are different from the objects (such as clip art and photographs) that are contained in the Media Gallery. Most of the objects in the Design Gallery are small parts of a publication, such as mastheads, captions, and calendars, that contain some text. (There are, however, some other objects, such as boxes and dots that can be used as borders or separators or for accent.) Using Design Gallery objects in your publications, rather than creating the objects from scratch, saves time and helps maintain consistency in your publications.

The Design Gallery is accessed by clicking the Design Gallery Object button on the Objects toolbar or by clicking Design Gallery Object... on the Insert menu. The Design Gallery is divided into three sections (tabs). The first tab, Objects by Categories, contains a list of the objects by types (categories), such as pull quotes, advertisements, and logos. When you click on a category, the available designs for that type of object are displayed in the gallery to the right. The second tab, Objects by Design, provides the same objects, organized by design sets. Choosing objects from the same design set maintains consistency in your publications. When you click on a design choice, various types of objects are displayed that have certain design elements, such as colors, in common. The Design Gallery also allows you to create or customize your own objects and save them for future use. The objects you create are stored under the third tab, Your Objects.

Once you have selected an object in the Design Gallery, you insert it into your publication by clicking it and then clicking the Insert button. Objects can be moved to the desired place within your publication by moving the frames around them. Publisher also allows you to change the default text (if any) within an object, as well as other characteristics of the object. Each time that a Design Gallery object is inserted in a publication, a Wizard button appears below the object. Clicking the Wizard button opens a task pane that gives you options for formatting the object.

HANDS On

Publisher BASICS

Inserting Design Gallery Objects

1. Click the Design Gallery Object button on the Objects toolbar.

2. Locate the desired object in the Design Gallery and click it.

3. Click the Insert button.

Inserting Objects from Design Gallery

In this activity, you will insert objects from the Design Gallery into the traveler newsletter.

1. Open the newsletter (the traveler), if it is not already open, and go to page 1.

2. Increase the Zoom to 75%.

3. Click the Design Gallery button on the Objects toolbar.

4. Click the Objects by Category tab and then click Table of Contents.

5. Select the Blocks Table of Contents (see Figure 4.49) and click Insert Object.

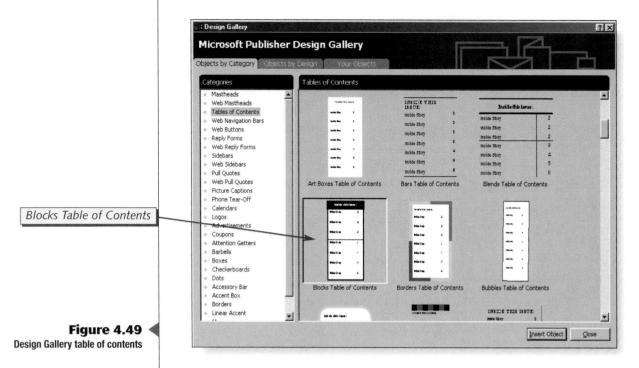

Figure 4.49
Design Gallery table of contents

Blocks Table of Contents

6. Move the Table of Contents so that the left side is even with the left blue margin line and the top is even with the green horizontal ruler guide as shown in Figure 4.50.

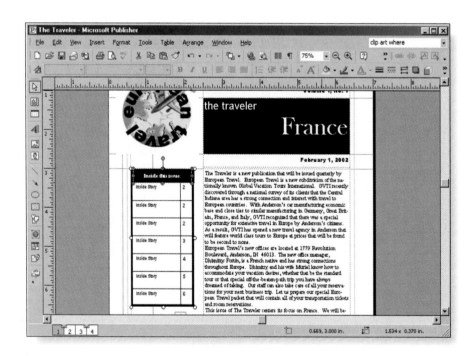

Figure 4.50
Table of contents from Design Gallery inserted into newsletter

7. Edit the default text in the Table of Contents to match the headings of the articles as shown below:

the traveler: France   1
The Bullet Train   2
The Eiffel Tower   2
Arc de Triomphe   3
French Food Delights   3
This Month's Tour   4

8. Save the newsletter.

The TOC contains an extra row that you don't need. Use the following steps to delete it.

9. Select the bottom row. On the Table menu, select Delete, then Rows.

10. Click the Design Gallery button 🖾, click Objects by Category, and then click Sidebars.

11. Select the Bars Sidebar as shown in Figure 4.51, and click Insert Object.

Another Way

- Click Table on the Standard toolbar and then click Delete Rows.

Bars sidebar

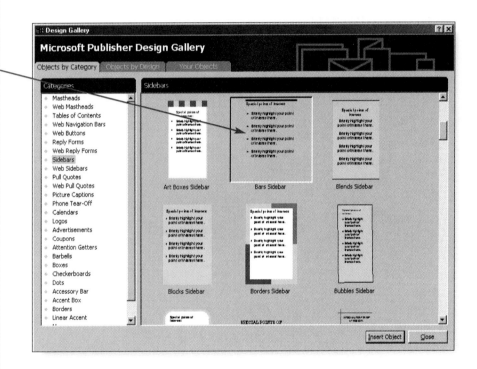

Figure 4.51
Sidebars selected from Design Gallery

12. Move the sidebar so that the left side is even with the left blue margin line and the top is just below the Table of Contents.

13. Resize the sidebar frame so that the bottom of the frame is even with the bottom blue margin line.

14. Keep the Special Points of Interest lead in. Edit the default bulleted list to read:
    GVTI forms new company in Anderson to feature European tours.
    France's bullet train is known for speed and safety.
    The Eiffel Tower sparkles nightly every hour on the hour.

The sidebar should appear as shown in Figure 4.52.

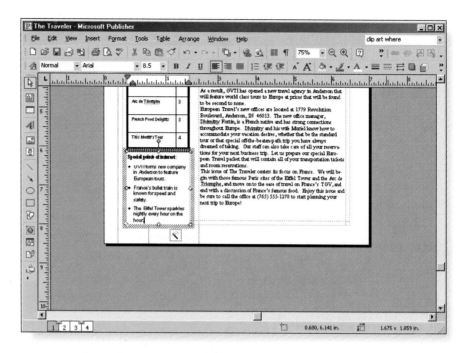

Figure 4.52
Sidebar for newsletter

15. Go to page 4 and change the Zoom to 75%, if necessary.

16. Save the newsletter.

17. Click the Design Gallery button ⊞, click Objects by Category, and then Calendars.

18. Select the Lines Calendar as shown in Figure 4.53 and click Insert Object.

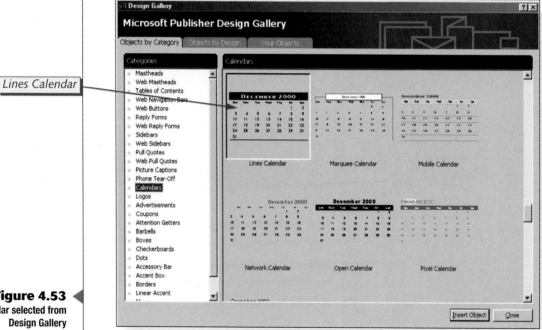

Lines Calendar

Figure 4.53
Lines Calendar selected from
Design Gallery

19. Click the Wizard icon below the calendar.

The Calendar Designs task pane appears.

20. Click the Change date range… button at the bottom of the task pane.

The Change Calendar Dates dialog box appears.

21. Change the Start date: to March 2002 and click OK.

22. Move the calendar to the bottom right corner where the blue margin lines intersect.

23. Resize the calendar by dragging the middle resize handle on the left side of the calendar frame until the left side of the frame is at the 2½-inch mark on the horizontal ruler. Resize the calendar again by dragging the middle resize handle on the top side of the frame to the 4¼-inch mark on the vertical ruler.

24. Click on the heading of the calendar.

25. Click in one of the date boxes in the calendar. Press Ctrl + A twice to select the text, and change the font size to 12.

The calendar appears as shown in Figure 4.54.

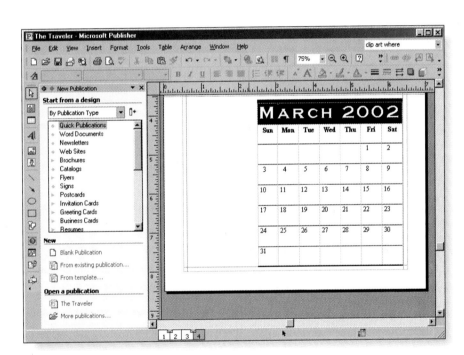

Figure 4.54
Calendar for March 2002

26. Save the newsletter.

You will now create an additional text box next to the calendar to highlight an upcoming trip to France.

27. Draw a text box with the left side of the text box even with the left blue margin line and the bottom side even with the bottom blue margin line. The top side should be even with the 4¾-inch mark on the vertical ruler, and the right side should be even with the 2¼-inch mark on the horizontal ruler.

28. Insert the March tour Word document on your Publisher Data CD.

Re-read step 26 under Creating Text Boxes and Inserting and Formatting Text, if you need help inserting text into the box.

29. Change the font and size to Times New Roman, 12.

30. Draw another text box with the left side even with the left blue margin line and the bottom side even with the top of the text box you created in step 27. The top side should be even with the 4-inch mark on the vertical ruler, and the right side should be even with the right side of the text box below it.

31. Change the font of this text box to Arial Black, 14, and type This issue's featured trip. **(See Figure 4.55.)**

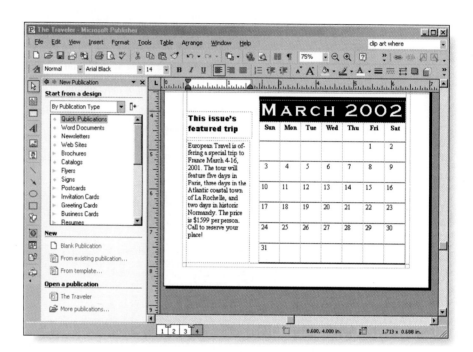

Figure 4.55
Text boxes inserted on page 4

32. Highlight March 4 through March 9 on the calendar by clicking on 4 and dragging to 9.

33. Click the down arrow next to Fill Colors on the Formatting toolbar and select the fifth box from the left to shade the date boxes in gray.

34. Highlight March 10 through March 16 and repeat step 33.

35. Select the text box to the left of the calendar and apply the same fill color as was used for the calendar.

36. Scroll to the top of the page.

37. Select european travel and change to Arial, 16.

38. Change the font and fill colors in this box so that the text is white on black.

39. Move the address box so that its top edge is even with the bottom edge of the european travel box.

40. Move the Phone/Fax/Email box down to the green ruler guide.

41. Insert a text box between the address and phone numbers.

42. Make the new box the same width as the address box.

43. Type Contact: and enter your name.

44. Change the font of the box to Arial, 12.

45. Save the newsletter.

Your completed page 4 appears as shown in Figure 4.56.

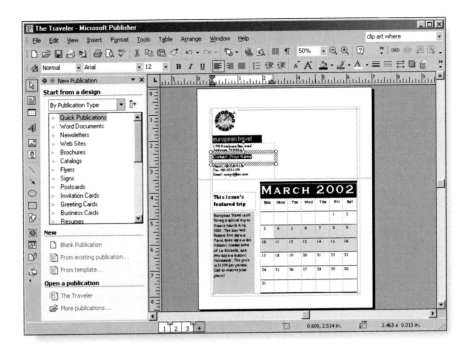

Figure 4.56
Completed page 4 of newsletter

EVALUATING THE DESIGN OF A NEWSLETTER

After you have completed a publication, you should evaluate the publication to see if there are any design problems and to make sure that the publication creates the impression you desire. The newsletter that you just created, with its block style, symmetry, and black and white color scheme, has a formal, serious look, in keeping with its emphasis on historic sites. Do you see any obvious problems with the design? Do you think there is sufficient white space, for example? The lack of white space, especially on the first page, could interfere with readability and discourage the reader. You may also wish to reconsider the font of the body text, which is a sans serif font, and the hyphenation of the paragraphs.

HANDS

Modifying the Newsletter

In this activity, you will make some modifications to your completed newsletter to improve its design.

1. Open the newsletter (the traveler), if it is not already open, and go to page 1.

2. Select all of the text in the main story box.

3. Add paragraph spacing by increasing the line spacing after paragraphs to 9 points.

Note   *Remember line spacing is adjusted on the Format menu.*

4. With the text still selected, turn off automatic hyphenation. (If you think that the right margin is too uneven without hyphenation, you may wish to manually hyphenate a word or two.)

5. Go to pages 2-3.

6. Select each of the story boxes and increase the line spacing after paragraphs to 9 points. (Because the hyphenation on these pages is not excessive, you may wish to leave the automatic hyphenation on.)

As you can see, adding paragraph spacing to the story box at the bottom of page 3 may cause the text to overflow the box. You will need to edit the text so that it fits the boxes. The next step contains possible edits:

7. Combine the first two paragraphs. Next, delete the sentence about French onion soup in the second paragraph. Finally, delete "while in Paris" from the end of the first sentence in the last paragraph. Be sure to keep the period at the end of the sentence.

8. Save the newsletter.

9. Go to page 4.

10. In the text box next to the calendar, add paragraph breaks and paragraph spacing by pressing [Enter⏎] once after the first sentence and once before the last sentence. Then change the line spacing between paragraphs to 9 points.

11. Save the newsletter.

USING DESIGN CHECKER

Publisher also provides a tool called **Design Checker** that can assist you in checking your publication for possible design problems. The types of problems that Design Checker looks for are listed below:

- Text in overflow area
- Disproportional pictures
- Empty frames
- Covered objects
- Objects partially off page
- Objects in nonprinting region
- Blank space at top of page
- Spacing between sentences
- Web sites unreachable by hyperlinks

Checking the Newsletter with Design Checker

In this activity, you will use Design Checker to check your publication for potential design problems. Keep in mind, however, that Design Checker may question elements in your publication that you have used deliberately and that do not need to be changed.

1. Open the newsletter (the traveler), if necessary.

2. On the Tools menu, click Design Checker….

The Design Checker dialog box appears.

3. Click the Options… button.

Using Design Checker

1. On the Tools menu, click Design Checker....

2. Click the Options... button.

3. Select Check all problems and click OK.

4. Under Check which pages? select All and click OK.

5. Click Change (or Delete) if a change is needed, or click Ignore if no change is needed.

4. Select Check all problems and click OK.

5. Under Check which pages? select All and click OK.

Design Checker begins to check your publication and notifies you of each potential problem it finds. If you agree that the problem should be corrected, click the suggested change. If you disagree (if you don't want Design Checker to make a change), click Ignore.

 *If Design Checker finds two spaces after a punctuation mark (a common problem), click Change.*

6. After Design Checker has finished checking your publication, save the publication again.

PREPARING PUBLICATIONS FOR OUTSIDE PRINTING

As you learned in Lesson 1, you may need to take your publications to a print shop or copy center for printing or duplication. Whether you will print your publications yourself, or take them to an outside printer, depends on several factors, such as:

■ How many copies of your publication do you need?

■ What kind of paper do you want to use?

■ Do you need to print in color or only black and white?

■ How high does the quality need to be?

■ What equipment do you have, and what are the capabilities of your equipment?

If you only need a few copies of a publication, you may be able to print your own copies using a laser or inkjet printer. On the other hand, if you need a large quantity of copies or if your equipment is not capable of the quality you want, you may need to have your publications printed by a commercial print shop.

If you will be taking your publication elsewhere to have it printed, some additional steps will be necessary to prepare your publication for printing. If the resolution of your own printer is good enough, you may be able to print a master copy of your publication and take it to the print shop for duplication. If you need a higher resolution than your printer can provide, however, you will need to take your publication to the print shop as a file or files. To help you prepare your files for outside printing, Publisher has a feature called **Pack and Go,** which lets you bundle and condense a publication's files to take to another computer. When you use Pack and Go, your publication will look exactly the same on the other computer as it does on your own, because Pack and Go bundles all of the graphics and fonts that go with your publication. Even if the other computer does not have the same fonts as your computer, Pack and Go makes it possible for the other computer to use the same fonts.

Note *In order for Pack and Go to work, Publisher must be installed on the other computer. Before you use Pack and Go to prepare your files for outside printing, you will want to verify that the print shop has the Publisher software.*

HANDS On

Publisher BASICS

Using the Pack and Go Wizard

1. On the File menu, click Pack and Go.

2. Click Take to a Commercial Printing Service....

3. Click Next.

4. Select A:\ (or another drive, if necessary) and click Next.

5. Make sure that all three choices are selected (checked) and click Next.

6. Click Finish to start the packing process.

7. Click OK to close the wizard.

Using Pack and Go

In this activity, you will pack your newsletter for outside printing. You will need to have a floppy disk or CD placed in the correct drive before beginning the packing process.

1. Open the newsletter (the traveler), if it is not already open.

2. On the File menu, click Pack and Go and then click Take to a Commercial Printing Service....

The Pack and Go Wizard dialog box appears and gives you a brief overview of Pack and Go's capabilities.

3. Click Next.

Publisher asks: Where would you like to pack your publication to?

4. Select A:\ and click Next.

 *You may need to modify step 4 if you do not have a floppy disk drive or if you will be writing the files to a CD. If necessary, change the destination drive from A to the appropriate drive letter.*

Publisher gives you choices for including fonts and graphics.

5. Make sure that all three choices are selected (checked) and click Next.

Publisher gives an overview of the packing process.

6. Click Finish.

Publisher begins to pack your publication. When the packing is finished, the message **Your publication is successfully packed** appears. Publisher also gives you the following explanation:

> The wizard copied Unpack.exe and your packed file into the directory you selected. Run Unpack.exe when you want to unpack your publication.

7. Click OK to close the wizard and print a copy of the publication on your own printer. If you don't want to print a copy, deselect (uncheck) Print a composite before clicking OK.

Test your knowledge by matching the terms on the left with the definitions on the right. See Appendix C to check your answers.

TERMS

_____ **1.** Clipboard

_____ **2.** Design Gallery

_____ **3.** landscape

_____ **4.** portrait

_____ **5.** WordArt

DEFINITIONS

a. page orientation where the top and bottom of the page are the longer sides of the paper

b. allows you to stretch, skew, or rotate text

c. contains objects, such as mastheads and calendars, that you can insert in your publication

d. allows items to be cut and pasted from one location to another

e. page orientation where the top and bottom of the page are the shorter sides of the paper

SAVING A PUBLICATION AS A WEB PAGE

You can save any publication created in Publisher as a Web page and publish it on an organization's intranet or on the Internet. Before you publish a Web page, however, you must save the publication in a form the Web can read. Web pages are written in *Hypertext Markup Language* (or *HTML*), which includes the codes for linking Web documents to each other. A set of rules called *Hypertext Transfer Protocol* (or *HTTP*) defines the way that hypertext links display Web pages. The Web would not exist without HTML or HTTP. A Publisher user, though, does not need to know HTML or HTTP to create a Web page. You can use Publisher features—the Save as Web Page command, for example—to code a publication with HTML and HTTP.

In this activity, you will convert the newsletter you created in this lesson to a Web page.

1. Open the newsletter *the traveler,* if it is not already open.

2. Click **Save As Web Page** on the File menu.

The Save as Web Page dialog box appears.

3. In the File name: box, change the name to *the traveler as Web Pages* and click **Save.** (See Figure 4.57.)

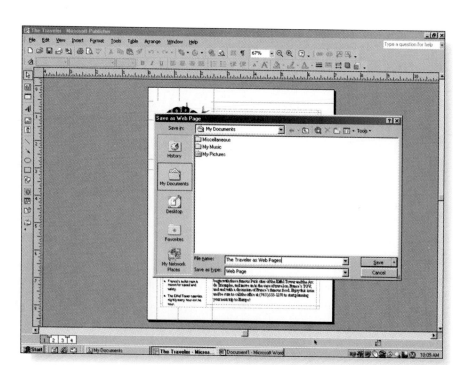

Figure 4.57 ◀
Save as Web Page
dialog box

4. Click **Save** 🖫.

The newsletter is now saved in HTML format.

You can enhance a Web page by adding a background color, along with an interesting texture or a pattern. Color and graphics are especially important in Web pages because black and white text alone can make your Web page look boring and not worth reading. In working with colors, however, remember that too many colors can be distracting. You want to draw attention to the content of the Web page, not the design of the page. As you change colors, make sure the text colors contrast with the background. If you use a dark blue background, for example, choose a light, bright color, instead of black, for the text.

Because the Web page you just created was based on a black and white publication, it needs to have color added.

5. Click **Color Schemes** on the task pane.

6. Under Apply a color scheme, click **Dark Blue.** (See Figure 4.58.)

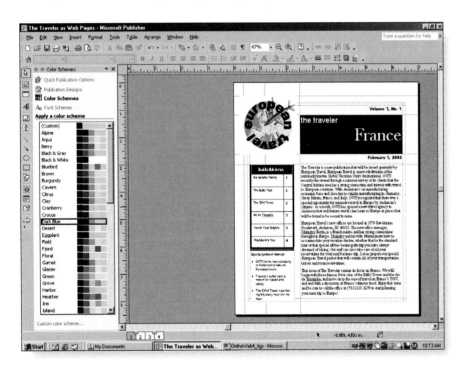

Figure 4.58 ◀
Applying a color scheme to
the traveler

7. Click **Background...** on the Format menu.

8. On the Background task pane, click **More backgrounds...**

9. On the Fill Effects dialog box, click the **Texture** tab, and then click the first choice in the third row as shown in Figure 4.59.

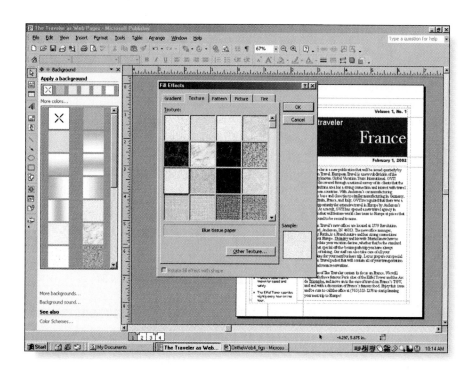

Figure 4.59 ◀
Fill Effects dialog box

10. Click OK.

The background texture is added to page 1.

11. Click pages 2–3.

On the Background task pane, under Apply a background, you will see that the background you selected is now one of the choices.

12. Move the pointer to this color choice.

A down arrow appears.

13. Click the down arrow.

A drop-down menu appears, as shown in Figure 4.60.

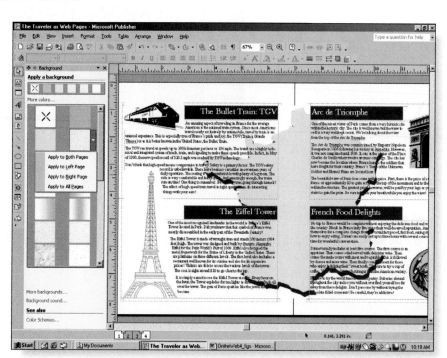

Figure 4.60 ◀
Drop-down menu for applying fill

14. Click **Apply to All Pages** on the drop-down menu.

The background texture is added to all pages.

When your newsletter is viewed through a Web browser, pages 2 and 3 will not be viewed together. As a result, only half of the map of France will be seen on each page, so the map should be deleted.

15. Select the map of France and then press the **Delete** key.

You may have noticed that the graphics still have white backgrounds. This is because their frames are opaque and are covering the new background. In the next few steps, you will correct this problem.

16. Click the Eiffel Tower picture on page 2.

17. On the Picture toolbar, click the **Set Transparent Color** button, as shown in Figure 4.61.

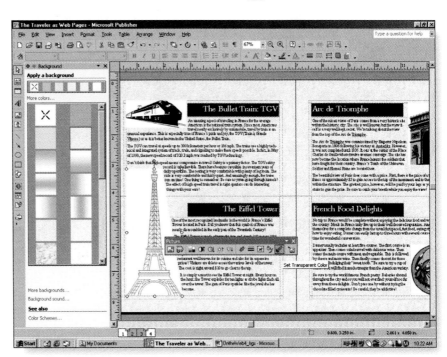

Figure 4.61
Setting Eiffel Tower graphic to transparent

The pointer changes to a small paint brush.

18. Click the Eiffel Tower picture with the paint brush pointer.

The background texture now shows through the Eiffel Tower picture, as shown in Figure 4.62.

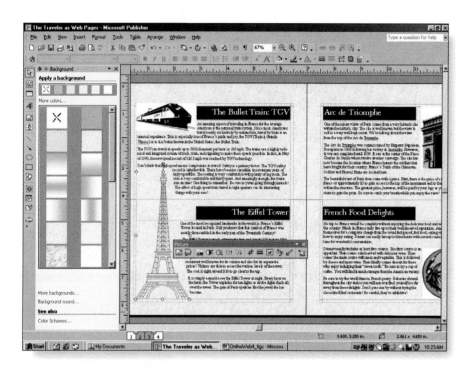

Figure 4.62 ◄
Eiffel Tower transparent
with background fill visible

19. Repeat steps 16–18 for each of the other graphics on pages 2–3.

20. Click **page 1.**

21. Right-click the *european travel* logo.

Its current file format does not allow you to change the background fill. The next series of steps allows you to resave the file in a TIF format that does support background fills.

22. Click **Save as Picture....**

23. In the File name: box, **type** european travel logo.

24. In the Save as type: box, select **Tag Image File Format.**

The Tag Image File format is commonly known as TIF.

25. Click the **Save** button.

You will now see two copies of the logo on the screen.

26. Select the old copy of the logo that is in place in the left corner of the page and press Delete.

27. Move the new logo into the space vacated.

28. Click **Save** 🖫.

29. Click **Select** on the Table menu and then click **Table.**

30. Click the down arrow next to the Fill Color button 🔲 ▾ on the Formatting toolbar.

31. Click **Fill Effects....**

32. Click the Texture tab, and then click the first color in the third row, as shown in Figure 4.63.

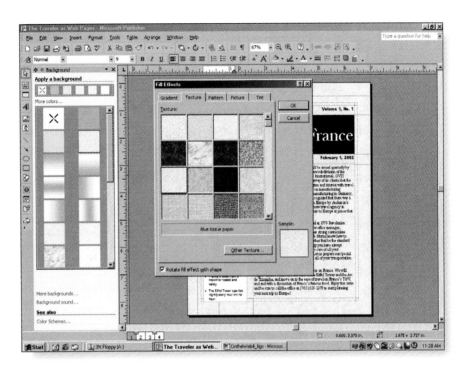

Figure 4.63
Table Fill Effects dialog box

33. Click **OK.**

The Fill color for the Table of Contents now matches the rest of the background.

34. Select the Special Points of Interest text box under the contents.

35. Change the fill color, following steps 30–33.

All of page 1 now has the same background color.

36. Copy the european travel logo from page 1.

37. Move to page 4 and paste the logo.

38. Delete the existing logo which does not accomodate the transparent background.

39. Move the pasted logo into the position vacated and resize as needed.

40. Click **Save** 🖫.

41. When asked if you want to save the modified logo to the Secondary Business personal information set, click **Yes.**

To move between pages on a Web site, the pages must be linked. You will learn how to add these links to your publication in Lesson 5. In Lesson 5, you will also learn how to preview your publication in a Web browser.

Lesson Summary & Exercises

SUMMARY

Now that you have learned some of the basics of design and are more familiar with the capabilities of Publisher, you may find that you wish to create some, or all, of your publications from scratch, without using Publisher templates. Before you can begin to create a publication from scratch, however, you need to plan the publication. After identifying the objective of the publication and its intended audience, you must consider how much you can afford to spend on the publication and how much information you need to include. These decisions will, in turn, determine other choices such as what format, paper, colors, and layout you will use.

Publisher gives you the flexibility to start with a blank publication and apply set-up, layout, and design elements to it. Some special features in Publisher can help with the design of certain parts of your publication. The WordArt Gallery contains preformatted text effects that you can use to create logos and other special kinds of text. The Design Gallery contains predesigned objects, such as mastheads, tables of contents, and calendars, that you can insert in your publication and then modify. Other Publisher features can help get your publication ready for printing. The Design Checker can assist you in checking your publication for possible design problems, and the Pack and Go Wizard can bundle and condense your publication's files to take to another computer for printing.

Now that you have completed this lesson, you should be able to do the following:

- Explain what factors must be considered when planning a publication.
- Choose appropriate formats and layouts for your publications.
- Change the page setup and margins of a blank publication.
- Create logos using WordArt.
- Rearrange layered objects in a stack.
- Create text boxes.
- Use layout guides and ruler guides to align text and graphics on a page.
- Change text wrapping.
- Choose and insert objects from the Design Gallery.
- Evaluate the design of a completed publication and make changes as needed.
- Use Design Checker to check for certain design problems.
- Explain what factors to consider when deciding how to print a publication.
- Use the Pack and Go feature to prepare a publication for outside printing.

CONCEPTS REVIEW

1 TRUE/FALSE

Circle T if the statement is true or F if the statement is false.

T   F   **1.** Your main objective when planning a publication is to get your intended readers to actually read your publication.

T   F   **2.** Three-column layouts are formal and serious-looking.

T F **3.** After you use ruler guides, you need to delete them so that they do not show when you print your publication.

T F **4.** When printing a double-sided publication, heavier paper may be needed so that text and graphics do not show through from one side to the other.

T F **5.** When you place a picture frame on top of a text frame, the picture covers the text.

T F **6.** Most of the objects in the Design Gallery are clip art and photographs.

T F **7.** Having plenty of white space makes your publication look "friendly."

T F **8.** When you use Pack and Go, your publication will look exactly the same on the other computer as it does on yours.

T F **9.** If your printer cannot handle 11" x 17" paper, you may still be able to use it by taking two 8½" x 11" sheets to a print shop for copying onto 11" x 17" paper.

T F **10.** Pack and Go will work on another computer, even if Publisher is not installed on the other computer.

2 MATCHING

Match each of the terms on the left with the definitions on the right.

TERMS DEFINITIONS

1. Design Checker

2. layout guides

3. legal size

4. letter size

5. Pack and Go

6. ruler guides

7. stacking

8. symmetrical

9. tabloid size

10. wrapping lines

a. 8½" x 11" paper

b. 8¼" x 14" paper

c. 11" x 17" paper

d. a layout where the text and graphics are balanced on each side of a page

e. placing frames on top of each other

f. green lines that allow you to align objects on a page

g. pink and blue dotted lines that indicate margin settings

h. red lines with black corner points between text and graphics

i. a Publisher feature that assists you in checking your publication for design problems

j. a Publisher feature that lets you bundle and condense files to take to another computer

Lesson Summary & Exercises

3 COMPLETION

Fill in the missing word or phrase for each of the following statements.

1. If you must use only black and white text and graphics, you can achieve some variety by using different shades of _____ or by printing on _____ paper.

2. When creating _____ pages, always consider the two pages together.

3. _____ layouts are less formal and often more interesting.

4. The _____ provides 30 preformatted designs of special text effects.

5. When you point at the green dot above a piece of WordArt, the _____ pointer appears.

6. As you move the mouse pointer, your place on the page is indicated by marks on the _____.

7. You can correct stacking problems by using commands on the _____ menu.

8. Each time that a Design Gallery object is inserted in a publication, a _____ button appears below the object.

9. Click the Text Wrapping button on the _____ toolbar to change text wrapping.

10. The Design Gallery is divided into three sections: Objects by _____, Objects by _____, and Your Objects.

4 SHORT ANSWER

1. What are some of the questions you need to consider when planning a publication?

2. How does the amount that you can spend on a publication influence the design?

3. How do you reverse the text and background colors from black on white to white on black?

4. How do you create and insert WordArt text into a publication?

5. What is the difference between layout guides and ruler guides?

6. How do you create and format text boxes?

7. Explain how to change the text wrapping around a picture.

8. Describe the kinds of objects that can be found in the Design Gallery and how the Design Gallery is organized.

9. What are some of the elements you need to examine when evaluating the design of a completed publication? How can Design Checker help?

10. What are some of the factors you need to consider when deciding how to print a publication?

5 IDENTIFICATION

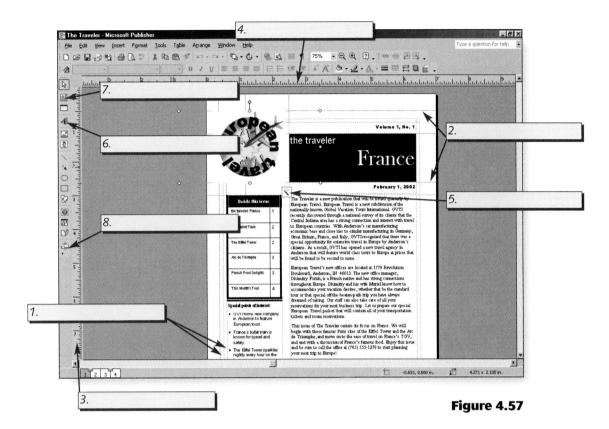

Figure 4.57

SKILLS REVIEW

Complete each of the Skills Review activities in sequential order to review the skills you learned in this lesson. In these activities, you will create the first page of a newsletter from a student named Andrew Jones, who is writing about his trip to France. In the process of creating the newsletter, you will review your skills to create page layouts using margin guides and ruler guides, insert text boxes and graphics, wrap text around graphics, rearrange the layering of objects, insert Design Gallery objects, use WordArt, reverse font and fill colors, and run Design Checker and the Pack and Go wizard.

1 Opening blank publication, checking page set up, changing margin settings, and inserting ruler guides

1. Open a new, blank publication.

2. For this newsletter, you will use 8½" x 11" paper and portrait orientation, which are default settings in Publisher. Verify that these are the current settings and change if necessary.

3. Change the margin settings to **0.8**" on all sides.

4. Insert horizontal ruler guides at the 3½-inch, 4-inch, 7-inch, and 7½-inch marks on the vertical ruler.

5. Save the newsletter as **My Trip to France.**

Lesson Summary & Exercises

2 Insert, move, resize and crop graphics

1. Insert the **French Countryside** graphic from your Publisher Data CD.

2. Move this picture to the top of the page and resize the picture to fit within the blue margin lines at the top and sides of the page.

3. Crop the top and bottom of the picture so that it will fit within the box created by the blue margin lines and the first green ruler guide. Crop the top of the picture so that the top of the tree is at the top edge of the picture and so that only a small amount of water is visible at the bottom.

4. Insert the **Fortins** graphic from your Publisher Data CD.

5. Resize the picture so that it is 4 inches wide. (Use the **Format Picture** button on the Picture toolbar. Make sure that **Lock Aspect Ratio** is checked.)

6. Move the picture to the lower left corner of the page and crop the bottom of the picture until it fits within the box created by the fourth green ruler guide and the blue margin lines at the bottom of the page.

7. Save the newsletter.

3 Rearrange the layering of objects

1. Insert the **Arc de Triomphe** graphic from the Publisher Data CD.

2. Resize the picture so that it is 1.25 inches wide.

3. Move the picture so that the upper right corner of the picture is in the corner created by the second green ruler guide and the right blue margin line.

4. Insert the **Eiffel Tower From Bottom** graphic from the Publisher Data CD.

5. Resize the picture so that it is the same size as the Arc de Triomphe picture (1.25 inches wide).

6. Move the picture so that the bottom of the picture is even with the third green ruler guide and so that the right side of the picture is at the 6½-inch mark on the horizontal ruler.

Note *The Eiffel Tower picture overlaps the Arc de Triomphe picture.*

7. Select the **Arc de Triomphe** picture and then click **Order** on the Arrange menu. Click **Bring to Front**.

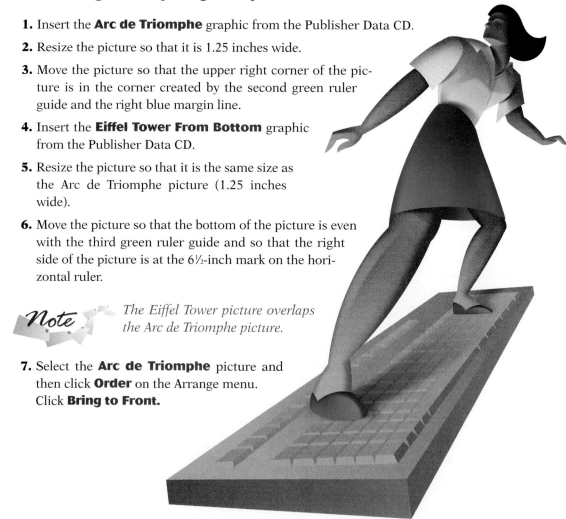

 *Now the Arc de Triomphe picture overlaps the sky in the Eiffel Tower picture. If any of the Arc de Triomphe picture overlaps the Eiffel Tower itself, crop the bottom of the Arc de Triomphe picture slightly.)*

8. Save the newsletter.

4 Use WordArt to create a masthead

1. Click the **Insert WordArt** button 📇, select the second WordArt style in the first row, and click **OK.**

2. Type My Trip to France in the Edit WordArt Text box.

3. Change the font to **Lucida Handwriting, 36,** and click **OK.**

 If Lucida Handwriting is not an available font, select another script font.

4. Click the **WordArt Shape** button 📇 on the WordArt toolbar and then click **Arch Up (Curve),** the first shape in the second row.

5. Change the fill and line color of the WordArt to a bright orange or yellow-orange color.

6. Move the WordArt to the top of the page and resize it so that the "M" in "My" and the "e" in France extend slightly beyond the left and right sides of the picture. The top of the WordArt semi-circle will also extend slightly above the top of the picture.

7. Save the newsletter.

5 Insert text boxes, resize and wrap text

1. Draw a text box in the middle of the page so that its top and bottom are the second and third ruler guides and so that its left side is the left blue margin and its right side is the left side of the Arc de Triomphe picture. (The text frame will overlap the Eiffel Tower picture.)

2. Insert the text file **Andrew Jones Intro** from the Publisher Data CD. When Publisher asks if you want to use autoflow, click **No.**

3. Change the font size of the text to **10.**

 Because the graphics were inserted before the text, the text does not wrap around the graphics.

4. To make the text wrap around the Eiffel Tower picture, select the text frame, and then click **Order** on the Arrange menu. **Click Send to Back.**

5. Draw a text box next to the Fortins picture at the bottom of the page. (The left side of the text box should be even with the right side of the Fortins picture. The top should be even with the fourth green ruler guide. The right and bottom sides of the text box should be even with the blue margin lines in the lower right corner of the page.)

6. Insert the text file **Andrew Jones European Travel** from the Publisher Data CD. When Publisher asks if you wish to use autoflow, click **No.**

7. Change the font size of the text to **10.**

8. Save the newsletter.

6 Add separators using the Design Gallery

1. Click the **Design Gallery Object** button on the Objects toolbar.

2. Click **Barbells** under Objects by Category, select **Balanced Barbell,** and then click **Insert Object.**

3. Move the barbell so that it is at the top edge of the first story box.

4. Resize the barbell frame so that the barbell extends from the left blue margin line to the right blue margin line.

5. Insert a second barbell separator so that it is at the *bottom* edge of the first story box. Resize it so that it also extends from the left to the right margin.

6. Save the newsletter.

7 Add headlines and a caption and reverse font and fill colors

1. Draw a text box to fill the space between the French Countryside picture and the first barbell separator.

2. Type A dream of a lifetime comes true!

3. Change the font to **Ravie, 18,** and center the text.

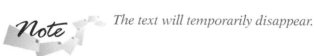 *If Ravie is not an available font, select another interesting font.*

4. Draw a text box to fill the space between the second barbell separator and the Fortins picture and second story box.

5. Type european travel made my trip a breeze!

6. Change the font of the words "european travel" to **Arial Black, 18,** and the font of the words "made my trip a breeze!" to **Ravie, 18.** Center the text.

7. Draw a text box in the space under the Arc de Triomphe picture and to the right of the Eiffel Tower picture.

8. Type My visit to Paris included stops at the Arc de Triomphe and the Eiffel Tower.

9. Change the font of the text in this box to **Arial.**

10. Change the font color of the text to white.

The text will temporarily disappear.

11. Change the fill color of the text box to **black** to make the words reappear.

12. Save the newsletter.

8 Add paragraph spacing, check for other design problems using Design Checker, and run the Pack and Go Wizard

1. Select the text in the first story box and add paragraph spacing (6 pt. after each paragraph).

2. Select the text in the second story box and add the same paragraph spacing.

3. Use **Design Checker** to check for other design problems and make corrections as necessary.

 Design Checker may question items that do not need to be changed. For example, Design Checker will question pictures whose proportions have been changed, but this does not need to be corrected if you have changed them deliberately—and carefully.

4. Check the newsletter for misspellings, make corrections as necessary, and then save the newsletter.

5. Print a copy of the newsletter and proofread it. Key any corrections and then save it again.

6. Run the **Pack and Go Wizard** to prepare the publication for outside printing.

LESSON APPLICATIONS

Complete the following activities in sequential order to build a flyer from scratch.

1 Create a flyer from a blank publication

Open a blank publication and check and change Page Set Up options to begin to build a flyer.

1. Click on Blank Publication in the New [or New from Existing] Publication task pane.

2. Click Page Set Up on the File menu.

3. Verify that the Publication type is full page and change the orientation to Landscape.

4. Change the paper size to Letter (8.5" x 11"), if necessary, and click OK.

2 Insert and format graphics on a flyer

Insert, move and resize graphics on a flyer. (Be sure to complete Lesson Application 1 above before beginning this application activity.)

1. Insert the *Map of France* graphic from the Publisher Data CD.

2. Move the map of France to the lower right corner of the page, so that the lower right corner of its frame is aligned with the intersection of the blue margin lines.

3. Insert the *Eiffel Tower* graphic from the Publisher Data CD.

4. Move the Eiffel Tower to the lower left corner of the page, so that the lower left corner of its frame is aligned with the intersection of the blue margin lines.

Lesson Summary & Exercises

5. Insert a horizontal ruler guide that is even with the 2½-inch mark on the vertical ruler.

6. Resize the Eiffel Tower graphic until the top of the Eiffel Tower is even with the horizontal ruler guide.

7. Save the publication as *Paris in the Spring flyer.*

3 Insert and format WordArt on a flyer

Insert a piece of WordArt, and change the color and move and resize the WordArt.

1. Open the *Paris in the Spring flyer,* if it is not already open.

2. Click the Insert WordArt button on the Objects toolbar.

3. Select the fifth WordArt style in the third row and click OK.

4. Edit the WordArt text to read: Paris in the Spring. Click OK.

5. Click the Format WordArt button on the WordArt toolbar.

6. On the Colors and Lines tab, click the down arrow next to Line Color.

7. Click More Colors…, select a green color from the color chart that will match, as far as possible, the color of the Map of France graphic, and then click OK.

8. On the Colors and Lines tab, click OK again.

9. Check the appearance of your WordArt. If the green color you selected does not match the color of the Map of France, repeat steps 4–7 and choose a different color.

10. Move the WordArt frame to the upper left corner of the flyer, so that the left side of the frame is even with the left blue margin line.

11. Insert a vertical ruler guide at the 5¹₂-inch mark on the horizontal ruler. (This is the center of your page).

12. Resize the WordArt frame so that the right edge of the "g" in "Spring" is even with the vertical ruler guide.

13. Adjust the WordArt (move and/or resize as necessary) so that it fits within the "box" created by the horizontal and vertical ruler guides and the blue margin lines. This should also align the "s" in the word "Paris" with the top of the Eiffel Tower.

14. Save the updated flyer.

4 Insert and format a Design Gallery Object on a flyer

Insert an object from the Design Gallery, move and resize it, and then edit and format its text.

1. Open the Paris in the Spring flyer, if it is not already open.

2. Click the Design Gallery Object button on the Objects toolbar.

3. Under Categories, click Attention Getters.

4. Select the Hollowed Starburst Attention Getter and insert it into your flyer.

5. Move the starburst to the upper right corner of the flyer so that it is centered within the "box" created by the green ruler guides and the blue margin lines.

6. Resize the starburst so that it fills most of the "box." (Leave some white space between the starburst and the WordArt so that they don't run into each other.)

7. Increase the Zoom so that you can read the text within the starburst, and change the text to read: Special trip `Enter↵` through `Enter↵` european travel

8. Change the font of the words "Special trip" and "through" to Baskerville Old Face, 16.

9. Change the font of the words "european travel" to Arial Black, 14.

10. Click the blue boxes under the "T" in "Through" and the "E" in "European", and undo the automatic capitalization.

11. Click the starburst and then click the Fill Color box on the Formatting toolbar.

12. Click the green color choice (which is the same color as the WordArt).

13. Save the updated flyer.

5 Insert and format a text box on a flyer

Draw a text box, enter text, and then format that text.

1. Open the Paris in the Spring flyer, if it is not already opened.

2. Draw a text box from the right edge of the Eiffel Tower frame to the right blue margin line. The top side of the text box should be even with the horizontal ruler guide and the bottom side should be even with the bottom margin line. (The text box will include the Map of France.)

3. Change the font of the text box to Baskerville Old Face, 16.

4. Press the `Enter↵` once and type the following text:

Join the staff of european travel for a once-in-a-lifetime trip to Paris! `Enter↵` `Enter↵`

Leave Indianapolis on May 10 and return on May 17. `Enter↵` `Enter↵`

Complete tour package including airfare from Indianapolis, hotel accommodations, meals, ground transportation, and sightseeing for only $899 per person. `Enter↵` `Enter↵`

Contact our office at 765-555-1278 or e-mail us at europe@last.com. `Enter↵` `Enter↵`

Let our staff of travel experts make your dream of a lifetime come true!
`Enter↵` `Enter↵` `Enter↵`

european travel `Enter↵`

1779 Revolution Boulevard `Enter↵`

Anderson, IN 46013

5. Undo the automatic capitalization of the "E" in "European travel" and "Europe@last.com"

6. Change the font of the words "european travel" to Arial Black.

7. Proofread and print the flyer.

8. Save the updated flyer.

Lesson Summary & Exercises

PROJECTS

1 What's in the Design Gallery?

Click each of the categories under Objects by Category and view the available designs in the Gallery to the right. List five categories whose objects contain text that must be edited, five categories whose objects are primarily ornamental, and five categories whose objects are specifically designed for use on Web pages.

Choose a masthead design that you particularly like and write its name. Click the Objects by Design tab and locate the design set that matches the masthead design you chose. List the other objects that are available in that design set.

2 Twelve Months Make a Year

The Design Gallery contains calendar designs for single months, but what if you need to create a 12-month calendar?

Open a new blank publication and change the page set-up to legal size paper and landscape orientation. Change the margins to 0.5 inches on all sides.

Using ruler guides, divide the page into six boxes of equal size.

(Hint: Divide the page in half using a vertical ruler guide, and then divide the page in thirds using horizontal ruler guides.)

Select a calendar style from the Design Gallery and insert it into the publication. Move the calendar object so that the upper left corner of the calendar is aligned with the blue margin lines in the upper left corner of the page. Resize the calendar to fit the box created by the ruler guides and the blue margin lines.

Select the calendar and make a copy of it using the Copy button on the Standard toolbar. Move the pointer to the upper right corner of the page and click the Paste button on the Standard toolbar. Move the copy of the calendar until it fits within the box in the upper right corner of the page. Make four more copies of the calendar object and move each one to fit within a different box on the page.

Select each calendar object and click the Wizard icon that is displayed. Change the dates on the calendars so that January and February are in the top boxes, March and April are in the middle boxes, and May and June are in the bottom boxes.

Insert a second page using the Page... command on the Insert menu. Indicate that 1 page is to be inserted after the current page. Select Duplicate all objects on page 1, and click OK. Note that page 2 has been created and a copy of page 1 has been inserted automatically on page 2. Change the month on each of the calendars on page 2 so that page 2 contains July through December.

Save the publication as 12 Month Calendar.

3 In Recognition

Because of your growing expertise with Microsoft Publisher, your boss asked you to present a workshop on the basics of Publisher to some of your co-workers. You have completed the workshop and would like to give certificates to each of the participants in the workshop. You can create a certificate from scratch using WordArt and Design Gallery borders.

Open a blank publication and change its orientation to landscape.

Choose a border from the Design Gallery and insert it into the publication. Move and resize the border to fit within the layout guides (margins) of your publication.

Open the WordArt Gallery and select a WordArt style that you think would be appropriate for a certificate. Edit the text to read: Certificate of Completion. Change the font to one that is more formal or ornamental, but still readable. Click OK to insert the text into your publication.

If the WordArt style you chose does not already have a semi-circular shape, change the shape using the WordArt toolbar. Move the WordArt so that the top of the semi-circle is about an inch from the top margin of the page, and so that it is centered horizontally on the page. Change the font size as necessary so that the left and right edges of the WordArt are approximately an inch from the side margins.

Draw a text box about an inch below the WordArt frame that is three inches long and approximately the same width as the WordArt frame. Type the following text in the frame:

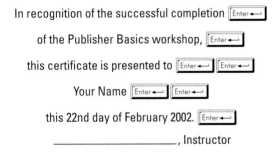

Center all of the lines of text, except for the last line. Right-align that line (the signature line). Change the font to Baskerville Old Face, 20 (or another formal-looking font). Make your name bold. (You can also experiment with making your name a larger or different font.)

Change the date to the current date. Create a line for a signature by pressing the underline key on your keyboard 24 times.

Undo the capitalization of the first letters of each line, if AutoCorrect has changed them to capital letters.

Save the certificate.

Lesson Summary & Exercises

4 Nothing but the Design Gallery

Did you know that it is possible to create a colorful postcard using nothing but Design Gallery objects?

Assume that you need to send a postcard to the members of a club at your school to remind them of an upcoming meeting or event. Open a blank publication and change the orientation to landscape. Insert a pull quote to use as a text box. Move the pull quote box to the left side of the card, and resize it to fill the left half of the card. Describe the event in this box (including the date, time, and location).

Insert a calendar with the month and year of the event at the top and the day of the event highlighted. This will emphasize the date and remind people to mark their calendars. Move the calendar to the upper right corner of the card and resize it to fill the top half of the right side of the card. If necessary, change the color of the calendar to match the color of the pull quote.

Insert an attention getter. Move it to the lower right corner of the card. Move and resize it to fit the remaining space on the card. Edit the text to say: Mark your calendars! Change the fill color of the attention getter to match the color of the pull quote and calendar.

Save the postcard.

5 Here's the Program

A club at your school is sponsoring a special meeting, where several people will make presentations. You have been asked to create the program for this meeting.

Open a blank publication and change the layout to Booklet and the orientation to Landscape. When Publisher asks if you wish to automatically insert pages, click No.

Select a border from the Design Gallery and insert it into your publication. Resize and move the border to fit within the margin lines on your publication.

On the Insert menu, click Page... and tell Publisher to insert three pages after the current page. Also click Duplicate all objects on page 1 and then click OK. Publisher inserts three pages with the same border as page 1. Go to pages 2–3 and delete the borders, but leave the border on page 4. The front and back of the program will now have the same border.

Lesson Summary & Exercises

Locate an appropriate graphic in the Media Gallery and insert it on page 1. Resize the graphic to fit the available space. Create text boxes above and/or below the graphic to give the title of the meeting and the date and location. Change fonts and sizes as necessary.

Include the agenda for the meeting on the inside pages (pages 2–3). Include such information as the time and title of each presentation and the name of the speaker. If the agenda is not long enough to fill two pages, put the agenda on page 3. Either leave page 2 blank or repeat the graphic from page 1.

On page 4 (the back), thank those who were involved in planning and preparing for the meeting. Also include information about your club, as space allows.

Proofread the program and use Design Checker to assist you in checking the program for any design problems. Make any necessary changes, and save the program.

Project in Progress

As you have prepared various promotional materials for your Friends of the Library group, you have become increasingly aware of the need for a logo for your organization and have decided to create one yourself.

Open a new, blank publication. Search the Clip Organizer or Design Gallery Live for a piece of clip art relating to books or reading. Use WordArt to add the name of your Friends of the Library group to the clip art. Group the clip art and WordArt as one logo. Save the new logo using the Save as Picture command. Save it in the JPEG File Interchange Format, under the name Friends Logo.

Open the Friends Newsletter that you created in Lesson 3. Go to the last page of the newsletter and click on the logo. Click the Wizard button and then click Logo Options on the Logo Designs task pane. Click Inserted picture, if it is not already selected, and then click Choose Picture.... When the Insert Picture dialog box appears, locate the Friends Logo that you just saved and insert it into your newsletter. Save the newsletter. When Publisher asks if you wish to save the new logo to the Other Organization personal information set, click Yes. The logo is now part of the personal information set and will be inserted automatically in future publications.

LESSON **5**

Creating a Web Site

CONTENTS

OBJECTIVES

After you complete this lesson, you will be able to do the following:

■ Explain what information is appropriate for a Web page.
■ Plan a Web site.
■ Create a Web site using design templates.
■ Link pages within a Web site and create links to other Web sites.
■ Add background sound to a Web page.
■ Check a Web site for design and linking problems.
■ View a Web site in Explorer.

This lesson explores how to use Microsoft Publisher to create a Web site. You will learn the characteristics of Web pages and how to plan a Web site. Then you will create a Web site using Publisher templates. This lesson teaches you how to create hyperlinks—both to link pages within a Web site and to create links to other sites. Finally, when the Web site is complete, you will learn how to check it for problems and how to preview it before publishing.

Conventions and tourism are big business all across the country. Millions of dollars are spent each year to attract people to a variety of destinations for business and pleasure. Bed and breakfast (B & B) owners use brochures and Web sites to showcase the features and explain the benefits of choosing B & B accommodations. Brochures and Web sites often feature drawings or photographs of the property, along with a list of amenities, price information, and driving directions. B & B owners, who often live on the premises, frequently strive to showcase the homelike atmosphere that distinguishes the property from a large hotel.

UNDERSTANDING THE BASICS OF PUBLISHING ON THE WEB

As you have seen by browsing the Web, people create and publish Web pages for various reasons. Companies often publish Web pages to promote their products or services or to provide customer support. Other organizations provide general types of information, such as the weather, news, or airline schedule information. Many individuals, like you, create Web pages too. Individuals may create Web sites to share news of trips or other interesting events in their lives. They also create sites to provide professional information and to express their interest and opinions on various issues.

When you are considering the need for a Web page, review the types of pages that you visit frequently. What types of information do they provide? How easy are they to navigate? What other features encourage you to return to the site? The following list shows some of the elements that create ongoing interest in a Web site.

- Information that interests a large number of people
- A sufficient quantity of information to encourage repeat visits
- Information that changes frequently
- Hyperlinks that are regularly updated and take readers to other related and useful sites
- Media that is interesting, timely, or useful, including pictures, sound clips, or motion clips

Among the reasons that individuals publish Web pages are:

- To make useful information available to many people including family and friends
- To publish information at a lower cost than printing the information
- To distribute time-sensitive information more efficiently

Remember that once you post a Web page, anyone who has access to the Internet will be able to read your page. Therefore, do not include information that you would not want the public to know. For example, if you create a personal Web page, you may want to provide your e-mail address for readers who want to contact you, but you should not give your telephone number. Because of the high visibility of a Web site, it is especially important that you carefully edit the page(s) to ensure quality and accuracy.

Don't forget that copyright laws apply to the Internet, just as they do to print publications. Before you use anyone else's text or graphics, make sure that you have the legal right to do so. Although government information is generally not copyright protected, resist the temptation to copy and paste information from government Web sites. Instead provide a hyperlink to connect users to the appropriate site.

Web pages must be written in Hypertext Markup Language (HTML) before they can be published on the Web. You do not need to know HTML to create a Web page, however. Publisher can handle this for you.

PLANNING A WEB SITE

Before you create a Web site, you should plan the content and layout. Decide on the basic elements that you want to include in your Web site by answering the following questions:

- What is the purpose or focus of my Web site?

- Do other sites exist that give the same, or similar, information. If so, how can I make my Web site unique?

- Who is my audience? What can I include to make visitors want to return to my site?

- Do I want or need to include more than one page? If so, what information appears on each page and how are the pages linked?

- Do I want or need to link to others' Web pages? If so, what is the address for each of those sites?

You can think of a Web page as being similar to a page in a book. However, a Web page can be any length needed to convey the information. When you are planning a page, however, you need to decide if it would be better to have one long page that readers will have to scroll through or multiple pages linked with hyperlinks. If you have clear divisions of information, it is usually better to create multiple pages.

If your Web site will have multiple pages, you should create a *map* of the Web site before you begin to build the actual site. Maps help you to plan the number of pages in the Web site and how the pages will be linked. Figure 5.1 shows the map for the Web site that you will create in this lesson, which is a Web site for *european travel,* the travel agency whose newsletter you created in Lesson 4. As you can see from the map, this Web site has ten pages. The first page, called the *home page,* contains links to five other pages. Four of these pages, in turn, contain a link to an additional page. Each of these additional pages is a calendar page that relates specifically to the page to which it is linked. For example, the calendar page that is linked to the Paris page is a calendar showing the dates of the next trip to Paris. Because these calendar pages are linked to specific pages, they are not accessed directly from the home page, but from the page to which they relate. The related links page, which contains links to *other* Web sites and to the *european travel* newsletter, can be accessed from all of the pages except the calendar pages.

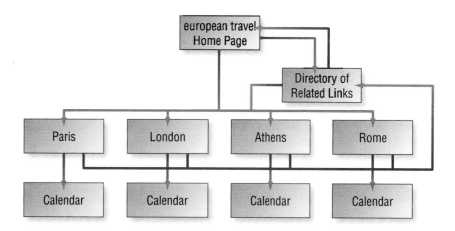

Figure 5.1
Web site map

Color and graphics are essential elements of Web pages. You can add graphics to your Web page, as you would in any publication, to complement or draw attention to text. You can also use graphics as hyperlinks to lead to another page in your Web site or to another Web resource. If you include graphics on a Web page, however, make sure they don't take too long to load. A reader may get impatient waiting for your page to load and decide to cancel the process. The smaller a graphic, the quicker it will load. Your goal is to create a visually interesting page that will load quickly.

You can also add background sounds and animation to Web pages. Sound clips and animation do not work in the Publisher window, but you can see how they will work online by previewing the Web page in a browser such as Explorer. You will learn more about adding background sounds and previewing Web pages later in this lesson.

Finally, consistency and white space are important on Web pages, just as they are in print publications. In fact, white space can be even more important on a Web page. Too much text, especially on the home page, may discourage an impatient Web surfer.

CREATING WEB SITES USING DESIGN TEMPLATES

Publisher simplifies the process of creating Web sites by providing Web page templates. The Publisher Web site designs start with only one page, the home page, but additional pages can be added. As each page is added, Publisher asks you to specify the type of page (story, calendar, event, special offer, price list, or related links). Each of these page types has a different template.

As Web pages are added, Publisher automatically supplies **navigation bars** on the left side and at the bottom of each page. A navigation bar allows you to move, or *navigate,* from page to page in your Web site. As each new page is added to a Web site, Publisher automatically updates the navigation bars to include the new pages, unless you indicate that you don't want a particular page to be included on the navigation bar. You can change the text and graphics on the navigation bar along the left side of each page, but the navigation bar at the bottom of the page cannot be changed. However, the bottom navigation bar updates automatically when the text on the left navigation bar is changed. In addition, because the text on the navigation bars is linked to the titles of each page, Publisher automatically updates both navigation bars when you change the title on a page.

 *Hyperlinks don't work while you're in the Publisher window. To actually use hyperlinks, you must view a Web page in your browser. You will learn how to preview Web pages in Explorer later in this lesson.*

Publisher BASICS

Choosing a Web Site Design

1. Click Web Sites under By Publication Type on the New Publication task pane.

2. Click on the design that is the most appropriate or closest to the final look that you wish to create.

3. Change the Personal Information Set, if necessary.

4. Change the Color Scheme, if desired.

Choosing a Web Site Design and Creating a Web Site Layout

In this activity, you will select a design for the european travel Web site and create the layout of the site.

1. Under Start from a design **on the New Publication task pane, click** By Publication Type, **and then click** Web Sites.

Thumbnail previews of available Web site designs appear in the Publication Gallery. You will select a Web site design that would be appropriate for a travel agency.

2. Scroll down until the Voyage Web Site appears and click it.

The Voyage Web Site template appears as shown in Figure 5.2. This design, with its travel motifs, is an obvious choice for a travel agency.

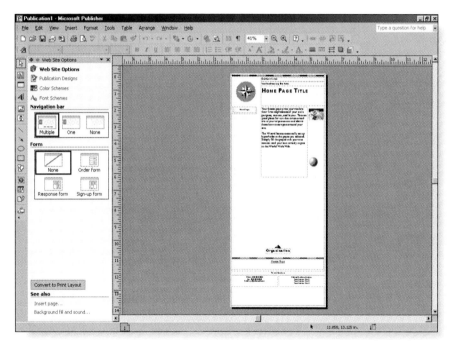

Figure 5.2
Voyage Web site template

3. On the Edit menu, click Personal Information....

4. Click Secondary Business.

The Personal Information set for european travel appears.

5. Under Color schemes, select Include color scheme in this set, **by clicking on the box until the check mark appears in the box. Then click the down arrow and scroll down until the Navy color scheme appears. Click it as shown in Figure 5.3.**

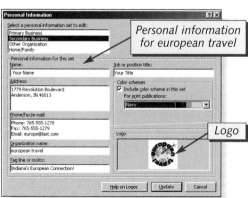

Figure 5.3
Updated Personal Information Set
for european travel

Creating a Web Site Layout

1. On the Web Site Options task pane, click Insert page....

2. Under Available page types on the Insert Page dialog box, click the down arrow and select the desired page type.

3. If you don't want the page to be included on the navigation bars, click the box in front of Add hyperlink to Web navigation bar to deselect it.

4. Click OK.

5. Repeat steps 1–4 for each of the other pages in your Web site.

Figure 5.4
Insert Page dialog box

6. Click Update.

The template for the Voyage Web Site appears with the Secondary Business information inserted.

7. On the Web Site Options task pane, click Insert page....

The Insert Page dialog box appears as shown in Figure 5.4.

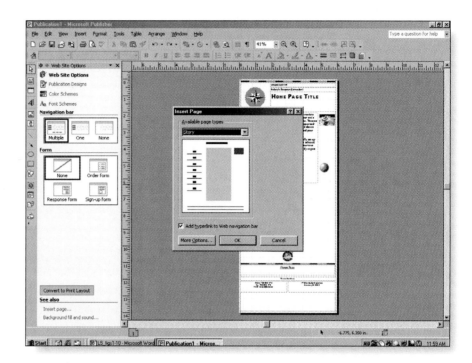

8. Under Available page types, Story is already selected. Because this is the type of page you will be creating, click OK.

Page 2 appears and a second page has been added to the page navigation information at the bottom of the Publisher window.

9. On the Web Site Options task pane, click Insert page... again.

10. On the Insert Page dialog box, click the down arrow under Available page types and select Calendar.

The Calendar page type appears. As you can see, the box in front of Add hyperlink to Web navigation bar is checked. Because you will be linking the calendar pages to specific pages, you do not want hyperlinks for the calendars to be added to the navigation bars.

11. Click the box in front of Add hyperlink to Web navigation bar to deselect it as shown in Figure 5.5.

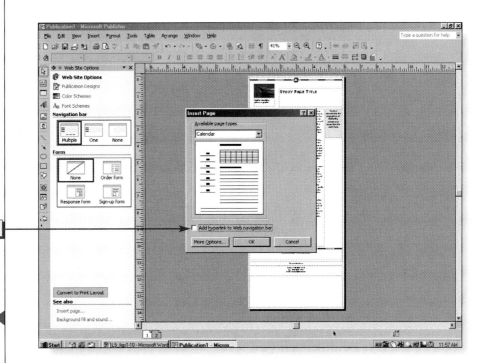

Figure 5.5
Add hyperlink to Web navigation
bar deselected

12. Click OK.

13. Repeat steps 7–12 three times to create six more pages.

Note   *Make sure that every other page is a calendar page.*

When you have completed this process, you should have 9 pages in your Web site as shown in Figure 5.6.

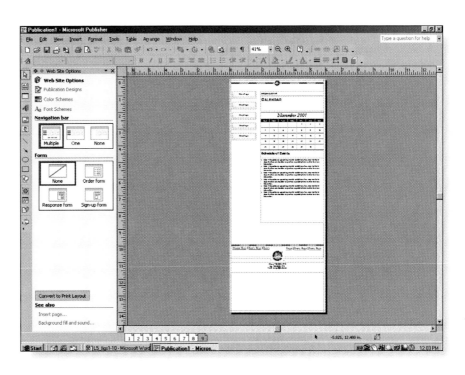

Figure 5.6
Nine-page Web site publication

14. On the Web Site Options task pane, click Insert page... one more time.

15. On the Insert Page dialog box, click the down arrow under Available page types and select Related links. (See Figure 5.7.)

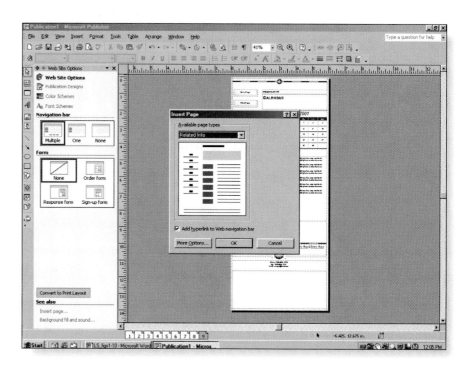

Figure 5.7
Insert related links page

16. Click OK.

You have now created a ten-page layout for your Web site.

17. Click the Save button 🖫.

18. On the Save As dialog box, type ET Web Site in the File name: box.

19. In the Save as type: box, select Web Page. (See Figure 5.8.)

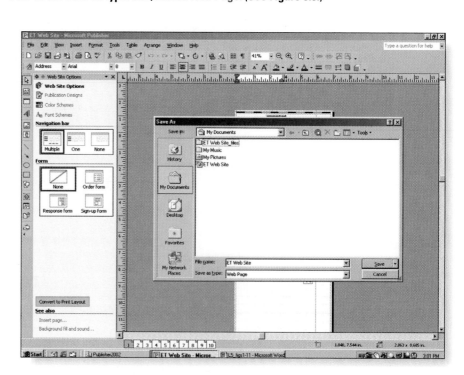

Figure 5.8
Save as dialog box

20. Click Save.

Notice the Publisher creates a folder titled ET Web Site_files. Within in the folder you will find separate HTML files for each page of the publication, numerous image files, and a master list of all the files connected with your Web site. Each of these files is known as an *asset.* Even simple one-page Web sites contain several assets.

You were not asked to save the file as a Publisher document. When you need to work on the Web site in Publisher, you may open the pubmaster HTML file that Publisher created when it saved the file as a Web page. Publisher will import the HTML file, and allow you to make changes. Each time you save the pubmaster file, new HTML files will be automatically created.

WEB SITE HOME PAGES

The home page is the first thing that people see when they visit your Web site. Careful design will create a good first impression. When businesses design Web sites, their home page design includes the corporate identity such as name and logo. They also carefully plan the placement of all elements to be as friendly as possible to Web site visitors.

HANDS On

Creating a Web Site Home Page

1. Open the pubmaster001 file **if it is not already open.**

Note   *If your copy of Publisher has been used to create other Web sites, the file name may have a different number. The key is to open the Pubmaster file located in the ET Web Site_files folder.*

2. Click Page 1.

3. Select (highlight) the words european travel **at the top of the Web page and change the font to** Arial Black, 10.

Note   *Zoom in as needed to view the text on the page.*

4. Click on Home Page Title.

5. Type Continental **and press** ⎡Enter⏎⎤. **Then type** Connection.

The title of your new Web site appears as shown in Figure 5.9.

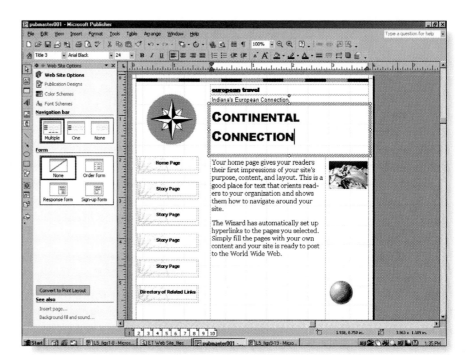

Figure 5.9
Web site title

6. Position your cursor in the story box beginning Your home page gives your readers . . . and press ⌨ Ctrl + A. With all the text selected, insert the text file Home page blurb that is found on the Publisher Data CD.

Publisher asks if you want to use autoflow as shown in Figure 5.10.

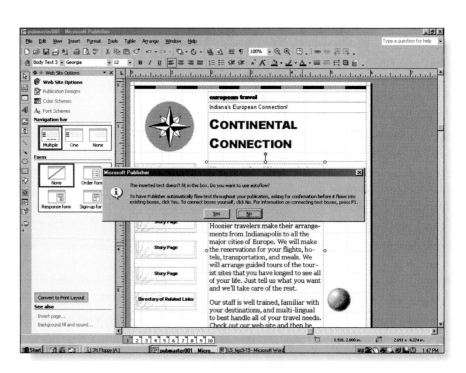

Figure 5.10
Autoflow warning box

7. Click No.

8. Resize the story box using the bottom resize handle so that all of the text fits in the story box. (See Figure 5.11.)

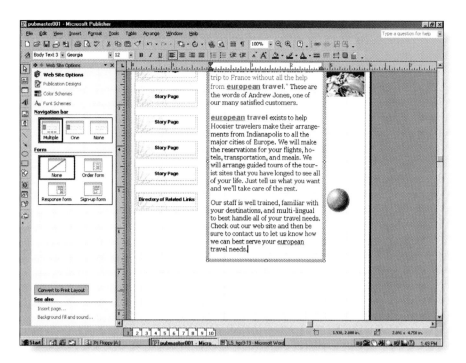

Figure 5.11
Resized story box

Another Way

Use Ctrl + A to select all the text in a text or story box.

9. Select all of the text in the story box and click the Align Left button ▤.

10. Move the globe picture on the right side of the page so that it is centered below the Directory of Related Links box on the navigation bar on the left side of the page, as shown in Figure 5.12.

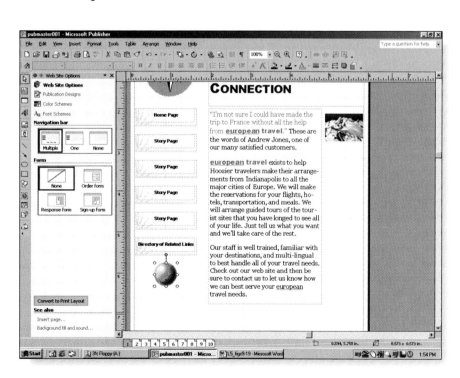

Figure 5.12
Repositioned globe

11. Click the default picture in the right margin and change the picture to Eiffel T on the Publisher Data CD.

12. Right-click and then click Format Picture…. (See Figure 5.13.)

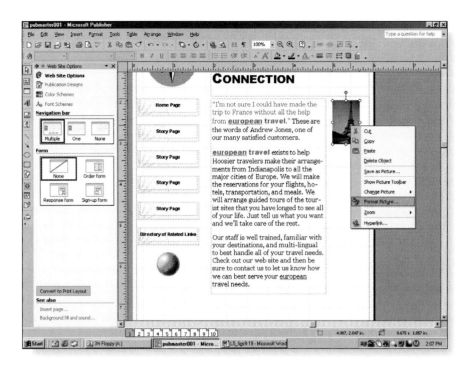

Figure 5.13
Format picture

13. On the Format Picture dialog box, click the Size tab and change the Height: box to 1.4. Make sure that the boxes in front of Lock aspect ratio and Relative to original picture size are both checked as shown in Figure 5.14.

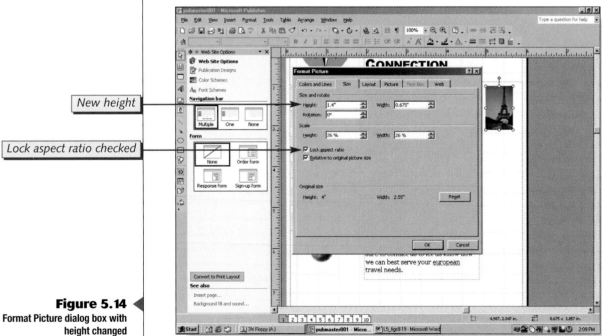

New height

Lock aspect ratio checked

Figure 5.14
Format Picture dialog box with height changed

14. Click OK.

15. Add a vertical ruler guide at the 5-inch mark on the horizontal ruler.

16. Move the Eiffel Tower picture so that the left side of the picture is on the vertical ruler guide and the top of the picture is even with the bottom of the Indiana's European Connection! text box, as shown in Figure 5.15.

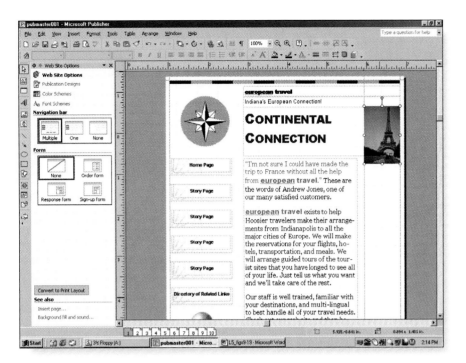

Figure 5.15
Eiffel Tower picture positioned

17. On the Insert menu, click Picture and then click From File….

18. On the Insert Picture dialog box, locate and click the file Big Ben on the Publisher Data CD, and then click Insert.

19. Change the size of the Big Ben picture so that its height is 1.4". (Refer to steps 12–14 above, if necessary.)

20. Move the Big Ben picture so that it is ¼-inch below the Eiffel Tower picture and so that the left side of the picture is on the vertical ruler guide.

Your home page should now look similar to Figure 5.16.

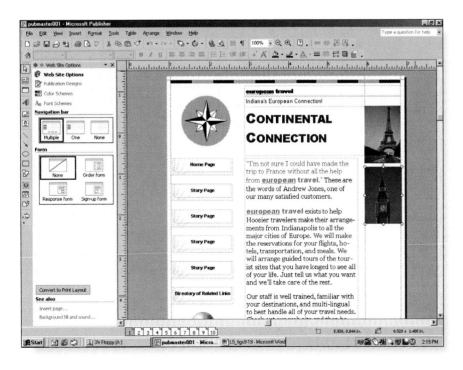

Figure 5.16
Big Ben inserted and positioned

21. Click Save ▦.

While saving you will see a message that indicates that the publication is being exported to HTML files.

22. Insert the picture Parthenon on the Publisher Data CD. (Refer to steps 17–18 above, if necessary.)

23. Change the size of the Parthenon picture so that its height is 1.4".

24. Move the Parthenon picture so that it is ¼-inch below the Big Ben picture and so that the left side of the picture is on the vertical ruler guide.

25. Insert the picture Colosseum on the Publisher Data CD.

26. Change the size of the Colosseum picture so that its height is 1.4".

27. Move the Colosseum picture so that it is ¼-inch below the Parthenon picture and so that the left side of the picture is on the vertical ruler guide.

28. Click Click Save ▦.

All of the text and pictures for the home page are now inserted. Your page should appear similar to Figure 5.17.

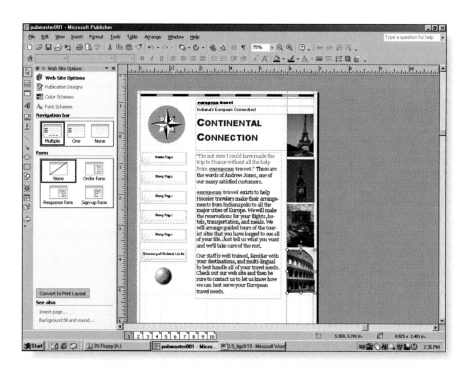

Figure 5.17
Home Page with text and pictures inserted

As you can see, there is still considerable white space after the story box on the home page. In the next few steps, you will move the *european travel* logo, navigation bar, and contact information at the bottom of the page so that they are directly below the story box.

29. Scroll to the bottom of the home page. Group the european travel logo, the black and blue bar, the navigation bar, and the contact information text boxes, so that they can be moved together.

If you do not remember how to do this: Click the european travel logo; press and hold the Shift key and click on each of the other elements (the black and blue bar, the navigation bar, the To contact us: text box, the Phone/Fax/Email text box, and the address text box) and click the Group Objects icon.

30. Move the grouped objects so that they are directly below the story box as shown in Figure 5.18.

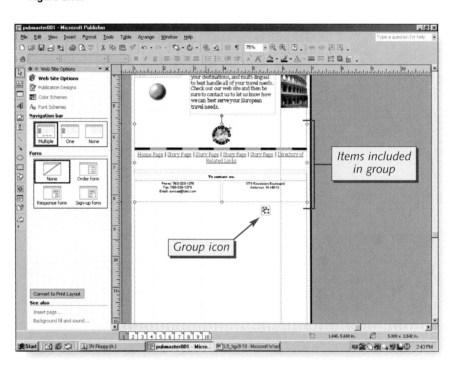

Figure 5.18
Grouped information moved
below story box

31. Select (highlight) the words europe@last.com in the contact information box.

32. Right-click and then click Hyperlink…, as shown in Figure 5.19.

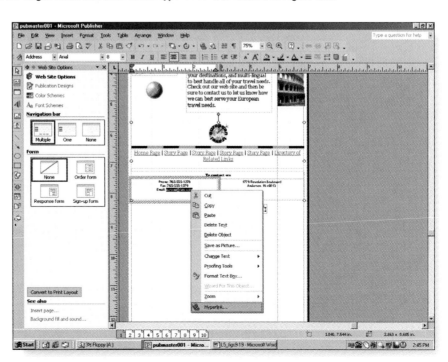

Figure 5.19
Changing E-mail address to
hyperlink

Adding a Hyperlink to an E-mail Address

1. Select the e-mail address.

2. Right-click and then click Hyperlink....

3. Under Link to (on the Insert Hyperlink dialog box), click E-mail Address.

4. Under E-mail address, type the e-mail address you selected.

5. Under Subject, type an appropriate phrase.

6. Click OK.

The Insert Hyperlink dialog box appears.

33. **Under Link to, click E-mail Address.**

34. **In the E-mail address: box, type** europe@last.com.

Note Publisher automatically adds mailto: before the words you just typed.

35. **Under Subject, type** Tour information request. **(See Figure 5.20.)**

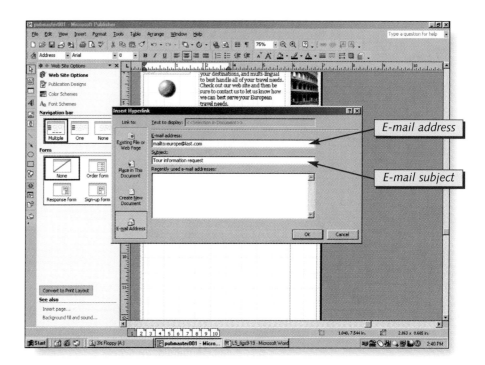

Figure 5.20
Insert hyperlink for e-mail address

36. **Click OK.**

The text europe@last.com now appears in blue and is underlined, indicating that it is now a hyperlink as shown in Figure 5.21.

Note You should always include a subject line with e-mail messages. This courtesy allows the people who receive your e-mail to quickly identify the purpose of your e-mail.

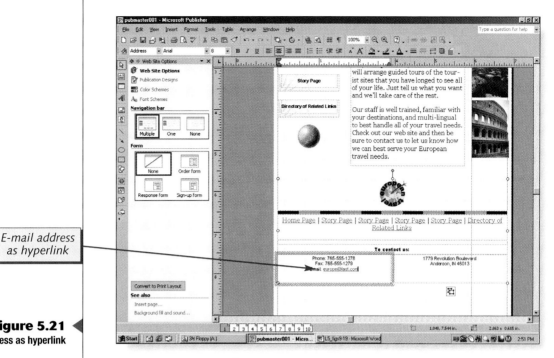

E-mail address
as hyperlink

Figure 5.21
E-mail address as hyperlink

37. Click Save 💾.

The home page is now complete. You are ready to enter content for the remaining pages of european travel's Web site.

ADDITIONAL WEB SITE PAGES

As a travel agency, **european travel** uses its Web site to inform readers of upcoming tours. Although the travel agency does not accept online reservations at this time, it does seek to provide the basic information that a tourist would need to determine the types of tours available and the dates of the tours. In this way, the Web site functions as an online newsletter. Unlike a newsletter, it can be updated as often as necessary to inform readers of new tour opportunities.

Notice that each page of the site includes the company's contact information. Since the primary purpose of the Web site is to generate tour request information, the contact information is vitally important. Good Web site design should complement the goals of the site.

As you visit sites, quickly evaluate them in terms of ease of use, type of content, and visual impression. These quick evaluations will help you plan and design effective Web sites.

Creating a Story Page

In this activity you will create the first story page that will link to the home page.

1. Open the ET Web Site file, if it is not already open.

2. Click page 2.

3. Select (highlight) the words Story Page Title at the top of the page and type Paris.

4. Replace the text in the story box that begins Developing a successful Web site requires . . . with the text in the file Trip to France on the Publisher Data CD.

5. Change the horizontal alignment of the story box to Align Left ▤.

6. Resize the story box using the bottom resize handle so that the extra white space at the end of the text box is eliminated, as shown in Figure 5.22.

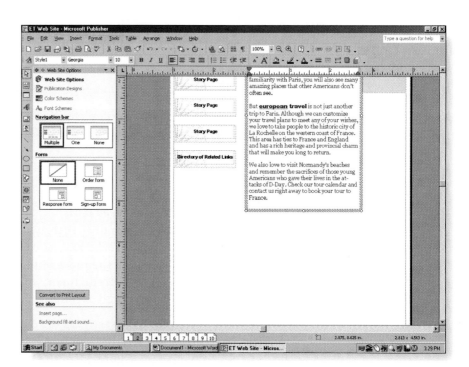

Figure 5.22
Story box resized

7. Select the phrase "Our tours to France include all the popular sites such as the Eiffel Tower, the Arc de Triomphe, the Louvre, and Notre Dame" and click the Copy button ▤ on the Standard toolbar.

8. Select all of the text in the pull quote box to the right of the story box and click the Paste button ▤.

The default pull quote text is replaced with the phrase you selected, and the Paste Options "smart tag" button appears below the pull quote. Smart tag buttons have menus that contain options specifically related to the action that was just performed.

9. Click the down arrow on the Paste Options button and then click Keep Text Only, as shown in Figure 5.23.

Figure 5.23
Keep text only

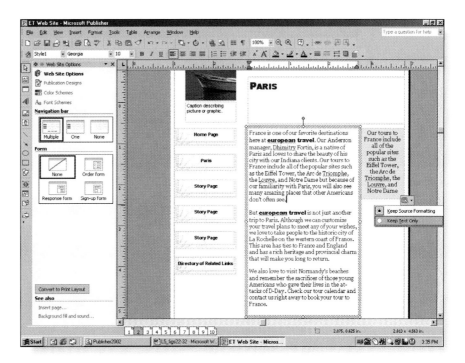

The text formatting changes back to the original pull quote formatting.

10. **Add a period at the end of the pull quote.**

The pull quote will appear as shown in Figure 5.24.

Figure 5.24
Pull quote

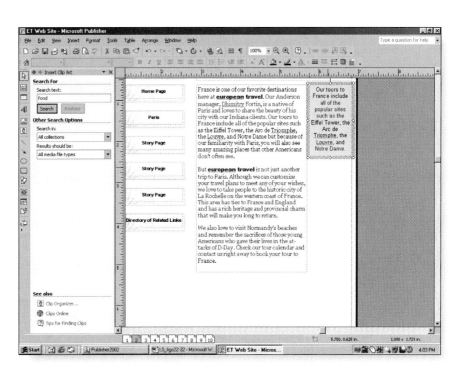

11. **Click on the picture in the upper left corner of the page and click the** Ungroup **icon**
to separate the picture from the caption text box.

12. **Right click on the picture and click on** Change Picture. **Select** La Rochelle **on the**
Publisher Data CD.

13. **Select the text in the caption box under the La Rochelle picture and type** The ancient harbor of La Rochelle on the west coast of France **[no period]**.

The picture and caption appear as shown in Figure 5.25.

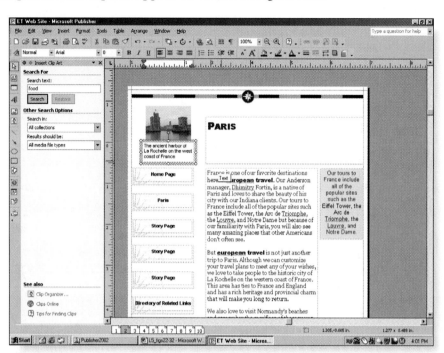

Figure 5.25
La Rochelle picture and caption inserted

14. **Regroup the picture and caption.**

15. **On the Insert menu, click** Picture… **then click** From File….

16. **Locate and click** Eiffel Tower from bottom **on the Publisher Data CD, and then click** Insert.

17. **Change the size of the picture so that its height is** 1.4".

18. **Move the picture so that it is above the pull quote and so that the right side of the picture is on the right blue margin line. (See Figure 5.26.)**

Another Way

To insert a picture, double click on the desired image from the Insert Picture dialog box.

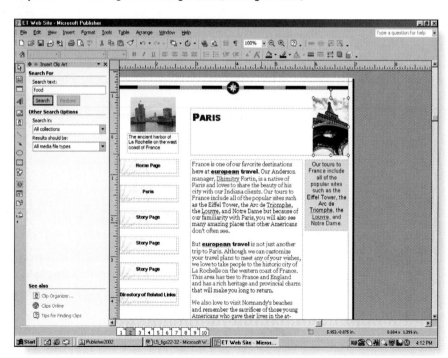

Figure 5.26
Eiffel Tower picture inserted

19. Insert a text box below the story box. The width of the new text box should be the same as the story box and the height should be ¾-inch, as shown in Figure 5.27.

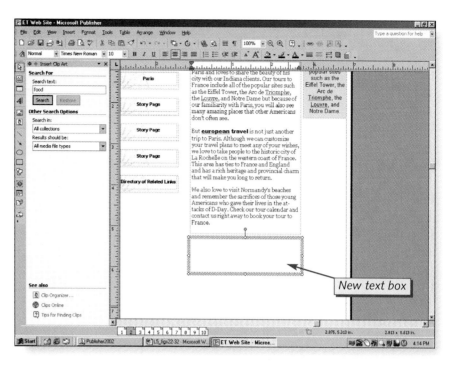

Figure 5.27
New text box

20. In the new text box, type Click here for more information on our March trip to Paris including dates, prices, and itinerary.

21. Select the text you just typed and change the font size to 12. (See Figure 5.28.)

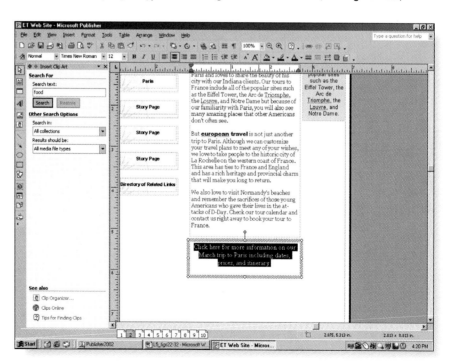

Figure 5.28
Text resized

Creating a Hyperlink to Another Page in a Web Site

1. Select the text that you wish to use as a hyperlink.

2. Right-click and then click Hyperlink...

3. Under Link to (on the Insert Hyperlink dialog box), click Place in This Document.

4. Under Select a place in this document, click the appropriate page.

5. Click OK.

Figure 5.29 ◀
Hyperlink to Another Page in
Document

Hints & Tips

Hyperlinks are used to connect to e-mail, connect pages within a Web site, and to connect to other Web sites.

22. Select the words Click here, right-click and then click Hyperlink....

23. Under Link to, click Place in This Document.

24. Under Select a place in this document, click Next Page, as shown in Figure 5.29.

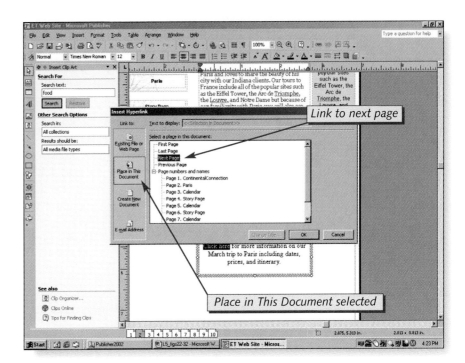

25. Click OK.

The text Click here is now blue and underlined, indicating that it is a hyperlink.

26. Scroll to the bottom of the page. Select the e-mail address. On the Insert menu, select Hyperlink. In the Edit Hyperlink dialog box, click on the recently used e-mail address for europe@last.com.

The e-mail address and Subject lines are automatically filed in.

27. Click OK.

28. Group and move the black and blue bar, the navigation bar, and the contact information at the bottom of the page so that they are directly below the Click here box, as shown in Figure 5.30.

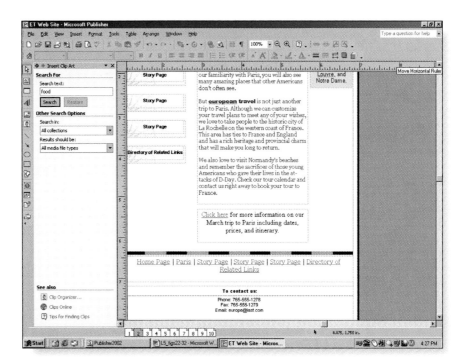

Figure 5.30

Completed page 2

29. Click Save 🖫.

Page 2 is now complete. Next you will create the calendar page that lets the reader know about the dates for upcoming trips to Paris.

Creating a Calendar Page

In the following activity, you will create a calendar page that can be accessed from the Paris story page.

1. Open the ET Web Site, if necessary.

2. Click page 3.

3. Click in front of the word Calendar in the first text box. Click the Center button 🗎 to center the word in the text box.

4. Type Paris. Press ⌜Enter⏎⌝. (See Figure 5.31.)

When you include date sensitive information on a Web site, be sure to update the site regularly to keep such information current.

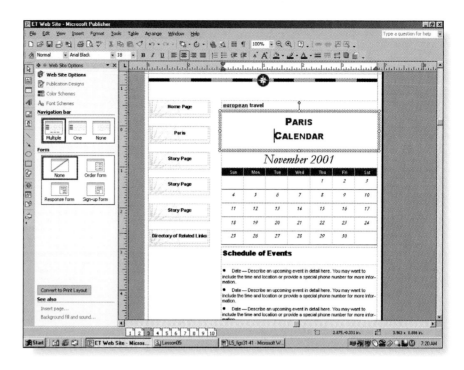

Figure 5.31
Paris calendar title

> *Note*
>
> *The month and year on the calendar show the current month and will differ from the month shown in Figure 5.31.*

5. Click the calendar and then click the Wizard button under the calendar.

The Calendar Designs task pane appears, as shown in Figure 5.32.

Calendar Designs task pane

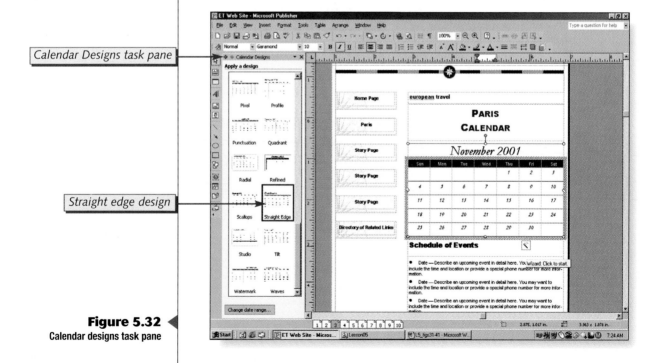
Straight edge design

Figure 5.32
Calendar designs task pane

6. Click Change date range….

The Change Calendar Dates dialog box appears.

7. Change the date to March 2003, **as shown in Figure 5.33.**

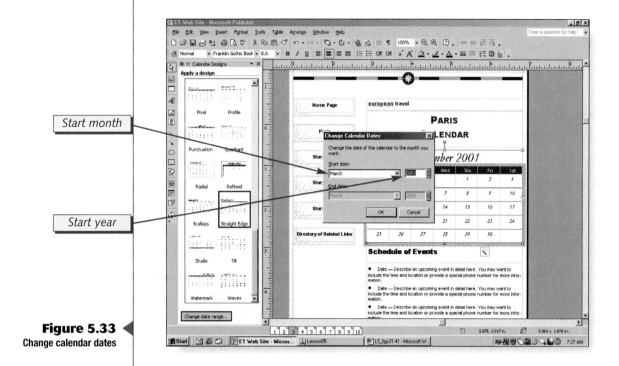

Start month

Start year

Figure 5.33 ◀
Change calendar dates

8. Click OK.

9. In the March 2003 calendar, select the dates 2–8 **and change the fill color to the fourth option (Accent 3/lavender) on the Fill Color drop down menu, as shown in Figure 5.34.**

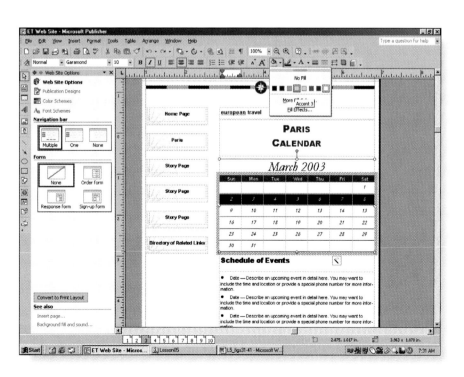

Figure 5.34 ◀
Accent 3 fill color

10. Select dates 9–15 and change to the same fill color.

11. Select the words Schedule of Events and type Trip Details:.

12. Select all of the text in the text box containing the bulleted list and change the text to France calendar highlights on the Publisher Data CD.

13. Select all of the text in this box and change the horizontal alignment to Align Left .

14. Ungroup the Trip Details and bullet point text boxes.

15. Resize the bulleted list text box to remove the extra space at the bottom of the text box. Then regroup the two boxes.

16. Move the european travel logo down so that it is positioned just below the e-mail address. Then group and move the european travel logo, the black and blue bar, the navigation bar, and the contact information so that they are directly below the bulleted list.

17. Select the europe@last.com e-mail address. Click the Insert Hyperlink button .

18. In the Edit Hyperlink dialog box, click on the recently used e-mail address for europe@last.com.

19. Click OK.

20. Click Save .

Page 3 is now complete and should appear similar to Figure 5.35.

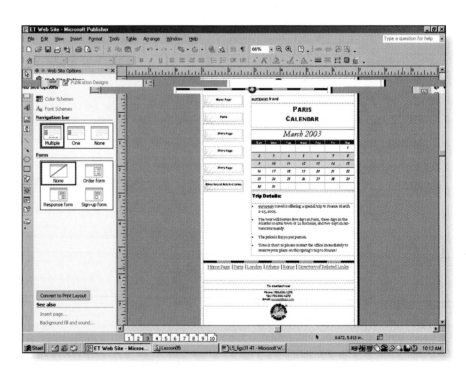

Figure 5.35
Completed page 3

Creating Pages 4–9 of the Web Site

In the following activity, you will work from the general directions provided to create the remaining story and calendar pages for the *european travel* Web site. If you need help with any of the specific directions to complete a step, refer to the last two hands-on activities.

1. Open the ET Web Site, if necessary.

2. Add content for pages 4–9 of the Web site, using following information. Refer to Figures 5.36 through 5.41 to see how the finished pages should look.

For page 4:

■ **Change the page title to** London.

■ **Change the text in the story box to the** London **Word file on the Publisher Data CD.**

■ **Align text to the left.**

■ **Change the spacing after paragraphs to** 11 pts. **Then resize the text box to remove the empty space.**

■ **Change the pull quote to** Your trip to London will include seeing the Tower of London, St. Paul's Cathedral, Westminster Abbey, and Buckingham Palace.

■ **Change the picture on the left to** Changing of the guard **on the Publisher Data CD.**

■ **Change the caption to** British pageantry at its finest!

■ **Insert the picture** London at night **on the Publisher Data CD and resize it to** 1.4" **high. Move it so that its right side is on the blue margin line and its bottom edge aligns with the bottom of the London title text box.**

■ **Add a text box under the story box and type** Click here for more information on our July trip to London including dates, prices, and itinerary. **Change the size of the type to** 12. **Add a hyperlink to the words** Click here **and link to the next page.**

■ **Change** europe@last.com **to an e-mail hyperlink.**

■ **Move the black and blue bar, the navigation bar, and the contact information so that they are directly below the Click here box.**

■ **Save your work.**

Your completed page should be similar to the page shown in Figure 5.36.

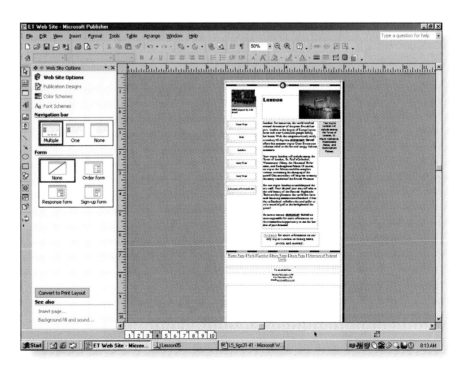

Figure 5.36 ◀
Completed page 4

For page 5:

- Center the Calendar heading. **Change the page title to** London Calendar, **and display the title on two lines.**

- **Change the calendar to** July 2003.

- **Shade the dates** July 14–26.

- **Change** Schedule of Events **to** Trip Details:.

- **Change the text in the bulleted list box to** London calendar highlights **on the Publisher Data CD. Left align the bullet points. Resize the list box only to remove any extra space.**

- **Change** europe@last.com **to an e-mail hyperlink.**

- **Move the european travel logo down so that it is positioned just below the e-mail address. Then move the logo, the black and blue bar, the navigation bar, and the contact information so that they are directly below the bulleted list.**

- **Save your work.**

Your completed page should be similar to the page shown in Figure 5.37.

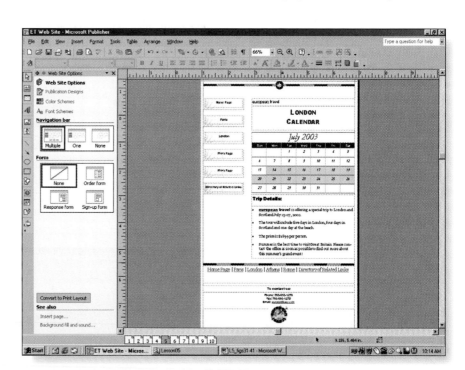

Figure 5.37
Completed page 5

For page 6:

- **Change the page title to** Athens.

- **Change the text in the story box to the** Athens **Word file on the Publisher Data CD.**

- **Align text to the left.**

- **Change the spacing after paragraphs to 11 pts. Then resize the text box to remove the empty space.**

- **Change the pull quote to** No trip to Athens would be complete without a visit to the Acropolis, the flat-topped hill featuring the remains of the world-famous Parthenon.

- **Change the picture on the left to** Acropolis **on the Publisher Data CD.**

- **Change the caption to** The ancient Acropolis overlooks the modern city of Athens.

- **Insert the picture** Athens restaurant **on the Publisher Data CD and resize it to** 1.4" **high. Move it so that its right side is on the blue margin line and its bottom edge aligns with the bottom of the Athens title text box.**

- **Add a text box under the story box and type** Click here for more information on our September trip to Athens including dates, prices, and itinerary. **Change the size of the type to** 12. **Add a hyperlink to the words** Click here **and link to the next page.**

- **Change** europe@last.com **to an e-mail hyperlink.**

- **Move the black and blue bar, the navigation bar, and the contact information so that they are directly below the Click here box.**

- **Save your work.**

Your completed page should be similar to the page shown in Figure 5.38.

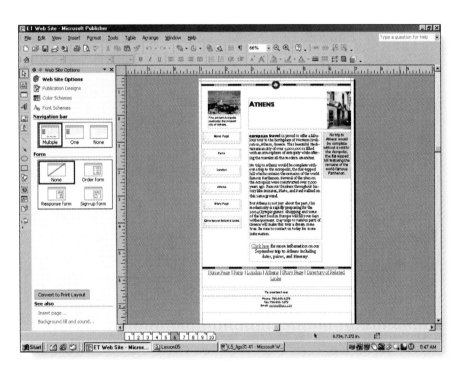

Figure 5.38
Completed page 6

For page 7:

- **Center the Calendar heading. Change the page title to** Athens Calendar, **and display the title on two lines.**

- **Change the calendar to** September 2003.

- **Shade the dates** September 8–20.

- **Change** Schedule of Events **to** Trip Details:.

- **Change the text in the bulleted list box to** Athens calendar highlights **on the Publisher Data CD. Left align the bullet points. Resize the list box only to remove any extra space.**

- **Change** europe@last.com **to an e-mail hyperlink.**

- Move the european travel logo down so that it is positioned just below the e-mail address. Then move the logo, the black and blue bar, the navigation bar, and the contact information so that they are directly below the bulleted list.
- Save your work.

Your completed page should be similar to the page shown in Figure 5.39.

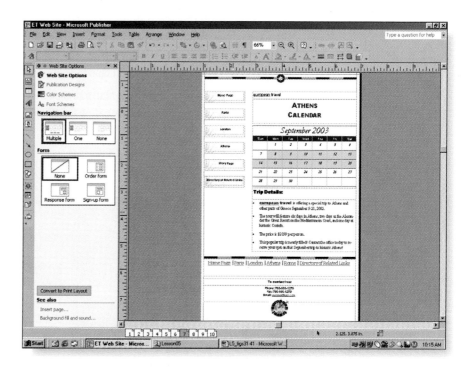

For page 8:

- Change the page title to Rome.
- Change the text in the story box to the Rome Word file on the Publisher Data CD.
- Align text to the left.
- Change the spacing after paragraphs to 11 pts. Then resize the text box to remove the empty space.
- Change the pull quote to Your trip will include a visit to the Pantheon, the Colosseum, and the Roman Forum.
- Change the picture on the left to St. Peter's Square on the Publisher Data CD.
- Change the caption to Vatican City is the caretaker for much of the world's greatest art.
- Insert the picture Venice on the Publisher Data CD and resize it to 1.4" high. Move it so that its right side is on the blue margin line and its bottom edge aligns with the bottom of the Rome title text box.
- Add a text box under the story box and type Click here for more information on our November trip to Rome including dates, prices, and itinerary. Change the size of the type to 12. Add a hyperlink to the words Click here and link to the next page.
- Change europe@last.com to an e-mail hyperlink.
- Move the black and blue bar, the navigation bar, and the contact information so that they are directly below the Click here box.

■ **Save your work.**

Your completed page should be similar to the page shown in Figure 5.40.

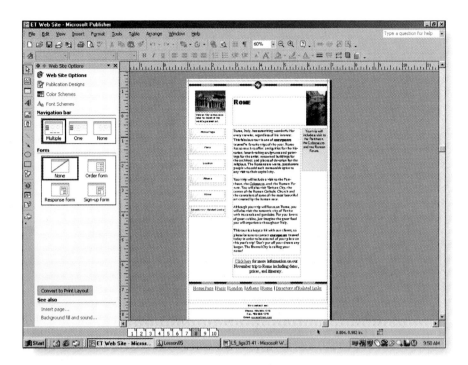

Figure 5.40
Completed page 8

For page 9:

■ **Center the Calendar heading. Change the page title to Rome Calendar, and display the title on two lines.**

■ **Change the calendar to November 2003.**

■ **Shade the dates November 17–29.**

■ **Change Schedule of Events to Trip Details:.**

■ **Change the text in the bulleted list box to Rome calendar highlights on the Publisher Data CD. Left align the bullet points. Resize the list box only to remove any extra space.**

■ **Change europe@last.com to an e-mail hyperlink.**

■ **Move the european travel logo down so that it is positioned just below the e-mail address. Then move the logo, the black and blue bar, the navigation bar, and the contact information so that they are directly below the bulleted list.**

■ **Save your work.**

Your completed page should be similar to the page shown in Figure 5.41.

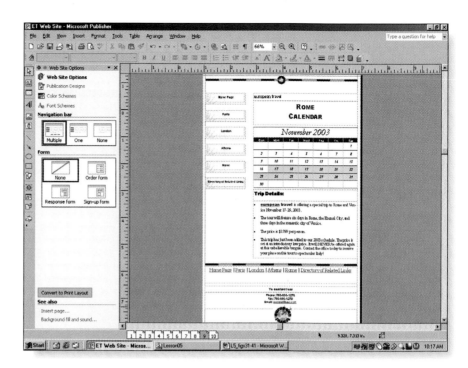

Figure 5.41 ◀
Completed page 9

All of your pages, except the related links page, are now complete.

Creating a Related Links Page

In this activity, you will create the final page of your Web site, a related links page. On this page you will provide external links. These are links to other Web sites that contain information that is related to your Web site.

1. Open the ET Web Site file, if it is not already open.

2. Click page 10.

3. Select the text box beginning Hyperlinks are electronic connections . . . and change the text to the Links introduction Word file on the Publisher Data CD.

4. When Publisher asks if you wish to use autoflow, click No.

5. Resize the text box slightly so that all of the text fits in the text box.

6. In the next text box, select the words Web site name and address hyperlink.

7. Type http://www.cia.gov/cia/publications/factbook/geos/fr.html

 *When typing Web site addresses, it is critical that you type the addresses perfectly. If you make any error or omission in typing the address, the hyperlink will not work.*

8. Click the down arrow on the AutoCorrect Options box and then Control AutoCorrect Options....

9. Click on the box beside Capitalize first letter of sentences to deselect it.

10. Click OK.

Publisher BASICS

Creating a Hyperlink to Another Web Site or File

1. Select the text that you wish to use as a hyperlink.

2. Right-click and then click Hyperlink....

3. Under Link to (on the Insert Hyperlink dialog box), click Existing File or Web Page.

4. If you are linking to another Web site, type the Web address for that Web site in the Address: box; or, if you are linking to another file, locate the file in the Look in: box and click on its name.

5. Click OK.

11. Change the font to Arial Black, 7.

12. Select the text beginning Briefly summarize why the information . . . and type Learn what the U.S. government has to say about France. **(See Figure 5.42.)**

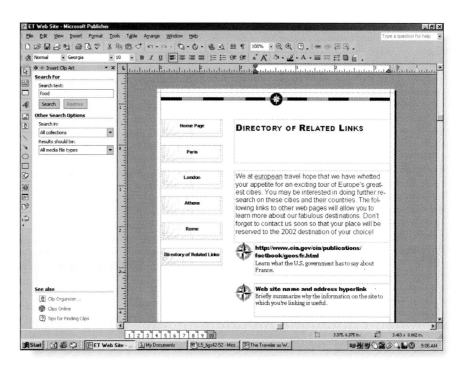

Figure 5.42

Link to the CIA World Factbook's France page

13. Repeat steps 6–9 for each of the next four text boxes, substituting the information below:

> http://www.cia.gov/cia/publications/factbook/geos/uk.html
> Learn what the U.S. government has to say about the United Kingdom.

> http://www.cia.gov/cia/publications/factbook/geos/gr.html
> Learn what the U.S. government has to say about Greece.

> http://www.cia.gov/cia/publications/factbook/geos/it.html
> Learn what the U.S. government has to say about Italy.

> http://travel.state.gov/travel_warnings.html
> This site gives you information on any country that the U.S. State Department believes is too dangerous for American citizens to visit.

When you have completed these additions, your screen page should appear similar to that shown in Figure 5.43.

You will have one remaining default text box. You will use it later in this lesson.

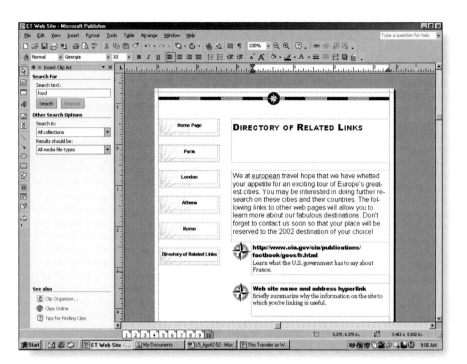

Figure 5.43
Related links information

14. **Select the Web address in the first text box:**

    http://www.cia.gov/cia/publications/factbook/geos/fr.html

15. **Click**  **+ C to copy the address. Then right-click and choose** Hyperlink....

Note *Keep the mouse pointer on the selected text as you right-click.*

The Insert Hyperlink dialog box appears.

16. **Under Link to, click** Existing File or Web Page, **as shown in Figure 5.44.**

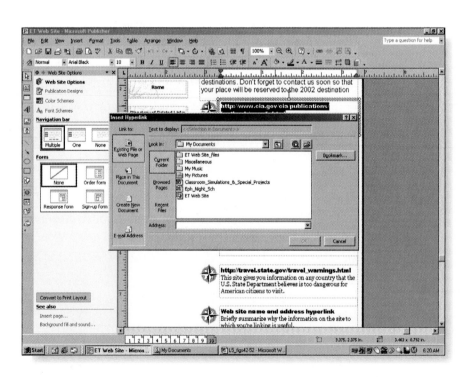

Figure 5.44
Insert Hyperlink dialog box

17. With the pointer in the Address: box, click  + V to paste the Web address (http://www.cia.gov/cia/publications/factbook/geos/fr.html)

> *Note*   *You can rekey the Web address, but by copying and pasting it you eliminate the problem of making a typing error. Remember that the link will only work if every element of the address is correct.*

18. Click OK.

The text turns to blue and is underlined indicating that a hyperlink exists.

19. Repeat steps 14–18 for each of the Web addresses.

20. Save the file.

HANDS On

Linking to Other Files

Not only can you insert hyperlinks to other Web sites, but you can also insert hyperlinks to other, related files. In this activity, you will link the newsletter *the traveler*, which you converted to Web pages in Lesson 4, to your Web site. If you did not convert the newsletter to a Web site, you should complete the On the Web activity on pages 186–191 before continuing with this activity.

1. Open the ET Web Site file, if it is not already open.

2. In the last text box on page 10, select the words Web site name and address hyperlink.

3. Type the traveler. Change the autocorrect capitalization of the "t."

4. Select the text beginning Briefly summarize why the information . . . and type This will link you with european travel's monthly newsletter, the traveler. This month's issue features the country of France.

5. Select the E in european which has been automatically capitalized and click on the blue bar that appears below the letter. From the AutoCorrect Options, select Change back to "european".

6. Select the words the traveler.

7. Right-click and choose Hyperlink….

8. On the Insert Hyperlink dialog box, click Existing File or Web Page.

9. In the Look in: box, locate the traveler as Web Pages file that you saved in Lesson 4 and click on it.

10. Click OK.

The newsletter *the traveler* is now linked to your Web site, as shown in Figure 5.45.

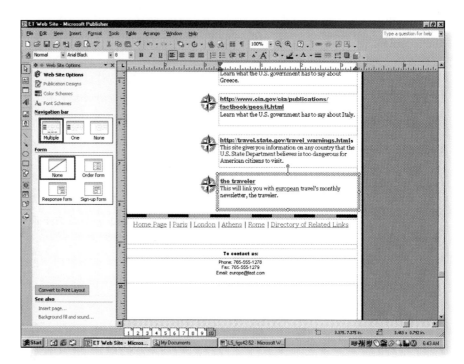

Figure 5.45
Link to *the traveler* newsletter

11. Scroll to the bottom of the page. Select the e-mail address. Right-click and choose Hyperlink… In the Link to: box, click on E-mail Address. Click on the address in the Recently used e-mail addresses: box. The information for europe@last.com will be inserted.

12. Click OK.

13. Save the file.

14. Close the file.

Adding Links Between Pages

Because The Traveler as Web Pages was created by saving a print publication as a Web page, navigation bars were not automatically supplied as they are when a Web site is created by using a Web site template. Without any links between pages, users cannot navigate from the first page of this newsletter to the other three pages.

In the following activity, you will add links among the pages of the newsletter so that you can move from page to page. You will also add *hot spots,* or areas that act as hyperlinks. The hot spot tool allows you to add a hyperlink to objects and graphics. When you click on a hot spot area, it acts as a hyperlink, connecting you to the linked page.

1. **Open** the traveler as Web Pages.

2. **On the Table of Contents, highlight The Bullet Train.**

3. **Right-click, click Hyperlink….**

4. **On the Link to: box, click Place in This Document.**

5. **Under Select a place in this document…, click Page 2. Page Title.**

Creating Hot Spots

1. On the Objects toolbar, click Hot Spot.

2. Under Link to (on the Insert Hyperlink dialog box), click Place in This Document.

3. Under Select a place in this document, click the appropriate page.

4. Click OK.

5. When the Hot Spot frame appears, move and resize it so that it covers the area that you wish to use as a hyperlink.

Figure 5.46 ◄
Enter Text dialog box

6. Click Change Title....

The Enter Text dialog box appears.

7. Type Page 2 **as shown in Figure 5.46.**

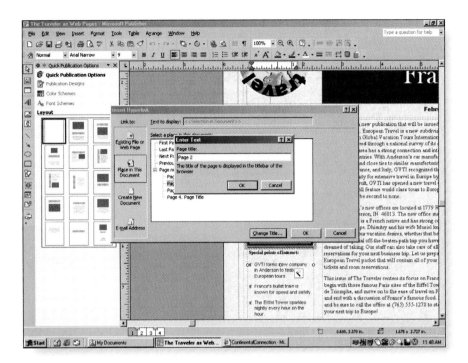

8. Click OK.

9. On the Insert Hyperlink dialog box, click OK **again.**

The text The Bullet Train is now blue and underlined, indicating that it is a hyperlink.

10. On the Objects toolbar, click Hot Spot .

The Insert Hyperlink dialog box appears.

11. On the Insert Hyperlink dialog box, click Place in This Document.

12. Under Select a place in this document:, click Page 2.

13. Click OK.

A frame appears as shown in Figure 5.47.

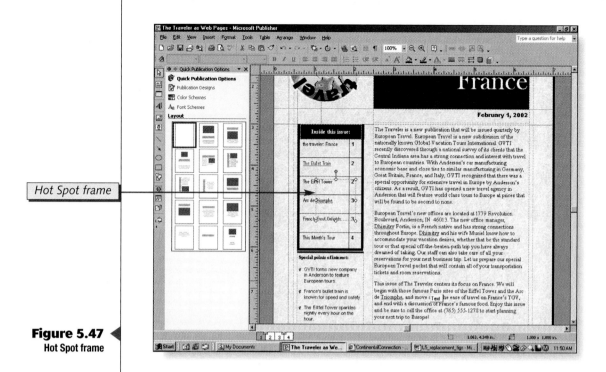

Figure 5.47
Hot Spot frame

14. Move and resize this frame so that it covers the two boxes in the Table of Contents that contain the number 2, as shown in Figure 5.48.

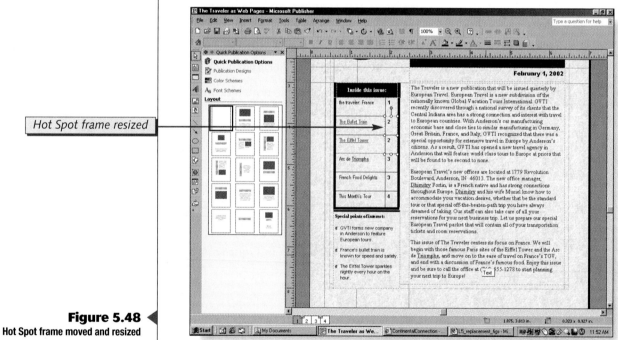

Figure 5.48
Hot Spot frame moved and resized

Note

Remember that none of these hyperlinks work in Publisher; they will only be active when the Web page is viewed in a browser. For now, you simply need to make sure that you have completed all the necessary steps to create the hyperlinks.

15. On the Table of Contents, highlight The Eiffel Tower.

16. **Right-click, click** Hyperlink….

17. **Under Select a place in this document…, click** Page 2. Page 2.

18. **Click** OK.

19. **Click Save** 🖫.

The text Eiffel Tower is now a hyperlink. Complete the following steps to add hyperlinks to the rest of the Table of Contents.

20. **Highlight** Arc de Triomphe **on the Table of Contents.**

21. **Right-click, and then click** Hyperlink….

22. **On the Insert Hyperlink dialog box, click** Place in This Document.

23. **Under Select a place in this document, click** Page 3. Page Title.

24. **Click Change Title**….

25. **Type** Page 3.

26. **Click** OK.

27. **Click** OK **to close the Insert Hyperlink box.**

28. **Use the steps you have just learned to create a hyperlink to Page 3 for French Food Delights.**

29. **Repeat steps 10–14 to add a hot spot to the boxes with the page number 3 on the Table of Contents. Under Select a place in this document (on the Insert Hyperlink dialog box), click** Page 3.

30. **Create a hyperlink for This Month's Tour, linking it to Page 4, using the steps you have already learned. Remember to change the title of the page to Page 4.**

31. **Add a hot spot to the box with the number 4 on the Table of Contents using the steps you have already learned. Be careful to create the link to page 4.**

32. **Click Save** 🖫.

Hyperlinks are now added to all of the text and numbers in the Table of Contents, making the Table of Contents function as a navigation bar. Each of the pages of the newsletter are now accessible from the first page. To create links between the other pages, complete the following steps.

33. **Click Design Gallery Object on the Objects toolbar.**

34. **Under Categories in the Design Gallery, click** Web Buttons.

35. **Scroll to the end of the Web Buttons and click the** Link Voyage **button, as shown in Figure 5.49.**

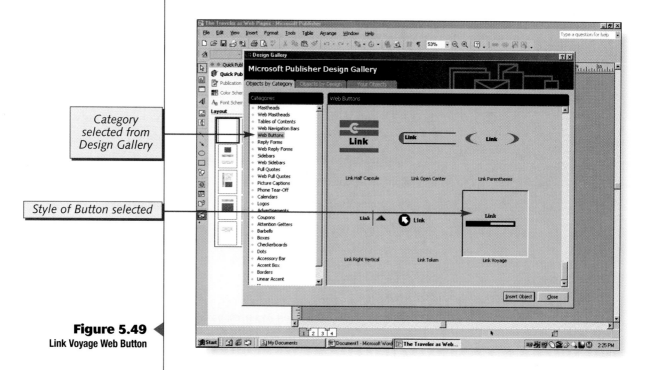

Figure 5.49
Link Voyage Web Button

36. **Click** Insert Object.

37. **Move the Web button to the lower right corner of the page.**

38. **Select the word** Link **on the Web button and type** Next Page, **as shown in Figure 5.50.**

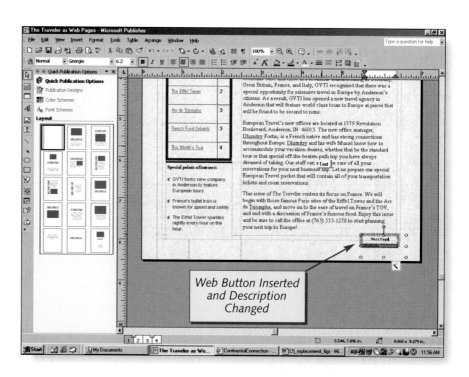

Web Button Inserted and Description Changed

Figure 5.50
Next Page inserted on Web Button

39. **Create a Hot Spot covering the Web button and link it to Next Page on the Insert Hyperlink dialog box. Be sure to cover the entire button, including the area where the words *Next Page* appear.**

40. **Select the words** Next Page **on the Web button and change the font size to** 9.

41. Repeat steps 28–35 for pages 2 and 3 of the newsletter.

 *You can also add links to move from each of these pages to the previous page and/or to the first page. Follow the same steps, but type Previous Page or First Page on the Web button. Then add a Hot Spot and link the Hot Spot to either Previous Page or First Page, as appropriate, on the Insert Hyperlink dialog box.*

42. Repeat steps 28–35 for page 4 of the newsletter, except make the link back to the first page of the newsletter.

43. Save the file.

44. Close the file.

BACKGROUND SOUND ON WEB PAGES

Sound can enhance a viewer's experience at your site. Some Web sites use sounds to indicate actions. For example, sounds can be added when the pointer selects a hot spot. Other Web sites play background sounds on one or more pages of the site. A site describing the various branches of the United States military, for example, might include the anthem of each service branch on the branch's pages.

Although sound can be a useful addition to Web pages, Web pages containing sound do take longer to download. When you are planning your Web sites, decide if sound is a good addition to the message you are trying to communicate. If sound does enhance the message, add it. If sound does not contribute significantly to the message, omit it. In other words, do not add sound just because technology makes it possible. Add sound to help you get your message across to viewers.

Adding Background Sound to a Web Page (Optional)

In this activity, you will learn how to import a sound clip from the Design Gallery Live and use it as background sound for the Paris calendar page in your Web site.

1. Open the ET Web Site file.

2. Click page 3 (the Paris calendar).

3. Click the Clip Organizer Frame button ⬛ on the Objects toolbar.

4. On the Insert Clip Art task pane, click Clips Online.

Publisher connects to the Internet, and the Design Gallery Live home page appears as shown in Figure 5.51.

 *If the Design Gallery License Agreement appears, click the Accept button.*

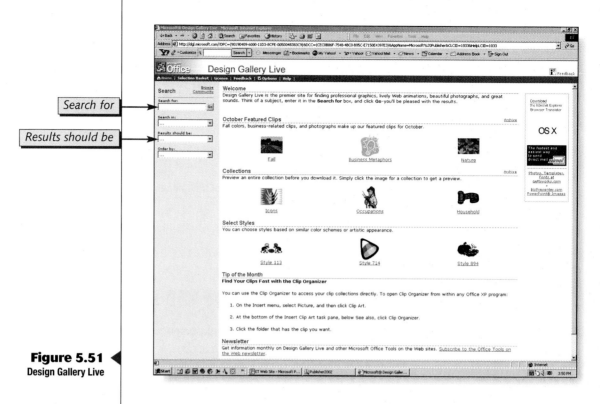

Search for

Results should be

Figure 5.51
Design Gallery Live

5. **In the Search for: box, type** French music.

6. **In the Results should be: box, select** Sounds.

7. **Click** Go.

The results of your search appear in the area to the right as shown in Figure 5.52.

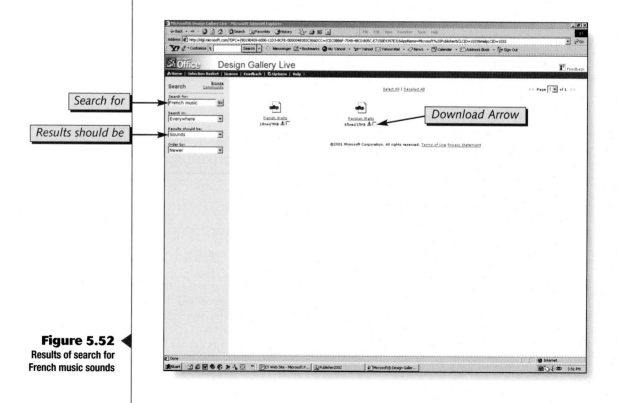

Search for

Download Arrow

Results should be

Figure 5.52
Results of search for
French music sounds

8. Click the Download arrow under the Parisian Waltz clip.

The sound clip is downloaded, and the Clip Organizer appears with the downloaded clip in the preview window, as shown in Figure 5.53.

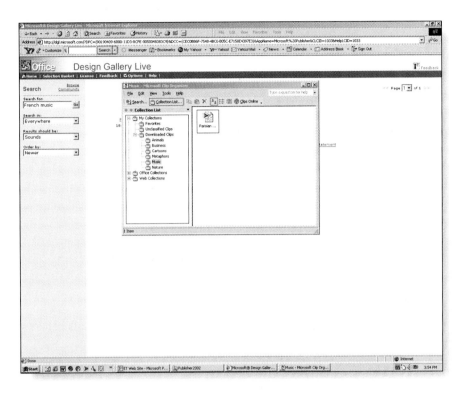

Figure 5.53
Download arrow selected

Publisher BASICS

Adding Background Sound to a Web Page

1. Open the Web page.

2. On the Web Site Options task pane, click Background fill and sound…

3. On the Background task pane, click Background sound…

4. On the General tab on the Web Options dialog box, click Browse… under Background sound.

5. Locate the appropriate music or sound file and click on its name.

6. Click Open.

7. On the Web Options dialog box, click Loop forever.

8. Click OK.

9. Click the down arrow on the right side of the clip and then click Preview/Properties.

The Preview/Properties dialog box appears. This box gives the name of the sound clip (BD00313_) and its file path (C:\My Documents\My Pictures\Microsoft Clip Organizer\BD00313_), which you will need in order to locate the sound clip. (If you wish, you can also listen to the sound clip by clicking the Play button.)

10. Close the Preview/Properties dialog box and then close the Clip Organizer.

11. Close the Design Gallery Live window and disconnect from the Internet.

Page 3 of the Web site reappears with the Insert Clip Art task pane displayed.

12. Click the down arrow next to Insert Clip Art and change the task pane to the Web Site Options task pane, as shown in Figure 5.54.

Publisher 2002 249
CREATING A WEB SITE

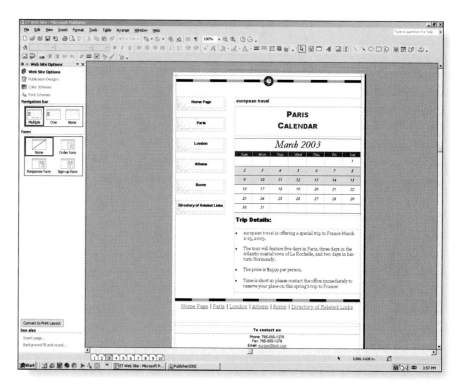

Figure 5.54
Web Site Options task pane

13. Click Background fill and sound… at the bottom of the Web Site Options task pane.

The Background task pane appears.

14. Click Background sound….

The Web Options dialog box appears.

15. On the General tab, click the Browse… button under Background sound.

The Background Sound dialog box appears.

16. Click the down arrow next to the Look in: box and locate the sound clip (using its file path).

 *The default path is My Documents/My Pictures/Microsoft Clip Organizer.*

17. Click on the file name (BD00313_) and then click Open.

18. On the Web Options dialog box, click Loop forever (if it is not already selected). (See Figure 5.55.)

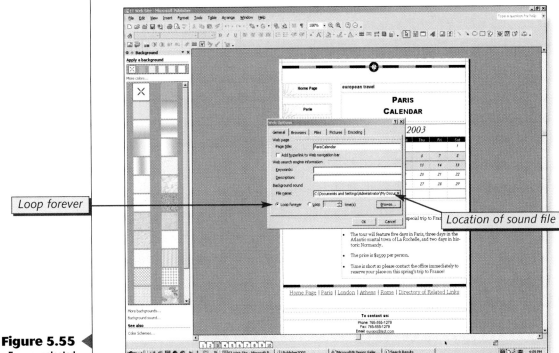

Loop forever

Location of sound file

Figure 5.55
Loop Forever selected

19. Click OK.

The Parisian Waltz file is now linked to the Paris calendar page on your Web site. When you access the Paris calendar page, the music will automatically begin to play. You cannot hear the music from within the Publisher window, however. You must preview the Web page in your browser to hear the music. You will learn how to do this at the end of this lesson.

20. Save the file.

CHECKING A COMPLETED WEB SITE FOR DESIGN PROBLEMS

Once a Web site is completed, you should proofread it carefully and make sure that all necessary links are in place. To check how the links will function, you must preview the Web page in your browser, which you will learn to do at the end of this lesson. The Design Checker tool that you learned about in Lesson 4 can assist you in checking for design problems in Web sites. When checking a Web site, Design Checker looks not only for problems that are common to all publications, but it also looks for problems specifically related to Web sites such as whether or not all of your pages are linked.

HANDS On

Using Design Checker

In this activity, you will use Design Checker to check for possible design problems in your Web site.

1. Click on page 1.

2. On the Tools menu, click Design Checker.

3. On the Design Checker dialog box, click Options....

4. On the Options dialog box, click Check all problems.

5. Click OK.

6. On the Design Checker dialog box, click OK again.

Design Checker begins to check your Web site. If Design Checker encounters any possible problems, it will give you messages about them. Evaluate the messages carefully. Remember that Design Checker may question design "problems" that are not really problems. If Design Checker questions something that is not really a problem, click Ignore. If it is a true problem, make the necessary correction.

7. If Design Checker tells you that an object such as one of the graphic icons is covering another object, you should click Ignore All, since this is not a problem.

8. Click Save ⊞.

VIEWING A WEB SITE IN EXPLORER

Before you a publish a page on the Web, you will want to see how it will look online. The Web Page Preview button 🔍 on the Standard toolbar displays a Web page in the Explorer browser.

In the browser, you can see and test all elements of the site, including:

- Examining the basic look and feel for good design characteristics.
- Verifying that animations and sound files work properly.
- Testing all internal links to make sure that they link to the proper place in the Web site.
- Testing all external links to make sure that the site they link to is active and that the link is to the desired location at the site.
- Verifying that the e-mail address launches an e-mail message.

Any problems that you detect or changes that you note cannot be made from the browser. You must return to the Publisher window to do the editing.

Using Web Page Preview

In this activity, you will display the ET Web Site in the Explorer browser and look for any possible problems. If any problems are found, you can return to Publisher and make the necessary changes.

1. Open the ET Web Site file, if it is not already open.

2. Click Web Page Preview 🔍 on the Standard toolbar.

The Web Page Preview dialog box appears.

3. Under Preview, click Web site, if it is not already selected, and then click OK.

Publisher opens Internet Explorer and shows how your Web page will look online.

4. Scroll to the bottom of the home page.

As you can see, the globe object is spinning. The globe is a piece of *animation.* Objects that are animated perform some kind of movement. You cannot see the animation in the Publisher window, but when a Web page is viewed in a browser, the animation is activated.

5. Click the link to the Paris page on the navigation bar.

The Paris page is displayed, as shown in Figure 5.56.

Figure 5.56
Paris page displayed in browser

6. Click the hyperlink that says <u>Click here</u> near the bottom of the page.

The Paris calendar page appears, and the Parisian Waltz begins to play (if you completed the optional section, Adding Background Sound to a Web Page).

7. Check the other links on the navigation bars by clicking on each of the hyperlinks to make sure that they lead to the intended pages.

Note *Do not check the external links on the Directory of Related Links page at this point. You will do that in the next activity.*

8. Check the links to the calendar pages by clicking the words <u>Click here</u> on the London, Rome and Athens pages.

9. Click the Close button to return to the Publisher window.

10. If any corrections to hyperlinks were needed, make the necessary edits in the Publisher window and then test the links again.

11. Click Save 🖫.

Checking External Links

Not only should you check the links within your Web site, but you should also check any external links (links to other Web sites) to make sure that they work as intended. In order to check these links, you must be connected to the Internet.

The Web is constantly changing. Thus, even if your external links work properly when you initially publish a Web site, they can get outdated. Therefore, it is important that you check the external links periodically to make sure that they continue to lead to functioning Web sites.

In this activity, you will check the links to other Web sites on the ET Web Site.

1. Open the ET Web Site, if it is not already open.

2. Click Web Page Preview 🔍 on the Standard toolbar.

3. On the Web Page Preview dialog box, click Web site and then click OK.

4. Click the link to the Directory of Related Links page.

5. On the Directory of Related Links page, click the first hyperlink.

If you are not already connected to the Internet, Explorer connects you. After the connection is made, the CIA World Factbook Web page for France should appear. If it does not, you may have made an error typing the address for this Web site.

6. Check each of the other hyperlinks on this page.

7. Check the links on the newsletter *the traveler.*

8. Click the Close button ❌ to return to the Publisher window.

9. If any corrections to hyperlinks are needed, make the necessary edits in the Publisher window and then test the links again.

10. Click Save 💾.

11. Close the ET Web Site file.

CORRECTING FORMATTING AND DESIGN PROBLEMS

When you checked the links on the newsletter *the traveler,* you probably noticed some formatting and design problems. The bullets on page 1 of the newsletter appear as question marks, and the graphics on pages 2 and 3 overlap the text. As you will recall, this newsletter was first created as a print publication and was then converted to HTML format using the Save as Web Page command. Not all of the formatting in print publications converts well, however. HTML does not support Publisher's bullets and, as you can see, text wrapping does not always work properly. You may also find that the placement of elements on a printed page does not work as well on a Web page. For example, most of the top of page 4 is blank because it was the mailing panel for the newsletter. As a Web page, however, this is a problem, because it forces the reader to scroll to the bottom of the page to see the calendar and trip information.

Changing the Traveler Web Site

In this activity, you will make some changes to The Traveler as Web Pages to correct the formatting and design problems.

1. **Open** the traveler as Web Pages **file.**

2. **On page 1, select the bulleted list under Special Points of Interest.**

3. **Click** Indents and Lists... **on the Format menu.**

4. **Under Indent settings on the Indents and Lists dialog box, click** Normal.

5. **Under Indents, change Left: to** 0, **as shown in Figure 5.57.**

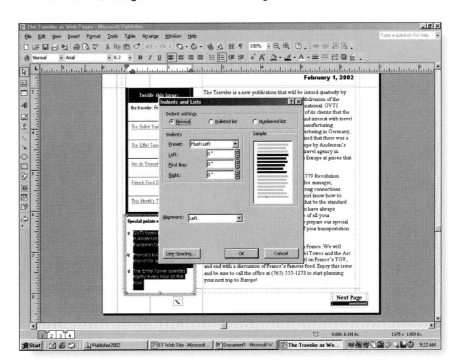

Figure 5.57
Indents and Lists dialog box

6. **Click** OK.

The bullets are removed and the indent settings are adjusted so that the items in the list will be left-aligned.

7. **Go to** page 2.

8. **Resize the first story box so that the left side of its frame is on the left blue margin line, if necessary.**

9. **Move the train graphic so that it is above the story box and resize it so that it fits on the page but does not overlap the story box.**

10. **Resize the second story box so that the left side of its frame is at the 2-inch mark on the horizontal ruler.**

11. **Move the Eiffel Tower graphic to the left and down and resize it so that it fits on the page but does not overlap either story box.**

12. **Go to** page 3.

13. Resize the first story box so that its right side is even with the 12¼-inch mark on the horizontal ruler.

14. Move the Arc de Triomphe graphic to the right side of the page and resize it so that it fits on the page but does not overlap the story box.

15. Resize the second story box so that its right side is even with 12¼-inch mark on the horizontal ruler.

16. Move the French Food graphic to the right side of the page and resize it so that it fits on the page but does not overlap the story box.

Your revised pages 2 and 3 should look similar to Figure 5.58.

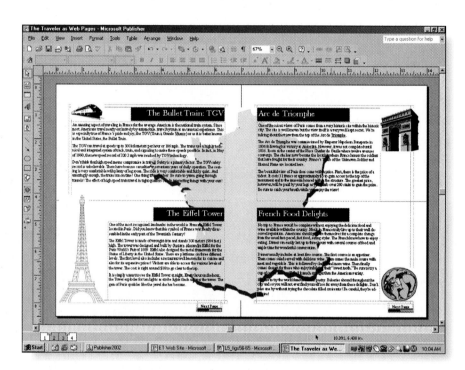

Figure 5.58
Revised pages 2 and 3

17. Go to page 4.

18. Group the european travel logo and the name, address and contact information that are at the top of the page, and move them to the left off the page (temporarily).

19. Group the calendar and the two text boxes that are to the left of the calendar, and move them straight up until their top edges are at the top blue margin line.

20. Move the european travel logo and the name, address and contact information so that they are just below the text boxes that are to the left of the calendar.

Your revised page 4 should look similar to Figure 5.59.

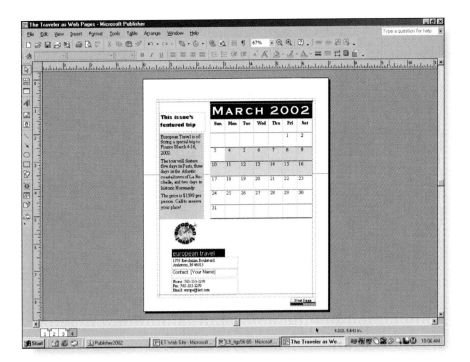

Figure 5.59
Revised page 4

21. Click Save .

22. Use Web Page Preview to view the results of your changes.

If any additional changes are needed, close the browser, make the corrections in Publisher and preview the site again.

Self CHECK

Test your knowledge by filling in the missing word or phrase in each of the following statements. See Appendix C to check your answers.

1. You can use graphics as _____ to lead to another page in your Web site or to another Web site.

2. As Web pages are added to a Web site, Publisher automatically supplies _____ on the left side and at the bottom of each page.

3. When you click on the part of an object that is a _____, it acts as a hyperlink, connecting you to a linked page.

4. The _____ on the Standard toolbar displays a Web page in the Explorer browser.

5. If you find any problems while previewing a Web site, you must return to the _____ to do any editing.

PUBLISHING A WEB PAGE

To be shared with others, a Web page must be ***published.*** Publishing involves storing your page on a ***server*** that has a permanent connection to the Web or an intranet. An ***intranet*** is a Web-like network used by the personnel of one organization. Information on the intranet is only available to others on the same intranet. Schools, for example, often have their own intranets. Most individuals do not have their own Web servers, so they choose to upload their page(s) to the Web server provided by their Internet service provider. Each Internet service provider charges a different fee (if any) and requires a different process to publish your page. Therefore, to publish a Web page, you need to contact the system administrator for your school or your Internet service provider.

For others to read your page, they must know that you have one. You can publicize your Web page in several ways:

- Exchange links with others who own pages. They provide a link on their home page that jumps to yours, and you include hyperlinks that jump to their pages. The more pages that contain links leading to your page, the more people will visit your site.

- Advertise in banners or sponsored links. Naturally, most Web page owners charge a fee for a banner ads and sponsored links, but depending upon potential revenue, a banner may be worth considering.

- Register your page with search engines and subject directories.

- Announce a new page at a newsgroup (discussion group, forum, or chat group) site.

Whatever methods you choose to publicize your Web page, the key to obtaining readers who will return regularly is to provide interesting, informative and up-to-date information on your page.

ON*the*WEB

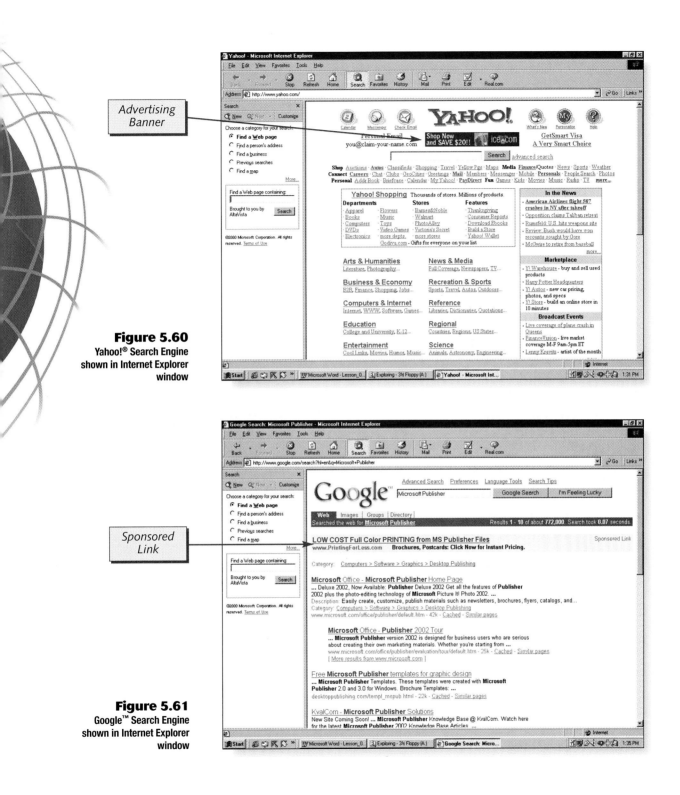

Figure 5.60
Yahoo!® Search Engine
shown in Internet Explorer
window

Figure 5.61
Google™ Search Engine
shown in Internet Explorer
window

SUMMARY

People create and publish Web pages for widely varied reasons. Publisher simplifies the process of creating Web sites, by providing Web page templates and by allowing publications to be saved in HTML format. Graphics, background sound, and animation can all be added to Web pages in Publisher. Hyperlinks allow you not only to link pages within a Web site, but also to link external sites or files. After a Web site is completed, you can view it in Explorer to test the links and to see how it will look when it is published. All changes or improvements must be made in Publisher.

Now that you have completed this lesson, you should be able to do the following:

- Explain what information is appropriate for a Web page.
- Plan a Web site and create a map of the site.
- Use Publisher templates to create a Web site.
- Link pages within a Web site and create links to external Web sites and files.
- Create hot spots as links.
- Add background sound to a Web page.
- Check a Web site for design and linking problems.
- View a Web site in Explorer.
- Make design changes to a published document to adapt it for viewing on the Web.

CONCEPTS REVIEW

1 TRUE/FALSE

Circle T if the statement is true or F if the statement is false.

T   F   1. Companies, organizations and individuals all create Web pages.

T   F   2. Because a Web page is not a print publication, you do not need to be concerned about copyright laws.

T   F   3. You must learn Hypertext Markup Language (HTML) before you can create a Web page.

T   F   4. Although graphics can enhance a Web page, they can also affect how long it will take the Web page to load.

T   F   5. You should include a lot of text on a Web page, especially on the home page.

T   F   6. When you add background sounds and animation to a Web page, you can see how they will work in the Publisher window.

T   F   7. To actually use hyperlinks, you must view a Web page in a browser.

T   F   8. When you create hyperlinks for other Web sites, it is critical that you type the addresses perfectly.

T   F   9. When checking a Web site, Design Checker only looks for problems specifically related to Web sites.

T   F   10. Once you have checked the hyperlinks in your Web site, they never need to be checked again.

Lesson Summary & Exercises

2 MATCHING

Match each of the terms on the left with the definitions on the right.

TERMS	DEFINITIONS
1. animation	**a.** Make your Web site available on others' computers
2. Design Checker	**b.** A computer permanently connected to the Web
3. home page	**c.** A Web-like network used by the personnel of one organization
4. Hot Spot tool	**d.** The main page of a multi-page Web site
5. hyperlinks	**e.** Allow you to move from page to page in a Web site
6. intranet	**f.** A tool that allows you to add a hyperlink to part of an object
7. navigation bars	**g.** A tool that can help you locate problems in a Web site
8. publish	**h.** Allows you to see how a page would look on the Web
9. server	**i.** When an object performs some kind of movement
10. Web Page Preview button	**j.** Connect you to other places in a Web site or to other Web sites

3 COMPLETION

Fill in the missing word or phrase for each of the following statements.

1. Web pages must be written in _____ before they can be published on the Web.

2. If your Web site will have multiple pages, you should create a _____ of the Web site before you being to build the actual site.

3. Insert page… is an option on the _____ task pane.

4. To save a publication in HTML format, select _____ in the Save as type: box on the Save As dialog box.

5. When text is _____ and _____, it indicates that the text is a hyperlink.

6. Without links between pages in a Web site, you cannot _____ from the first page to the other pages when you preview or publish the Web site.

7. The Hot Spot button is on the _____ toolbar.

8. Web Buttons is a category in the _____.

9. To check how hyperlinks will function, you must _____ the Web page in your browser.

10. If you create a personal Web page for yourself, you may want to provide your _____, rather than your telephone number, for readers who want to contact you.

4 SHORT ANSWER

Write a brief answer to each of the following questions.

1. Name at least four characteristics that a Web page should have.

2. Name five factors to be considered in planning a Web site.

3. Name at least three things that you can add to a Web page to enhance its appearance or to make it more interesting.

4. What are the six page types that are available in Publisher?

5. Briefly describe how to add a hyperlink to text.

6. Name three ways that you can use hyperlinks (three places/things that you can link to).

7. Briefly describe how to add background sound to a Web page.

8. What does Web Page Preview allow you to do? What can't you do when you are previewing a Web page?

9. How is an intranet like the Internet? How are they different?

10. What is the key to obtaining readers who will return regularly to your Web page?

5 IDENTIFICATION

Label each of the elements in Figure 5.62.

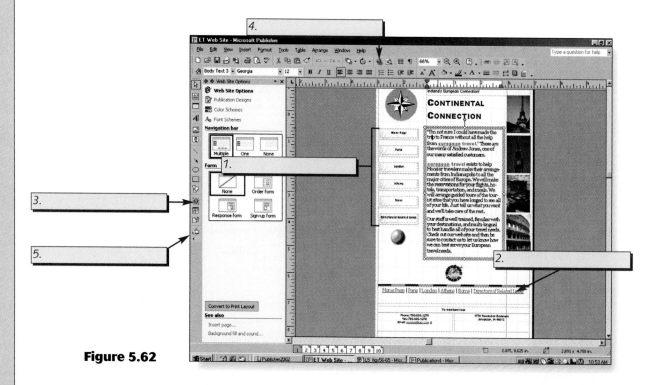

Figure 5.62

SKILLS REVIEW

Complete each of the Skills Review problems in sequential order to review your skills to create a Web site and add hyperlinks, both to pages within the Web site and to other Web sites.

1 Choose a Web site design and create a Web site layout

1. Click **Web Sites** under **By Publication Type** on the New Publication task pane.

2. Click the **Bubbles Web Site.**

The Personal Information for Anderson Pet Mall should be automatically inserted. If it is not, edit the Primary Business personal information set, following the steps for creating a personal information set on pages 25 and 26 of Lesson 1.

3. On the Web Site Options task pane, click **Insert page....**

4. Under Available page types, click **Price list** and then click **OK.**

5. On the Web Site Options task pane, click **Insert page...** again.

6. Under Available page types, click **Calendar** and then click **OK.**

7. On the Web Site Options task pane, click **Insert page...** a third time.

8. Under Available page types, click **Related links** and then click **OK.**

9. Save the Web site as **APM Web Site.** Be sure to change the Save as type: box to **Web Page.**

2 Create a Web site home page

1. Click **Page 1.**

2. Change Home Page Title to **Anderson Pet Mall.**

3. Delete the small frame (under the title frame) that says Anderson Pet Mall.

4. Select the text box beginning Your home page gives your readers . . . and change the text to *Text for Panel One for Lesson 2* on the Publisher Data CD.

 This is the same text that you used for one of the panels on the Anderson Pet Mall brochure.

5. Change the horizontal alignment of this text box to **Align Left.**

6. Use the Enter key ⌨Enter◄┘ to add a blank line between the two paragraphs.

7. Change the font size to **14.**

8. Change the picture in the right margin to the **Pet Store** picture on the Publisher Data CD.

9. Scroll to the bottom of the page and group the Anderson Pet Mall logo, the row of dots, the navigation bar and the contact information boxes.

10. Move the grouped objects so that they are directly below the main text box and centered on the page.

11. Save the Web site.

Lesson Summary & Exercises

3 Add a hyperlink to an e-mail address

1. Highlight **ruffmeow@anderson.net** in the contact information box on page 1.
2. Right-click and then click **Hyperlink....**
3. Under Link to, click **E-mail Address.**
4. Under E-mail address, type ruffmeow@anderson.net.
5. Click **OK.**
6. Repeat steps 1–5 on the other pages of the site.
7. Save the Web site.

4 Create other pages in a Web site

1. Click **page 2.**
2. Edit the default text in the price list table as follows:

Dog shampoo	$9.99
Puppy treats	4.99
Dog sweater	29.99
Leather collar	6.99
Pet bowl	8.99
Cat toy	4.99
Cat litter	5.99
Litter pan	4.99
Hamster wheel	3.99
Turtle food	1.99
Bird treats	4.99
Bird vitamins	8.99

3. Delete the phrase **"Include a description if necessary"** from each box in the table.
4. Change the font size of the table to **14.**
5. Group the Anderson Pet Mall logo, the row of dots, the navigation bar, and the contact information boxes and move the grouped objects so that they are just below the price list and centered on the page.
6. Save the Web site.
7. Click **page 3.**
8. Change the page title (Calendar) to **This Month at APM.**
9. Click the calendar and then click the **Wizard button** .
10. Click **Change date range...** on the Calendar Designs task pane.
11. Change the date to **July 2003.**

12. Select the bulleted list under Schedule of Events and type the following information:

July 4—Start your Independence Day celebration by entering your pet in our History Pet Costume Contest. There is a $100 grand prize, and the winning pet will be featured in the area newspaper.

July 12—Shot Day at Anderson Pet Mall. Dr. Rangu will be here to update your pet's immunization history. Prices are radically reduced.

July 21-27—Anderson Pet Mall's annual summer sale. There will be a 20% discount on everything in the store.

13. Change the font size of the bulleted list to **14.**

14. Resize the bulleted list frame to remove the extra space at the bottom of the frame.

15. On the July 2003 calendar, click on the **4** box and then click the down arrow next to **Fill Color** on the Formatting toolbar.

16. Select the fourth fill color option (red).

17. Add the same fill color to the boxes for July 12 and July 21–27.

18. Group the Anderson Pet Mall logo, the row of dots, the navigation bar, and the contact information boxes and move the grouped objects so that they are just below the bulleted list and centered on the page.

19. Save the Web site.

5 Create a related links page

1. Click **page 4.**

2. Select the first text box (beginning Hyperlinks are electronic . . .) and type As a service to our pet-loving customers, we have included this page of other excellent Web sites. We hope you enjoy your browsing, and be sure to come see us soon at Anderson Pet Mall!

3. Change the font size to **14.**

4. In the next text box, select Web site name and address hyperlink.

5. Type http://www.akc.org

6. Select the text beginning **Briefly summarize . . .** and type American Kennel Club.

7. Press the Enter key and then type This site has everything you ever wanted to know about dogs.

8. Repeat steps 4–7 for the next two text boxes, substituting the information below:

http://www.addl.purdue.edu
Animal Disease Diagnostic Laboratory at Purdue University
Is your pet feeling sick? Check out this site.

http://www.apapets.com
American Pet Association
This site has a lot of information for people like you who love their pets.

9. Select the Web address in the first box (http://www.akc.org).

10. Right-click and then click **Hyperlink....**

11. Under Link to (on the Insert Hyperlink dialog box), click **Existing File or Web Page.**

12. In the Address: box, type the same Web address and click **OK.**

13. Repeat steps 9-12 for the other two Web addresses.

14. Change the default graphics to the left of each box as follows:

For the first graphic, change to the graphic *Man and dog* on the Publisher Data CD.

For the second graphic, change to the graphic *Cat and dish* on the Publisher Data CD.

For the third graphic, change to the graphic *Smiling cat* on the Publisher Data CD.

15. Delete the next two text boxes. Also delete the default graphics next to these two boxes. Move the bottom text box up to remove the extra space.

 *This should leave one text box and graphic that you will edit in the next section.*

16. Save the Web site.

6 Save a publication as a Web page and link it to your Web site

1. Locate and open the file Pet Periodical 1-1 that you created in Lesson 3.

2. On the File menu, click **Save as Web Page....**

3. On the Save as Web Page dialog box, change File name: to **Pet Periodical Web Pages** and then click **Save.**

4. Close the Pet Periodical Web Pages file and open the **APM Web Site** file.

5. Click on **page 4.**

6. In the last text box, select Web site name and hyperlink and type Pet Periodical.

7. Select the text beginning **Briefly summarize . . .** and type This will link you to Anderson Pet Mall's monthly newsletter, Pet Periodical. Keep informed about what's going on at APM and learn more about pet ownership and care.

8. Select the words **Pet Periodical.**

9. Right-click and then click **Hyperlink....**

10. On the Insert Hyperlink dialog box, click **Existing File or Web Page.**

11. Locate the Pet Periodical Web Pages file that you just saved and click on it.

12. Click **OK.**

13. Change the default graphic to the left of this box to the **Anderson Pet Mall logo** on the Publisher Data CD.

14. Group and move the row of dots, the navigation bar, and the contact information so that they are just below the last text box and centered on the page.

15. Save the Web site.

7 Add links between pages

1. Close the APM Web Site file and open the **Pet Periodical Web Pages** file.

2. On the Table of Contents, select **INDIANA STATE BIRD: THE CARDINAL.**

3. Right-click and then click **Hyperlink....**

4. On the Insert Hyperlink dialog box, click **Place in This Document.**

5. Click **page 2** under Select a place in this document....

6. Click **OK.**

7. Repeat steps 2–6 for the next two items on the Table of Contents.

8. For the remaining items on the Table of Contents, repeat steps 2–6, but click the appropriate page number (rather than Page 2) under Select a place in this document....

9. Click **Design Gallery Object** on the Objects toolbar.

10. Under Categories, click **Web Buttons.**

11. Click the **Link Framed Oval Button.**

12. Click **Insert Object.**

13. Move the Web button to the lower right corner of the page.

14. Select the word **Link** on the Web button and type Next Page.

15. Click the **Hot Spot button** [icon] the Objects toolbar.

16. On the Insert Hyperlink dialog box, click **Place in This Document** and then click **Next Page.**

17. Click **OK.**

18. Move and resize the Hot Spot frame so that it covers the Next Page button.

19. Select the words **Next Page** on the Web button and change the font size to **10.**

20. Repeat steps 9–19 for pages 2 and 3 of the newsletter.

21. For page 4, follow the same steps but type First Page on the Web button. Link the Hot Spot to Page 1 on the Insert Hyperlink dialog box.

22. Save the file.

8 Preview a Web site and check hyperlinks

1. Click **Web Page Preview** [icon] on the Standard toolbar.

2. Under Preview: on the Web Page Preview dialog box, click **Web site** and then click **OK.**

3. Check each of the links on the navigation bars.

4. Check each of the links on the Related Links Page.

5. Check the links on the Pet Periodical Web Pages.

6. Click the **Close button** [X] to return to the Publisher window and make any necessary edits.

Lesson Summary & Exercises

LESSON APPLICATIONS

Complete the following activities in sequential order to create an online thank you card that can be linked to **european travel's** Web site.

1 Create a greeting card and save it as a Web page

1. Under By Publication Type on the New Publication task pane, click Greeting Cards.

2. Click the Globe and Flower Thank You Card.

3. Click Page 4.

4. On the Edit menu, click Delete Page.

Publisher asks: Delete this page?

5. Click OK.

6. Click Page 2.

7. On the Edit menu, click Delete Page.

8. On the Delete Page dialog box, click Left page only and then click OK.

Publisher reminds you that you are viewing a two-page spread and asks if you really want to delete this page.

9. Click OK.

Your greeting card now has two pages.

10. On page 2, change the default text to read: A WORLD OF GRATITUDE FOR YOUR BUSINESS.

11. Draw a second text box on page 2 and type: FROM THE STAFF OF [Enter⏎] [Enter⏎] european travel.

12. Center both lines of text and use the Format Painter to change the font of the first line (FROM THE STAFF OF) to match the text in the first text box.

13. Select the words "european travel" and change the font to Arial Black, 12, and the font color to the same color as the rest of the text.

14. Using the Save As Web Page command on the File menu, save the card under the name *ET Web Card.*

2 Add a piece of animation to a Web card

1. Locate the Voyage Web Site template in the Publication Gallery and click on it.

2. Click the globe object on this template and then click the Copy button on the Standard toolbar.

3. Close this template.

4. Open the **ET Web Card** file that you created in the previous activity (if it is not already open) and go to page 2.

5. Click the Paste button on the Standard toolbar.

6. Resize the globe object so that it is 1-inch high and 1-inch wide.

7. Drag the globe picture so that it is centered in the space above the words "A WORLD OF GRATITUDE FOR . . ."

8. Save the Web card.

3 Add links between pages on a Web card

1. Open the **ET Web Card** file, if it is not already open, and go to page 1.

2. Click the Design Gallery Object button on the Objects toolbar and then click Web Buttons.

3. Click Link Framed Oval and then click Insert Object.

4. Move the Link Framed Oval object to the lower right corner of page 1, so that its right edge is even with the right blue margin line and so that its top edge is on the bottom blue margin line.

5. Change the word "Link" to read: Go to next page.

6. Click Page 2.

7. Repeat steps 2–3.

8. Move the Link Framed Oval object to the lower left corner of page 2, so that its left edge is even with the left blue margin line and so that its top edge is on the bottom blue margin line.

9. Change the word "Link" to read: Previous page.

10. Select the words "Previous page."

11. Right-click, click Hyperlink..., and then click Place in This Document.

12. Click Previous Page on the Insert Hyperlink dialog box and then click OK.

13. Click Page 1.

14. Select the words "Go to next page."

15. Right-click, click Hyperlink..., and then click Place in This Document.

16. Click Next Page on the Insert Hyperlink dialog box and then click OK.

17. Save the Web card.

4 Add an e-mail button to a Web card

1. Open the *ET Web Card* file, if it is not already open, and go to page 2.

2. Click the Design Gallery Object button and then click Web Buttons.

3. Click Email Framed Oval and then click Insert Object.

4. Move the Email Framed Oval object to the lower right corner of page 2.

5. Select the word "E-mail" on the object.

6. Right-click, click Hyperlink…, and then click E-mail Address.

7. In the E-mail address: box, type europe@last.com (or select europe@last.com from the list of recently used e-mail addresses). Click OK.

8. Save the Web card.

5 View the Web card in Explorer

1. Open the *ET Web Card* file, if it is not already open.

2. Click the Web Page Preview button.

3. Click Web site and then click OK.

4. Check all of the links on your Web card and view the animation on page 2.

5. Click the Close button to return to the Publisher window.

PROJECTS

1 Check it out!

When you previewed the ET Web Site in this lesson, you discovered that the globe object was actually an animation. In fact, each of the Publisher Web site designs contains an animated object. To find out what other kinds of animation are available, click Web Sites under By Publication Type on the New Publication task pane. Scroll down the list of Web site templates in the Publication Gallery and choose ten of them. Write each of their names and then click on each one. After each of the templates is open, click Web Page Preview. Locate the animated object on each template and write a brief description of the animation.

2 Website Creations

You have been hired as a marketing assistant at the fast-growing Website Creations. Your organization offers professional design and consulting services for businesses that operate an intranet and/or do business on the Internet. You have learned that new intranet users are often confused about the types of documents to publish on their networks, and you would like to provide this information on your company's Web site.

Create a Web page starting from a blank publication. Draw a full-page text box on the blank page, using the blue margin lines as your guide. Inside the text box, type a message to intranet users. Use a memorandum format, such as:

To: Intranet Users
From: Website Creations
Date: July 31, 2003
Re: CONFUSED?

Indicate five selection criteria for documents to be published. Let the users know that Website Creations can give them much more information on the subject and hands-on help. Provide an e-mail address that they can use to get more information.

Save the memorandum as a Web page. Add a hyperlink to the e-mail address. Enhance the appearance of the page by adding a background color or texture. Save again and preview it on the Explorer browser.

3 Plan ahead

Abby Steer, the owner of Sharp Shots Photography, will be at Website Creations for a first consultation this afternoon. Abby uses digital cameras and, naturally, wants her new Web site to include examples of her work. Make a list of questions to guide you as you interview Abby and as you plan the site. Sketch a home page layout to use as a starting point. Draw circles, rectangles, squares, and so on, to represent photographs. Show links to other pages at the site and to other sites that you propose. Suggest fonts and background colors for the site.

4 My resume

Many of your friends are finding jobs by posting their resumes on the Web, so you have decided to give it a try. Under By Publication Type on the New Publication task pane, click Resumes and then click Entry Level. Choose a resume design and open the template. Change the personal information set to Home/Family and edit the information to give your name, address, and contact information. Click Update.

Edit the resume template to list your education, work experience, references, and so on. Save the resume as a Web page. Add Web buttons at the bottom of each page and then add Hot Spots to the Web buttons so that they can be used to navigate between the pages. Add a hyperlink to your e-mail address. Save again, and use Web Page Preview to check the links on your resume.

Lesson Summary & Exercises

5 A testimonial from a satisfied customer

If you completed the Skills Review activities for Lesson 4, locate the newsletter My Trip to France that you created in those activities. Save the newsletter as a Web page. Open the ET Web Site that you created in this lesson. Select the name Andrew Jones on the first page of the Web site and add a hyperlink to the My Trip to France Web page. Save the ET Web Site.

Go to the Paris page on the ET Web Site. Draw a text box under the pull quote box and type: Click here to read the newsletter of a satisfied customer. Using the Format Painter, change the formatting of the new text box to match the formatting of the pull quote box. Select the words "Click here" and add a hyperlink to the My Trip to France Web page. Save the ET Web Site again. Use Web Page Preview to check the links you just created.

6 Venus links

Note
You must complete the On the Web project in Lesson 4 before completing this project.

Open the Venus Web page that you saved in Lesson 4. Draw a text box at the bottom of the page and type Links to Helpful Sources. Then type the addresses of the four Web sites that you chose in the On the Web project in Lesson 2. (If you did not complete that project, or if you no longer have the addresses, search the Web for information about the planet Venus and locate four helpful Web sites. Refer to the instructions on pages 80 and 81, if necessary.)

Select each of the four Web site addresses. Right-click and then click Hyperlink.... When the Insert Hyperlink dialog box appears, click Existing File or Web Page. In the Address: box, type the selected address, and then click OK.

Save the updated Web page. Use Web Page Preview to check your hyperlinks.

Project in Progress

Your efforts to increase the visibility of your local Friends of the Library group are paying off. Membership has doubled, and donations for the annual book sale are at an all-time high. You are looking for a way to continue the momentum and to provide more timely information to the group's members than you can provide through your quarterly newsletter. Based on a recent survey of your members, you know that most of them are Internet users, so you have decided that it is time to create a Web site for your organization.

Create a map of the Web site to help you plan what information you will include on each page and how the pages will be linked. Choose a Web page design and create the home page of the Web site. (If necessary, edit the Other Organization personal information set, following the instructions in Lesson 1 and adding the logo you created in Lesson 4.) Incorporate promotional text from the tri-fold brochure and newsletter than you created in Lessons 2 and 3. Create a calendar page, highlighting the dates of the annual book sale. Create other pages, as necessary, to complete your site.

Save the Web site as Friends Web Site.

Creating Business Forms, Business Cards, and Letterhead

CONTENTS

OBJECTIVES

After you complete this lesson, you will be able to do the following:

- Select a design set and modify its color scheme.
- Change and save a color scheme in a personal information set.
- Use design sets to create business cards, letterhead, fax cover sheets, and business forms.
- Use Mail Merge to create mailing lists and then merge the information onto letters and other publications.
- Create, edit, and fill in tables.
- Add borders and shading to tables.
- Create electronic forms for Web pages.

In this lesson, you will learn how to use Publisher's design sets to create a variety of business forms that have consistent design elements. You will also learn how to use Publisher's Mail Merge feature to merge mailing list data onto letters and other publications. Finally, you will learn how to create and edit tables, which are the basic elements of many business forms.

HANDS
On

USING PUBLISHER DESIGN SETS TO CREATE BUSINESS FORMS

In previous lessons, you learned the importance of using design elements consistently within a publication. Consistency is also important when you are designing business forms and other materials, such as letterhead and business cards, for a business or organization. When the same design elements, such as logos and color schemes, are used in all of an organization's publications, people begin to identify those design elements with the organization.

Publisher makes it easy to achieve this consistency, by providing design sets. Design sets are collections of publications that share common design elements. In this lesson, you will use Publisher's design sets to create a set of forms for a single business.

Many of the business forms contain tables. Tables are a convenient way to organize data that is best presented in tabular format. The Publisher Design Sets include preformatted grids with columns of various widths and rows of various heights.

Choosing and Modifying a Design Set

In the following activity, you will choose, and then modify, a design set for the travel agency, european travel, whose newsletter and Web site you created in Lessons 4 and 5.

1. With the New Publication task pane displayed, click the down arrow under Start from a design, and then click By Design Sets.

A list of design sets appears in the task pane.

2. Click Axis under Master Sets.

Thumbnail previews of the publications available in this set appear in the Publication Gallery, as shown in Figure 6.1. Scroll through the various publications to see what types of forms can be created. Although you will only work with a few of these forms in this lesson, you can see the variety of forms available.

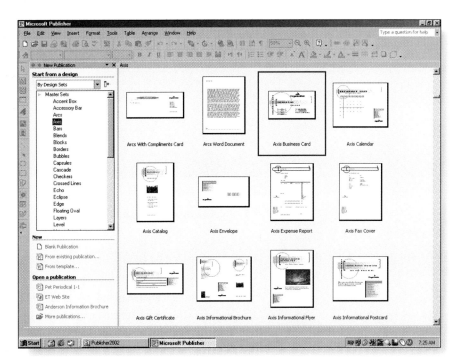

Figure 6.1
Thumbnail previews of
available publications

3. **Click the** Axis Business Card.

The template for the business card appears, as shown in Figure 6.2. As you can see, information for Anderson Pet Mall has been automatically inserted. To replace this information with the information for european travel, you will need to change the personal information set.

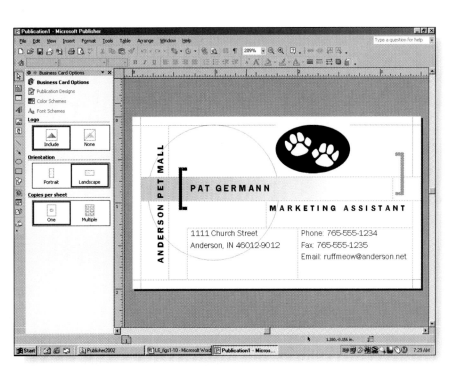

Figure 6.2
Business card template

4. Click **Personal Information...** on the Edit menu.

5. Select the **Secondary Business** option and then click **Update**.

 *If the Secondary Business personal information set does not contain the information for* european travel, *edit the information set following the instructions on pages 145–146 in Lesson 4. Then click Update.*

The information for european travel is inserted in the business card template. You will now select a color scheme specifically for european travel.

6. Click **Color Schemes** on the Business Card Options task pane.

All of the color schemes that are available in Publisher are displayed in the task pane under the heading Apply a color scheme. As you can see, the color schemes are sorted alphabetically by the name of the color scheme.

7. Scroll through the list of color scheme options until the Eggplant color scheme appears. This color scheme emphasizes black and gray while adding a bit of color, which will coordinate well with the black and gray european travel logo.

8. Click the **Eggplant** color scheme option.

The color scheme on the business card changes to the Eggplant color scheme, as shown in Figure 6.3.

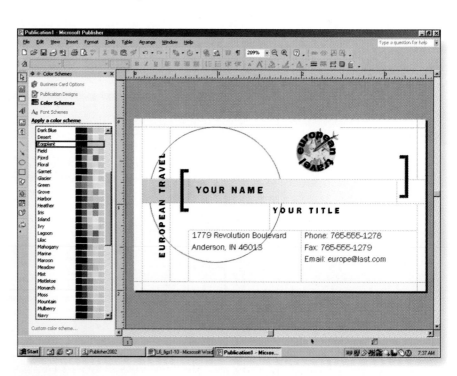

Figure 6.3
Eggplant color scheme applied to business card

Although you have changed the color scheme on the business card, the color scheme will not be permanently saved as part of the information set for european travel unless you tell Publisher that you wish to have it saved. In order to use the same color scheme throughout all of european travel's publications, you need to update the personal information set.

Changing and Saving the Color Scheme in a Personal Information Set

1. Open the personal information set you wish to change.

2. Under Color schemes, click the down arrow and scroll through the options until the desired color scheme appears.

3. Click the desired color scheme.

4. Make sure that the box in front of Include color scheme in this set is checked.

5. Click Update.

Figure 6.4 ◀
Eggplant color scheme in Personal Information dialog box

9. Open the personal information set for european travel (the Secondary Business set).

10. Under Color schemes, click the down arrow and scroll up until the Eggplant color scheme appears, as shown in Figure 6.4.

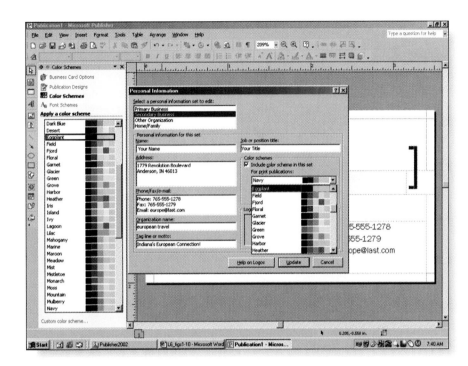

11. Click on the Eggplant color scheme. Make sure that the box in front of Include color scheme in this set is checked. (This will ensure that Publisher retains the new color scheme as part of the information set.)

12. Click Update.

The Eggplant color scheme is now saved as part of the european travel personal information set. Whenever this personal information set is used, the Eggplant color scheme will be automatically used as well.

13. Save the publication as european travel business card.

CREATING BUSINESS CARDS

In the previous activity, you began to create a business card using a template from a design set. Because a business card is a very small and simple publication, Publisher is able to do most of the work for you, once you have chosen a design set and the correct personal information set. There are, however, a few additional decisions that you must make when creating business cards. First, you should evaluate the font size that Publisher has used for the business card. If there is enough extra space on the card, you may wish to increase the font size to make the information on the card as easy to read as possible. Second, you may wish to add other information, such as additional contact numbers, that may not be in the personal information set. Finally, you will need to decide how the cards will be printed.

If you will be printing the cards yourself on a laser or inkjet printer, you will need to purchase perforated card stock or find some way to cut the cards apart. Printing multiple copies of a business card on the same sheet is no problem, however. Publisher can handle this for you.

Completing and Printing Business Cards

In this activity, you will complete the business card that you started in the previous activity. Then you will print multiple copies of the business card on a single sheet of paper or card stock.

 *It is not necessary to have perforated card stock to complete this activity. You can print the completed cards on plain paper to see how they will look. Of course, they will not be true "cards" unless they are printed on card stock. Check with your instructor to find out if you need to use card stock and if it is available in your computer lab.*

1. **Open the european travel business card file, if it is not already open.**

2. **Click Business Card Options on the task pane, if it is not already the current task pane.**

3. **Click Multiple under Copies per sheet.**

When you print the business card, Publisher will automatically print multiple copies of the business card on a single sheet.

4. **Click at the end of the fax number and press** Enter⏎ **to create a new line. Then type** Cell: 765-555-1280, **as shown in Figure 6.5.**

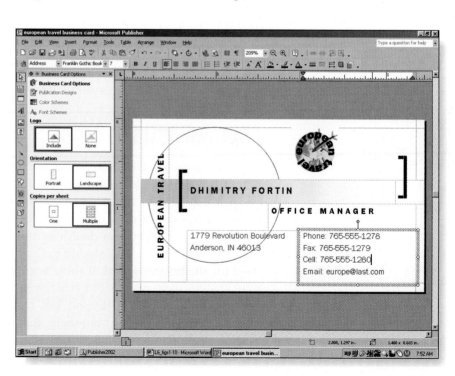

Figure 6.5
Additional contact information added to business card

5. Select the words "EUROPEAN TRAVEL" on the left side of the card.

As you may recall from previous lessons, the name european travel is usually in Arial Black and lowercase. Because the template automatically uses Franklin Gothic Demi and uppercase, you will need to change the font.

6. Right-click, point to Change Text, and then click Font....

The Font dialog box appears.

7. Under Font, locate and click Arial Black.

8. Under Effects, click the box in front of All caps to remove the check mark from this box, as shown in Figure 6.6.

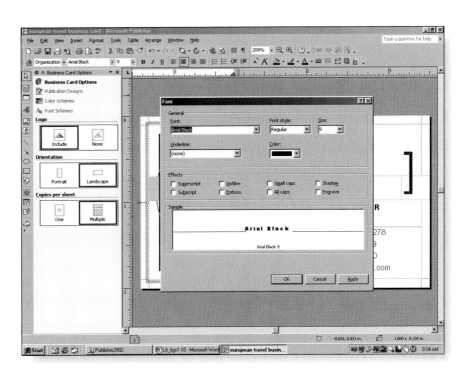

Figure 6.6 ◀
Font dialog box with changes for european travel logo

9. Click OK.

The business card template reappears with the font changed.

10. With the words european travel still selected, increase the font size using the Increase Font Size button **A'** on the Formatting toolbar.

This button allows you to increase the font size one point at a time, so that you can determine how large you can make the font size before the words overflow the text frame. When the text overflows the frame, use the Decrease Font Size button **A'** to reduce the font size by one point, so that the font size is the maximum size possible for the frame.

11. Repeat step 10 for each of the other text frames.

Publisher **BASICS**

Determining the Maximum Font Size for a Frame

1. Select the text to be resized.

2. Click the Increase Font Size button repeatedly until the words overflow the text frame.

3. Click the Decrease Font Size button once to reduce the font size to the maximum size for the frame.

12. Save the business card file.

You will now make one final change to the business card. Because the circle on the business card is black, it interferes with the readability of the address text. In the next few steps, you will change the color of the circle to match the fill color of the name text box. This will also add a bit more color to the business card.

13. Click the circle at a point above the name text box.

Handles appear around the circle.

14. Right-click and then click Format AutoShape…, as shown in Figure 6.7.

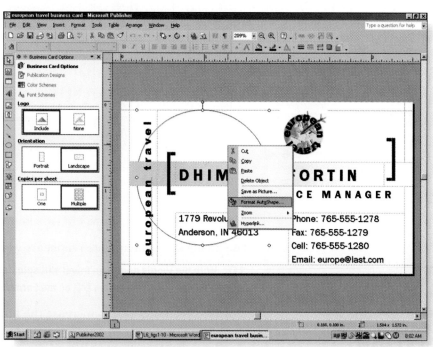

Figure 6.7
Format AutoShape selected

The Format AutoShape dialog box appears.

15. Click the Colors and Lines tab, if it is not already on top.

16. Under Line, click the down arrow next to Color and then click the third color choice (tan).

17. Click OK.

The circle is now the same color as the name text box.

18. With the circle still selected, click Order on the Arrange menu, and then click Send to Back, as shown in Figure 6.8. (This puts the address text on top of the circle.)

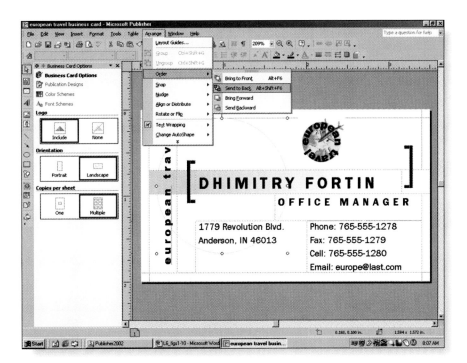

Figure 6.8
Send to Back

The business card is now complete and should appear as shown in Figure 6.9.

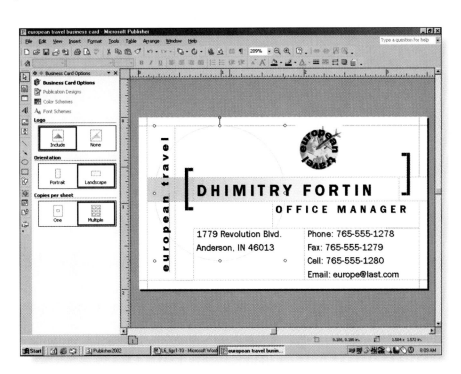

Figure 6.9
Completed business card

19. Save the business card.

1. Click the Print Preview button.

2. Click the Print button on the Preview window to proceed with printing.

3. Click Close on the Preview window to return to the Publisher window.

20. Click the Print Preview button  on the Standard toolbar to see how the business cards will print.

Publisher automatically creates ten copies of the business card, as shown in Figure 6.10.

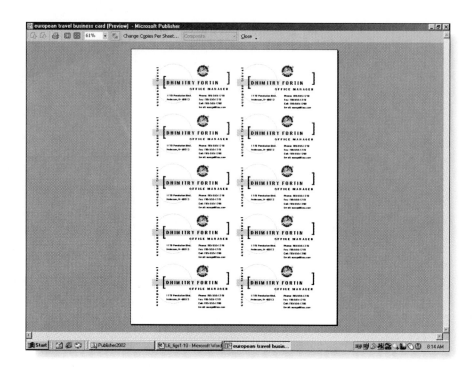

Figure 6.10
Print Preview of european travel business cards

Note *If you will be using card stock, load the card stock in your printer before completing the next step.*

21. Click the Print button 🖨 on the Preview window to print the business cards.

22. Click the Close button ☒ on the Preview window to return to the Publisher window.

CREATING LETTERHEAD

Nearly all businesses and organizations use ***letterhead*** to provide basic contact information (name, address, and phone numbers) on every letter. Letterheads are important because they often create the first impression of a business or organization. For that reason, they are often printed on special paper. Publisher design sets simplify the process of creating letterheads and ensure that the letterhead design is consistent with the organization's other publications.

Using Design Sets to Create Letterhead

In this activity, you will create a letterhead for european travel that is consistent with the design of its business cards.

1. **Open Publisher. Click** By Design Sets **on the New Publication task pane, if it is not already selected.**

2. **Click** Axis **under Master Sets and then click the** Axis Letterhead.

The Axis Letterhead template appears with information for the Anderson Pet Mall inserted.

3. **Change the personal information set to the information set for european travel. (Read steps 4 and 5 under Choosing and Modifying a Design Set, if necessary.)**

4. **Select the words** european travel **at the top of the letterhead and then right-click.**

5. **Point to** Change Text **and then click** Font....

6. **On the Font dialog box, change Font: to** Arial Black, **change Size: to** 18, **and deselect (remove the check mark) from** All caps.

7. **Click** OK.

8. **Increase the size of the logo on the letterhead so that it is approximately the same width as the text box underneath, as shown in Figure 6.11. (As the logo is resized, you will need to move it so that it stays centered over the text box.)**

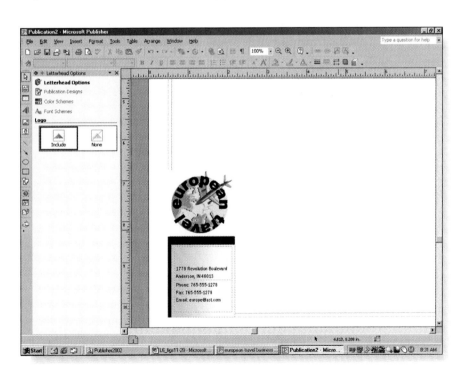

Figure 6.11
Logo resized

9. **Increase the font size of the address and contact numbers to** 9. **You will need to abbreviate "Boulevard" as "Blvd." as you did on the business card.**

10. Change the circle color at the top of the letterhead to match the fill color of the organization name text box, following steps 13–17 under Completing and Printing Business Cards.

The letterhead is now complete, as shown in Figure 6.12.

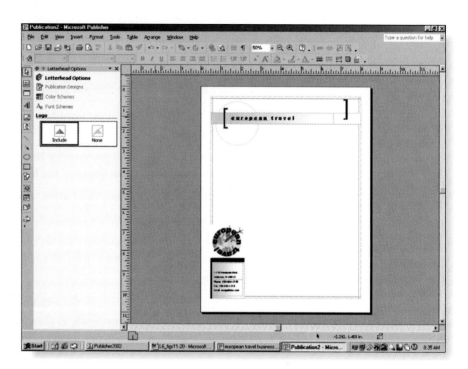

Figure 6.12
Completed letterhead

11. Save the publication as european travel letterhead. Close the publication.

USING MAIL MERGE

Now that you have created letterhead, you are ready to create an actual letter. As you are probably aware, letters consist of several parts besides the letterhead, including the date, the recipient's name and address, the salutation, the body of the letter, and the closing. Businesses and organizations frequently send the same letters to many different people, but they must address each letter individually.

If you were planning to send the same letter to 500 people, you would not want to retype the entire letter 500 times. In addition, if you send multiple mailings to the same 500 people, you would not want to retype their addresses each time. With Publisher's *Mail Merge* feature, you can enter the addresses only once and then *merge* the addresses onto letters, envelopes, postcards, and any other publications that have address blocks or mailing panels.

The mail merge process begins with two documents: the *main publication,* such as a letter or postcard, and the mailing list (called the *data source*). You identify the pieces of data in the mailing list with *field codes* (such as Name, Address, City, State, and Zip Code) and then insert the field codes into the main publication. When Publisher completes the mail merge, it replaces the field codes in the main publication with actual address information from the data source. The process saves time and reduces errors.

Creating and Merging Address Data onto Letterhead

In this activity, you will create and then merge address data onto the letterhead you created in the previous activity.

1. Open the european travel letterhead, if it is not already open.

2. Draw a text box starting at the 2½-inch mark on the horizontal ruler and at 3-inch mark on the vertical ruler. The right side and the bottom of the text box should be on the blue margin lines, as shown in Figure 6.13.

Publisher BASICS

Creating a Mailing List Using the Mail Merge Wizard

1. On the Tools menu, click Mail Merge, then click Mail Merge Wizard.

2. Under Select recipients, click Type a new list.

3. Click Create....

4. Fill in the contact information.

5. Click New Entry.

6. Repeat steps 4–5 until all of the names and addresses are entered.

7. Click Close.

8. Save the mailing list.

9. On the Mail Merge Recipients dialog box, change the sort if necessary.

10. Click OK.

Figure 6.13
Text box added to letterhead

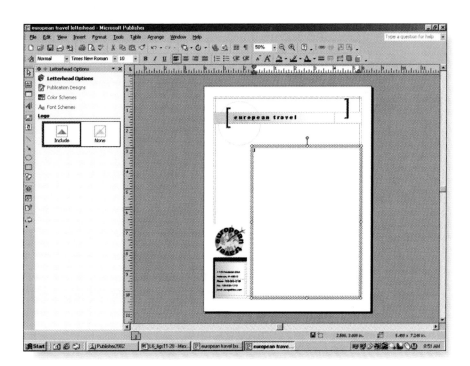

3. On the Tools menu, click Mail Merge and then click Mail Merge Wizard.

The Mail Merge task pane appears.

4. Under Select recipients, click Type a new list.

5. Under Type a new list, click Create....

The New Address List dialog box appears.

6. In the Title box, type Ms.; in the First Name box, type Sherrie; in the Last Name box, type Lightner; in the Address Line 1 box, type 6789 Pennsylvania Ave.; in the City box, type Shirley; in the State box, type IN; and in the Zip Code box, type 47384. (See Figure 6.14.)

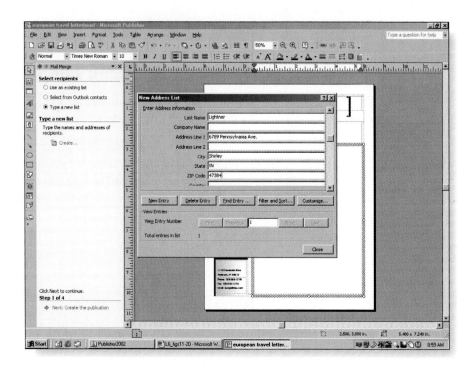

Figure 6.14
New Address List dialog box

The New Address List dialog box contains more fields than you need for the personal addresses you will be entering. Be careful to enter the name and address information in the correct fields.

Use the Tab key to move from line to line in the New Address List dialog box.

7. Click New Entry.

Publisher saves the information you just typed and gives you a new, empty form in which to type your next address.

8. In the Title box, type Mr.; **in the First Name box, type** Rocky; **in the Last Name box, type** Rhodes; **in the Company Name box, type** Brainchild, Inc.; **in the Address Line 1 box, type** 1595 BSU Circle; **in the City box, type** Muncie; **in the State box, type** IN; **and in the Zip Code box, type** 47302.

9. Click Close ☒.

The Save Address List dialog box appears.

10. In the File name: box, type european travel mailing list. **(See Figure 6.15.)**

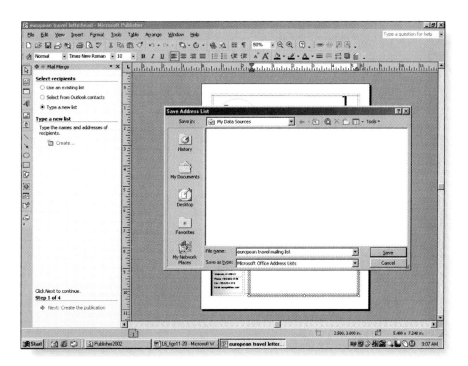

Figure 6.15 ◀
Save Address List dialog box

11. **Click** Save.

The Mail Merge Recipients dialog box appears, as shown in Figure 6.16. Read the paragraph at the top of the dialog box. Mail Merge allows you to sort your list by any of the mailing list fields. This sort feature is very helpful when creating large mailing lists. For example, if you use a bulk-mailing permit, you will need to sort your mailing list by zip code in order to comply with postal regulations.

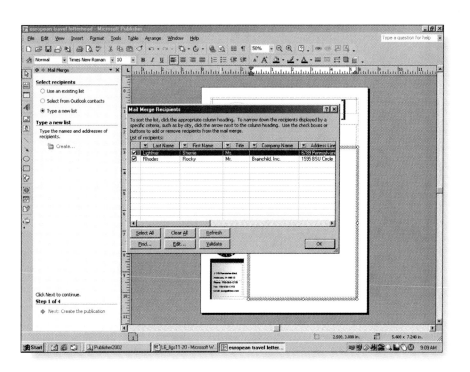

Figure 6.16 ◀
Mail Merge Recipients dialog box

12. **Click** OK.

Merging Mailing List Data

1. After creating a mailing list, click Next: Create the publication.

2. Click the place in the letter where you want to put the address information.

3. Click Address block... on the Mail Merge task pane.

4. Change the format of the address block, if necessary.

5. Click OK.

6. Press Enter twice at the end of <<AddressBlock>> on the letter to create a blank line.

7. Click Greeting Line... on the Mail Merge task pane.

8. Change the default settings on the Greeting Line dialog box, if necessary.

9. Click OK.

10. Type the rest of the letter.

Figure 6.17 ◄
Insert Address Block dialog box

13. At the bottom of the Mail Merge task pane, click Next: Create the publication.

14. Read the information under Create the publication on the Mail Merge task pane. Then click in the text box that you created earlier and click Address block... on the task pane.

The Insert Address Block dialog box appears, as shown in Figure 6.17. This dialog box allows you to change the format of your address block in various ways. For this activity, however, you will use the default settings.

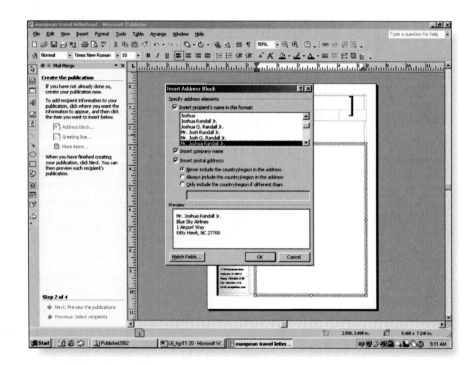

15. Click OK.

The letterhead reappears with the field code <<AddressBlock>> inserted.

16. Press ⌷Enter↵⌷ twice at the end of <<AddressBlock>> to create a blank line.

17. Click Greeting Line... on the Mail Merge task pane.

The Greeting Line dialog box appears, as shown in Figure 6.18. This dialog box allows you to change the wording of the greeting in various ways. Again, for this activity, you will use the default settings.

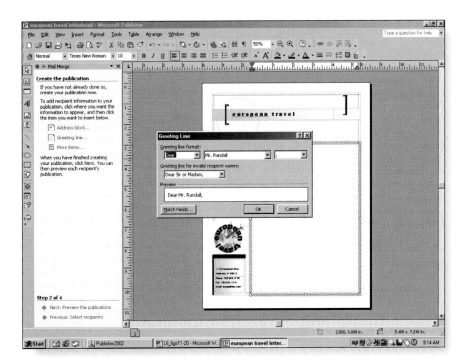

Figure 6.18 ◄
Greeting Line dialog box

18. Click **OK**.

The letterhead reappears with the field code <<GreetingLine>> inserted, as shown in Figure 6.19. You could now type the body of a letter in the text box.

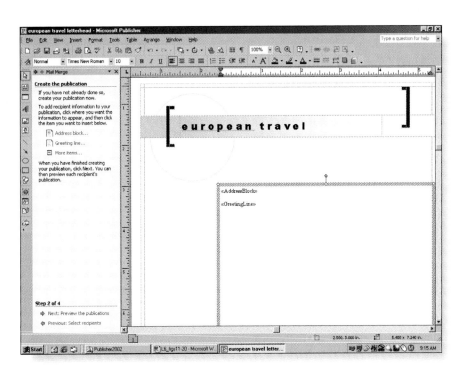

Figure 6.19 ◄
Letterhead with address and greeting field codes

19. To complete the Mail Merge process, click **Next: Preview the publications** under Step 2 of 4 on the Mail Merge task pane.

Mail Merge inserts the name and address information for your first recipient into the letter, as shown in Figure 6.20.

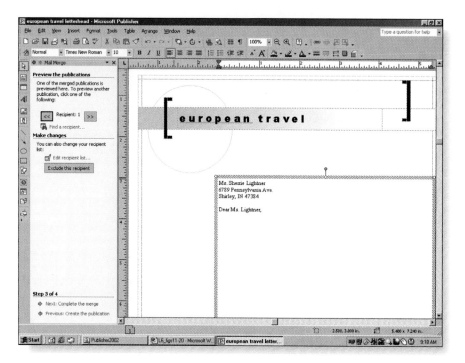

Figure 6.20
First recipient's name and address
inserted in letter

20. **To preview the letter with the next recipient's information inserted, click the forward double-arrow button** `>>` **on the Mail Merge task pane.**

The second recipient's information now appears in the letter preview.

21. **Click Next: Complete the merge under Step 3 of 4 on the Mail Merge task pane.**

Mail Merge is now ready to produce (print) your publication.

22. **Click Print... on the Mail Merge task pane.**

The Print Merge dialog box appears and allows you to specify whether you wish to print all of the entries or only selected ones.

23. **Click OK.**

Mail Merge will print two copies of your letter with the two different recipients' information inserted.

24. **Save and close the publication.**

CREATING FAX COVER SHEETS

When businesses and organizations send faxes, they often send a *fax cover sheet* as the first page to introduce the rest of the fax. Like letterhead, fax cover sheets often provide the first impression of a business or organization. Fax cover sheets are organized like a memorandum, with To, From, and Date information. Contact information is normally also included, as well as the total number of pages in the fax. Most of the specific transmittal information is handwritten on a fax cover sheet. Companies print many copies of the cover sheets and keep supplies near the fax machines.

Using a Design Set Template to Create a Fax Cover Sheet

In this activity, you will create a fax cover sheet for european travel. It will be used by all employees to provide a consistent first impression of the business.

1. With the New Publication task pane displayed, open the template for the Axis Fax Cover.

2. Change the personal information set to the information set for european travel.

3. Change the font and font size of the business name (european travel) to Arial Black, 18.

4. Increase the font size of the words "Fax Transmittal Form" to 14.

5. Change the font size of the other text boxes, including the address and contact information in the lower left corner, to 8.

6. Delete Dhimitry Fortin from the From box since all employees will use this fax cover sheet.

7. Increase the size of the logo, as you did for the letterhead.

8. Move the logo down so that it is directly above the address and contact information in the lower left corner.

The fax cover sheet is now complete, as shown in Figure 6.21.

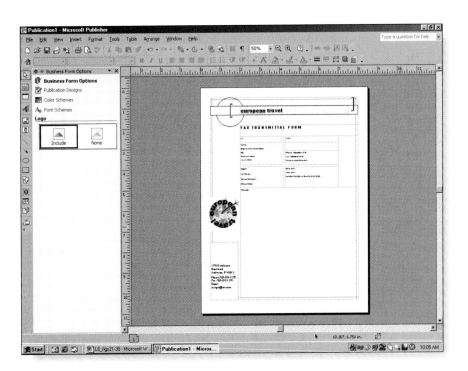

Figure 6.21
Completed fax cover sheet

9. Save the publication as european travel fax cover.

10. Close the publication.

CREATING BUSINESS FORMS WITH TABLES

Businesses use many different forms—to bill their customers, to order supplies, and to keep track of inventory or other internal information. Publisher design sets provide many of these forms, including invoices, purchase orders, inventory lists, and expense reports. Although the forms share certain characteristics, such as fonts and logos, with other design set publications, the largest part of each form is a *table* that is designed to hold the necessary information.

Tables arrange information in columns and rows. As noted earlier, many of the forms in the Publisher design sets contain tables that can be edited to fit the needs of a particular business. Tables can also be created from scratch, using commands on the Table menu.

HANDS On

Creating a Purchase Order Form

In this activity, you will create an order form by editing the tables in a design set template. Then you will create a table from scratch.

1. With the New Publication task pane displayed, select the template for the Axis Purchase Order from the Axis design set.

2. Change the personal information set to the information set for european travel.

3. Change the font and font size of the business name (european travel) to Arial Black, 18.

4. Change the font size of the words "Purchase Order" to 14.

5. Change the font size of the rest of the text in the top and the address and contact parts of the purchase order to 8.

6. Increase the size of the logo, as you did for the letterhead and fax cover sheet.

7. Move the logo down so that it is directly above the address and contact information in the lower left corner.

8. After Bill To: press ⟦Enter ◄─⟧ and then type european travel.

Note — *If the first letter of european changes to a capital letter, click on the blue bar below the letter and click Stop Automatically Correcting "european."*

9. After Ship To: press ⟦Enter ◄─⟧ and then type european travel.

10. In the mailing address and shipping address boxes, type european travel's address (1779 Revolution Boulevard, Anderson, IN 46013), **as shown in Figure 6.22.**

Another Way

- Because the address has been inserted in the lower left corner of the form, it would also be possible to copy and paste this address into the mailing and shipping address boxes.

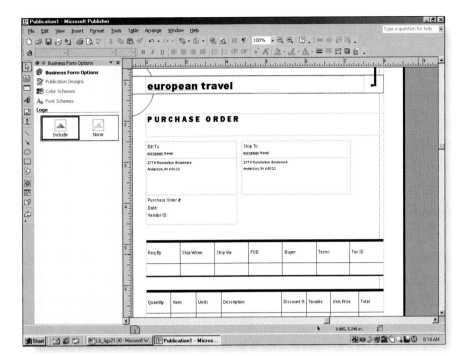

Figure 6.22
european travel's address entered
on purchase order

11. In the lower right corner of the form, change Miscellaneous to Other and Balance Due to Total.

This form contains two tables, one for the shipping instructions and one for the actual order information. Each of the tables contains boxes, called cells, which are formed by the intersection of a column and a row. In the next few steps, you will delete unnecessary cells from the first table.

12. Click the cell that contains the letters FOB, hold down ⬆Shift and click on each cell to the right the four cells. (FOB, Buyer, Terms, and Tax ID are highlighted.)

13. Click Delete on the Table menu, and then click Columns. (See Figure 6.23.)

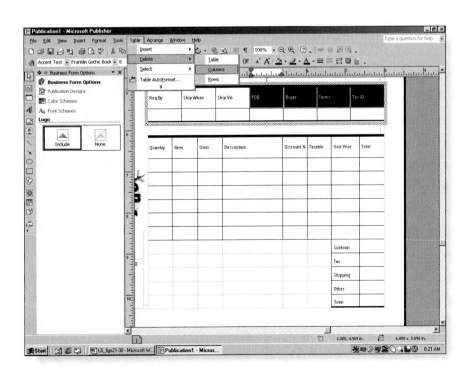

Figure 6.23
Deleting columns from a table

Publisher BASICS

Deleting a Column in a Table

1. Click any cell in the column.

2. On the Table menu, click Delete and then click Columns.

Another Way

- Select the cells that you wish to delete and then right-click. Click Change Table and then click Delete. Click Columns to delete entire columns or Rows to delete entire rows.

The four cells that you selected are deleted, as well as the cells below (cells in the same columns).

14. **Resize the table frame, using the right resize handle, so that it is the same width as the table below, as shown in Figure 6.24.**

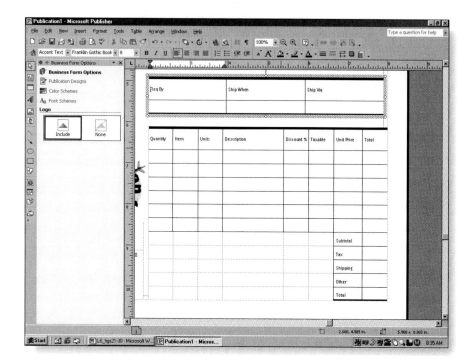

Figure 6.24 ◀
Resized table frame

15. **Save the form as** european travel purchase order.

16. **Close the publication.**

FILLING IN FORMS

Once a form is created, it can be printed and filled in by hand, or it can be filled in by typing in the cells and then printed. If a form will be printed and filled in by hand, cells may need to be enlarged to provide sufficient space for handwriting. If a form is filled in by typing directly into the form, cells can be smaller. When you type in a cell, the text wraps around in that cell, instead of wrapping to the next row. You use [Tab] or the arrow keys to move from column to column, and arrow keys to move from row to row. Pressing [Tab] at the end of a row moves the insertion point to the first cell in the next row. Pressing [Enter←] inserts a blank line in a cell, instead of advancing to the next cell. You can also use your mouse to click any cell in the table.

Moving Around in a Table

1. To move from column to column, use the Tab key or the arrow keys.

2. To move from row to row, use the arrow keys.

3. To move from the end of a row to the first cell in the next row, press the Tab key.

Filling in a Purchase Order Form

In this activity, you will type data in the european travel purchase order form.

1. Open the european travel purchase order, if it is not already open.

2. Click in the cell under "Req By", type Your Name, and then press Tab to move to the next cell.

3. In the cell under "Ship When" type 2/4/02 and press Tab.

4. In the cell under "Ship Via" type Ground Shipping.

5. Type the following information in the first two rows of the second table. Leave the Discount and Taxable columns blank.

Quantity	Item	Units	Description	Unit Price	Total
2	CP1102	Case	8.5 x 11 copy paper	$20.99	$41.98
1	CP2031	Each	Heavy-duty paper cutter	$29.99	$29.99

6. At the bottom of the Total column, type the following information:

Subtotal	$71.97
Tax	$3.60
Shipping	Free
Total	$75.57

In the next few steps, you will increase the font size of the text and change the cell alignment to make the purchase order easier to read.

7. Select the two figures under Unit Price and click the Align Right button.

8. Select all of the cells in the Total column, except the header row, and click the Align Right button.

Your purchase order should look similar to the one shown in Figure 6.25.

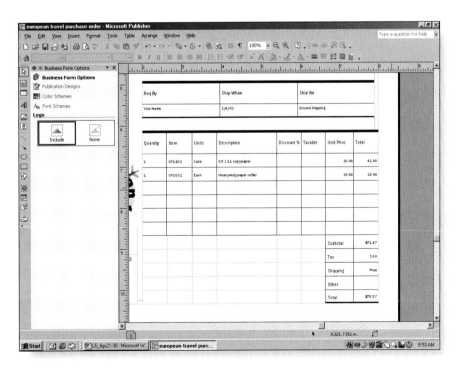

Figure 6.25
Purchase order with amounts right aligned

Selecting an Entire Table

1. Click any cell in the table.

2. On the Table menu, point to Select, then click Table.

9. On the Table menu, point to Select and then click Table.

10. With the entire table selected, change the font size to 8.

11. Click anywhere in the first table (the shipping information table), point to Select on the Table menu and then click Table.

12. Change the font size to 8.

13. Scroll to the top of the purchase order. Change the Purchase Order #/Date/Vendor ID box so that it contains the following information:

Purchase Order #: P12362
Date: 1/21/02
Vendor ID: 024568

> *Note* — *You cannot click, and then type, after the words Purchase Order # and Date. You must retype the words Purchase Order #, Date, and Vendor ID, along with the above information.*

The purchase order is now complete and ready for printing.

14. Save the completed purchase order.

15. Print the completed purchase order.

16. Close the publication.

CREATING A TABLE FROM SCRATCH

Although it is convenient to use the tables already created in the design sets, you may need to create a table that does not resemble any of the tables on the predesigned forms. There are two different ways to create a table. You can *insert* a table by clicking Insert Table on the Table menu, or you can *draw* a table by clicking the Insert Table button 🔲 on the Objects toolbar. Both methods cause the Create Table dialog box to appear, where you can specify the number of rows and columns you need and what Table format you prefer. Once the table is inserted, you can then edit and format the table to hold whatever information you need.

HANDS On

Creating and Editing a Table

In this activity, you will create a table using commands on the Table menu.

1. Open Publisher and create a new blank publication.

2. On the Table menu, point to Insert and then click Table.

The Create Table dialog box appears.

3. Change the Number of rows to 4 and the Number of columns to 6.

4. In the Table format box, scroll down until List with Title 3 appears.

5. Click List with Title 3, as shown in Figure 6.26.

Creating a Table

1. Click Insert Table on the Table menu, or click the Insert Table button on the Objects toolbar.

2. Specify the number of rows and columns and the desired table format.

3. Click OK.

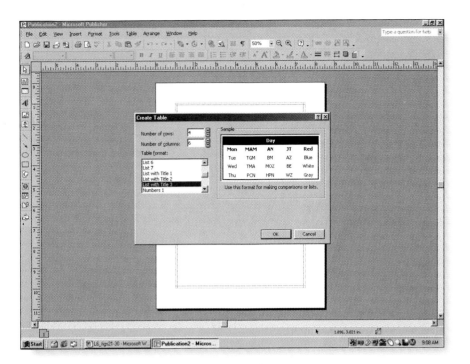

Figure 6.26
Table format dialog box

6. Click OK.

A table is inserted in the blank publication.

7. Move the table to the top of the page.

8. Select the entire table and change the font to Arial.

As you can see, the first row in the table contains a single cell, which is designed to hold the title for the table.

9. Click this row and type Tour Registration List.

You will use the second row as a **_header row._** Header rows contain headings for each column.

10. Click the first cell in the second row and type Tour.

11. Press [Tab] to move to the second cell in this row and type Participant.

12. Using [Tab] to move from cell to cell, insert the following headings in the remaining cells in this row: Deposit, 1st installment, 2nd installment, Final installment.

You may have noticed that the headings for 1st, 2nd, and Final installments have been automatically hyphenated. You can eliminate automatic hyphenation in a table, just as you can in text boxes.

13. Select the three installment headings and then point to Language on the Tools menu.

14. Click Hyphenation…, deselect Automatically hyphenate this story, and then click OK.

You have now completed the header row for your table.

15. Click the first cell in the next row.

16. In this row, **type** France under Tour, **type** Tom Hunt **under Participant, type** $500 **under Deposit, and type** $500 **under 1st installment. Leave the other cells blank and press** [Tab] **or use the arrow keys to move to the first cell in the fourth row.**

17. In the fourth row, **type** Italy under Tour, **type** Angie Swincher **under Participant, and type** $500 **under Deposit.**

18. Save the table as Tour registration list.

Inserting Rows and Columns in a Table

To insert a row:

1. Click the row that is above or below the place where you want to insert the new row.

2. On the Table menu, point to Insert.

3. Click either Rows Above or Rows Below, depending on where the row needs to be inserted.

To insert a column:

1. Click the column that is either to the left or to the right of the place where you want to insert the new column.

2. On the Table menu, point to Insert.

3. Click either Columns to the Left or Columns to the Right, depending on where the column needs to be inserted.

Another Way

• Click the row or column where you wish to insert a new row or column and then right-click. Click Change Table and then click Insert. Click Columns to the Left or Columns to the Right, or Rows Above or Rows Below, depending on your needs.

Inserting Rows and Columns and Adjusting Column Widths

While completing a table, you may discover that you need to insert additional rows or columns. To insert a row, click the row that is above or below the place where you want to insert the new row, and then point to Insert on the Table menu. Click either Rows Above or Rows Below, depending on where the new row needs to be inserted. To add a column, click the column that is either to the left or to the right of the place where you want to insert the new column, and then point to Insert on the Table menu. Click either Columns to the Left or Columns to the Right, depending on where the new column needs to be inserted.

In this activity, you will modify the tour registration list table by adding a row and a column and by adjusting the width of columns.

1. Open the Tour Registration List, if it is not already open.

2. Click the first cell in the fourth row (the cell that contains the word "Italy") and then point to Insert on the Table menu.

3. Click Rows Above.

A row is inserted between the third and fourth rows.

4. Click the first cell in this row and type France. Press ⌨Tab to move to the next cell and type Susan Goff. Press ⌨Tab again and type $500 under Deposit.

5. With the insertion point still in the Deposit column, point to Insert on the Table menu and then click Columns to the Left.

A column is inserted between the Participant and Deposit columns.

6. Click the first cell in this column (the cell in the header row) and type Telephone.

7. Save the table.

The table now has a column where participants' telephone numbers can be entered.

When Publisher inserts a table, it makes all of the columns in the table the same width by default. You may find, however, that some columns need to be wider than others. For example, in the table you just created, the participant column should be wider than the other columns because some participants' names may become too long to fit on a single line.

8. Point to the vertical line between the Participant and Telephone columns.

A two-way arrow appears.

9. With the two-way arrow displayed, click and drag about ¼" to the right.

All of the participants' names should now be on one line, but the table extends beyond the blue margins on the page. You can reduce the width of other columns slightly to keep the table within the page margins.

10. Point to the vertical line between the Tour and Participant columns.

11. With the two-way arrow displayed, click and drag about ¼" to the left.

12. Resize the remaining columns to constrain the width of the table to the blue margin guidelines, as shown in Figure 6.27.

Adjusting Column Width in a Table

1. Point to the vertical line on the right side of the column that needs to be adjusted.

2. With the two-way arrow displayed, click and drag to the right to make the column wider; or

3. Click and drag to the left to make the column narrower.

Figure 6.27
Tour registration list table with resized columns

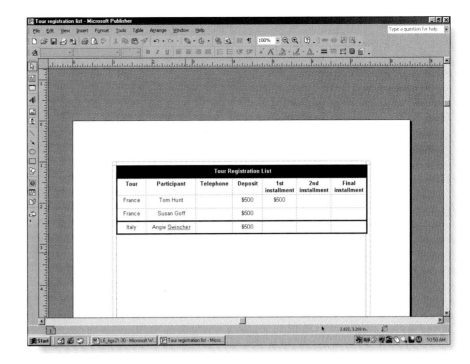

13. Save the table.

HANDS On

Adding Gridlines to a Table

1. Click any cell in the table.

2. On the Table menu, point to Select and then click Table.

3. Right-click and then click Format Table…

4. Click the Colors and Lines tab, if it is not already on top.

5. Under Presets: click the third button (gridlines).

6. Under Line, click the down arrow next to Color: and then click the black option.

7. Click OK.

Adding Borders and Shading to a Table

You can enhance a table with borders or with shading. Borders and shading not only make a table more attractive, but they can also make a table easier to read. The outlines around each cell in a table are visible on your computer screen but will not print unless borders, called gridlines, are added. Shading can also make a table easier to read when applied selectively. Shading unifies related cells, while separating them from unshaded cells. When a table is printed, it can be difficult to follow across the rows if the table does not have gridlines or shading.

1. **Open the Tour Registration List, if it is not already open.**

2. **Click any cell in the table, point to Select on the Table menu, and then click Table.**

3. **With the entire table selected, right-click and then click Format Table….**

The Format Table dialog box appears.

4. **Click the Colors and Lines tab, if it is not already on top.**

5. **Under Presets: click the third button (gridlines).**

6. **Under Line, click the down arrow next to Color: and then click the black option, as shown in Figure 6.28.**

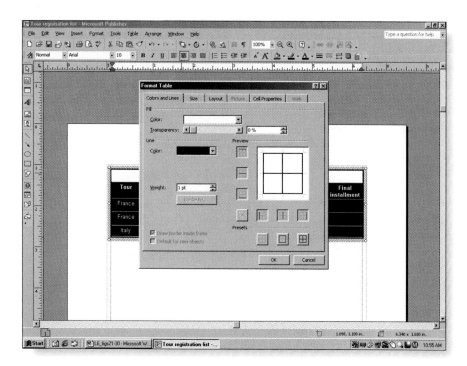

Figure 6.28 ◀
Format Table dialog box

7. Click OK.

Gridlines surround all of the cells in your table.

8. Select the two cells that contain the word "France."

9. Point to Select on the Table menu and then click Row.

Both rows are selected.

10. With the two rows selected, right-click and then click Format Table….

11. Under Fill on the Colors and Lines tab, click the down arrow next to Color: and then click the gray option.

12. Click OK.

The two France rows are shaded, and your table is now complete, as shown in Figure 6.29.

Be careful to select shading that will not obscure the text in the cells. Even if the text is still readable on the screen, it may print out darker. Shading should be used to improve readability, not hinder it.

Publisher BASICS

Adding Shading to a Table

1. Select the cells you wish to shade.

2. Right-click and then click Format Table…

3. Under Fill on the Colors and Lines tab, click the down arrow next to Color:

4. Click the appropriate fill color.

5. Click OK.

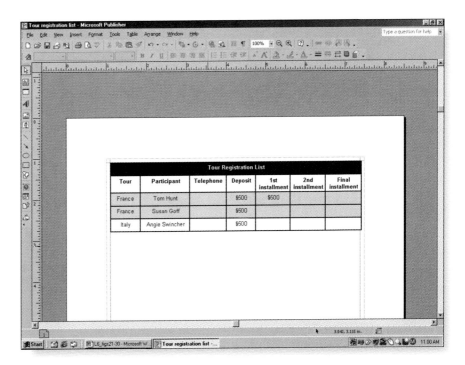

Figure 6.29
Completed tour registration
list table

13. Save and print the table.

14. Close the publication.

Test your knowledge by circling T or F as the correct answer for each of
the following questions. See Appendix C to check your answers.

T F 1. Letterheads and fax cover sheets often create the first impression of a
business or organization.

T F 2. Mail Merge allows you to sort your mailing list by zip code but not by
name.

T F 3. Once a fax cover sheet is saved, it can be used repeatedly and
customized for each fax.

T F 4. If a form will be printed and filled in by hand, cells in a table may need
to be enlarged to provide sufficient space for handwriting.

T F 5. In a table, you can use either the Tab key or the arrow keys to move
from column to column.

ON*the*WEB

CREATING ELECTRONIC FORMS FOR POSTING ON THE WEB

Businesses often need to provide forms on their Web sites to allow visitors to their sites to place orders online or communicate their need for more information. Publisher simplifies the process of creating these ***electronic forms*** by providing three Web Reply Forms in the Design Gallery. The three basic forms (Order Form, Response Form, and Sign-Up Form) can be customized to meet the needs of a particular business. These forms are also available on the Web Site Options task pane.

The Web Reply Forms contain one or more of the following ***form control*** elements: Single-line Text Box, Multiline Text Box, Checkbox, Option Button, List Box, and Command buttons. These form control elements allow data to be captured and submitted online. Double-clicking each form control element causes a dialog box to appear, which allows you to control how the data will be retrieved. Not only are these form control elements part of the Web Reply Forms, but they are also available as objects under Form Control on the Objects toolbar. As Web Reply Forms are customized, additional form control elements can be added by clicking the Form Control button and then selecting the needed element. Electronic forms can also be designed from scratch, using these same form control elements from the Objects toolbar.

In the following activity, you will add a Web Reply Form to european travel's Web site and then modify the form to allow visitors to request more information about particular trips.

1. Open the *ET Web Site* file that you created and saved in Lesson 5.

2. Click page **10** (the last page of the Web site).

3. On the Web Site Options task pane, click **Response form.**

An additional page, containing the Response Form, is added to the Web site.

4. Click on the page **11,** which should appear as shown in Figure 6.30.

If necessary, delete the spinning globe from page 11 so that it does not interfere with the navigation bar.

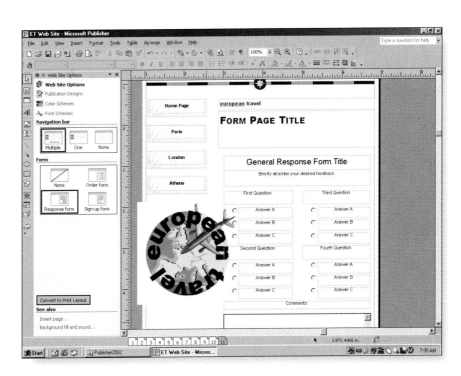

Figure 6.30 ◀
Response form added to
european travel's Web site

5. Resize the european travel logo and move it down, as necessary, to keep it from interfering with any information on the form, as shown in Figure 6.31.

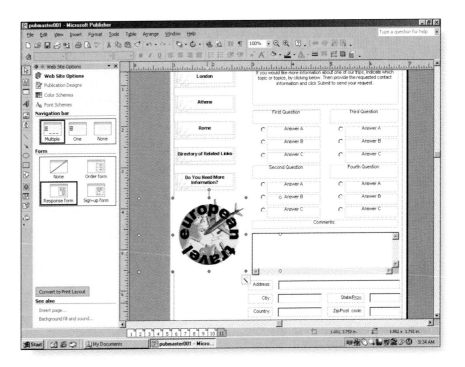

Figure 6.31 ◀
european travel logo moved and
resized

6. Change **FORM PAGE TITLE to read:** DO YOU NEED MORE INFORMATION?

7. **Delete the General Response Form Title box.**

8. **Resize the next box ("Briefly describe your desired feedback.") to fill the empty space above it.**

9. **Change the text in this box to read:** If you would like more information about one of our trips, indicate which topic or topics, by clicking below. Then provide the requested contact information and click Submit to send your request.

10. **Change "First Question" to read:** France. **Change "Answer A" to** Paris, **"Answer B" to** La Rochelle, **and "Answer C" to** Normandy.

11. **Change "Second Question" to read:** Great Britain. **Change "Answer A" to** London, **"Answer B" to** Scotland, **and "Answer C" to** Golf packages.

12. **Change "Third Question" to read:** Greece. **Change "Answer A" to** Athens, **"Answer B" to** Ancient Greek ruins, **and "Answer C" to** Greek islands.

13. **Change "Fourth Question" to read:** Italy. **Change "Answer A" to** Rome and Vatican City, **"Answer B" to** Florence, **and "Answer C" to** Venice.

14. **Double-click the first option button (Paris).**

The Option Button Properties dialog box appears.

15. **In the boxes under Return data with this label and Option button value, type the button name (Paris), as shown in Figure 6.32. Click OK.**

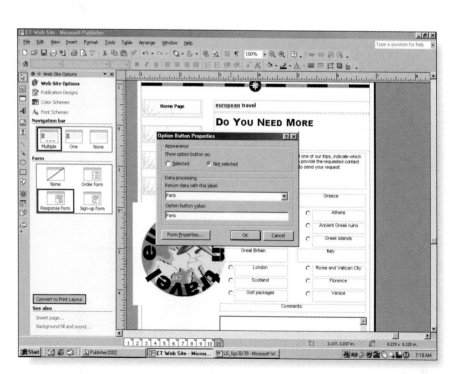

Figure 6.32 ◀
Option Button Properties
dialog box

16. Repeat steps 14–15 for each of the option buttons, changing the Return data with this label and Option button value boxes to the match the button name.

Your completed form should appear as shown in Figure 6.33.

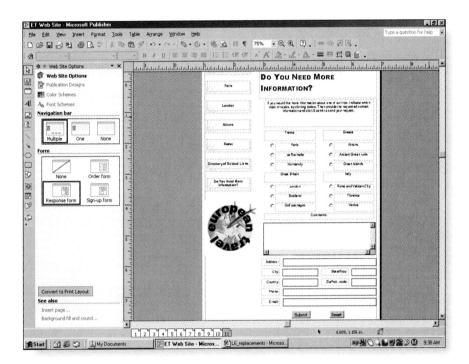

Figure 6.33 ◀
Completed form

17. Save the Web page.

Publisher asks:

To correctly process your form on page 11, you must fill in the Action box with a program from your ISP or choose a different data retrieval method. Do you want to specify the action now?

18. Click No.

The form you create will not function properly in the Web browser until you get information from your Internet service provided (ISP). Data collected from the forms may be saved on a Web server, sent to you via e-mail, or may be collected using a program your ISP provides.

Lesson Summary & Exercises

SUMMARY

In this lesson, you learned how to use Publisher design sets to create a consistent image for a business or organization. You selected a design set and modified its color scheme and then used this design set to create various forms and promotional materials, including business cards and letterhead, for a business. You also learned how to use Publisher's Mail Merge feature to create mailing lists and merge the names and addresses onto letters and other publications. Finally, you learned how to create and edit tables, which are the basic elements of many business forms.

Now that you have completed this lesson, you should be able to do the following:

■ Select a design set and modify its color scheme.

■ Change and save a color scheme in a personal information set.

■ Use design sets to create and print multiple copies of business cards.

■ Use design sets to create letterhead and fax cover sheets.

■ Use Mail Merge to create mailing lists and then merge the information onto publications that have address blocks or mailing panels.

■ Use design sets to create purchase orders and other business forms.

■ Create and fill in tables.

■ Insert rows and columns in tables and adjust column width.

■ Add borders and shading to tables.

■ Create electronic forms on Web pages

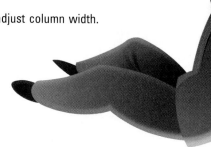

CONCEPTS REVIEW

1 TRUE/FALSE

Circle T if the statement is true and F if the statement is false.

T F 1. When the same design elements are used in all of an organization's publications, people begin to identify those design elements with the organization.

T F 2. Pressing the Tab key at the end of a row in a table moves the insertion point to the first cell in the next row.

T F 3. Pressing the Enter key in a cell moves the insertion point to the next cell.

T F 4. Printing multiple copies of a business card on the same sheet is a difficult process in Publisher.

T F 5. Publisher design sets include many different business forms, as well as letterhead and business cards.

T F 6. The field codes that are inserted by the Mail Merge Wizard are just place holders and must be typed over.

T F 7. The outlines around each cell in a table are visible when the table is printed.

T F 8. When you create a business card using a template from a design set, Publisher is able to do most of the work for you.

T F   9. When a table is printed, it can be difficult to follow across the rows if the table does not have gridlines or shading.

T F 10. Publisher provides electronic "Web Reply" forms in the Design Gallery, but these forms cannot be modified.

2 MATCHING

Match each of the terms on the left with the definitions on the right.

TERMS	DEFINITIONS
1. Cells	**a.** Collections of publications that share common design elements
2. Cover sheet	**b.** Provides basic contact information on a letter
3. Design sets	**c.** Identify pieces of data in a mailing list
4. Field codes	**d.** Allows you to create and insert mailing list information into publications
5. Gridlines	**e.** Introduces a fax
6. Header rows	**f.** Arrange information in columns and rows
7. Letterhead	**g.** Boxes formed by the intersection of columns and rows in a table
8. Mail Merge	**h.** Contain headings for each column in a table
9. Print Preview	**i.** Borders around each cell in a table
10. Tables	**j.** Allows you to see how a publication will look when it is printed

3 COMPLETION

Fill in the missing word or phrase for each of the following statements:

1. To print more than one copy of a business card on the same sheet, click _____ under Copies per sheet on the Business Card Options task pane.

2. The _____ and _____ buttons on the Formatting toolbar are used to increase and reduce font size one point at a time.

3. Gridlines are added on the _____ tab on the Format Table dialog box.

4. If you use a bulk-mailing permit, you will need to sort your mailing list by _____ in order to comply with postal regulations.

5. Fax cover sheets are organized like a _____ with To, From, and Date information.

6. The largest part of most business forms is a _____ that is designed to hold the necessary information.

7. On the Create Table dialog box, you specify the number of _____ and _____ you need and what Table format you prefer.

8. The mail merge process begins with two documents: the _____ and the _____.

9. _____ unifies related cells in a table, while separating them from other cells.

10. If you print business cards on a laser or inkjet printer, you need to purchase _____ or find some way to cut the cards apart.

4 SHORT ANSWER

1. How do you change and save the color scheme in a personal information set?

2. What are three factors that you should consider when creating business cards?

3. How do you adjust font size incrementally to find the maximum font size for a frame?

4. How can the Mail Merge feature save you time when doing large mailings?

5. Summarize the Mail Merge process.

6. Name the two different ways to create a table.

7. How do you insert a row in a table? A column?

8. How do you adjust the width of a column in a table?

9. Explain the purposes of borders and shading in a table.

10. Name the six form control elements that Publisher uses to capture and submit data on electronic forms.

5 IDENTIFICATION

Identify the cell, column, row, header row, gridlines, Print Preview button, Increase Font Size button, Decrease Font Size button, and Form Control button.

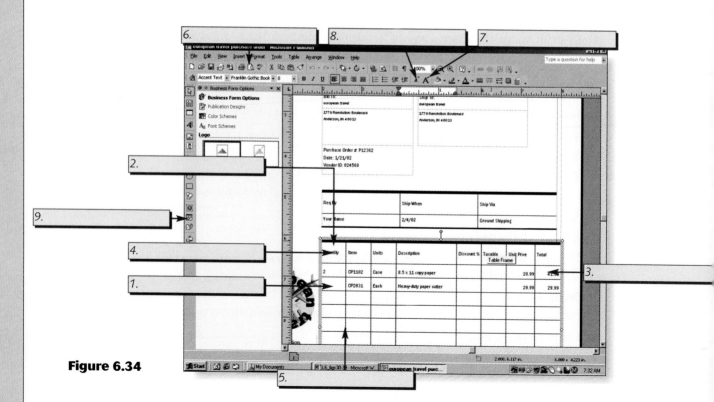

Figure 6.34

SKILLS REVIEW

Complete each of the Skills Review activities in sequential order to review the skills you learned in this lesson. In these activities, you will create business cards, letterhead, a purchase order form, and a product list table for Anderson Pet Mall. In the process of creating these materials, you will review your skills to select design sets, change color schemes, use Print Preview, create mailing lists using the Mail Merge Wizard, print merged letters, and create, edit and enhance tables.

1 Select a design set and change its color scheme

1. Select **By Design Sets** on the New Publication task pane.
2. Click **Bubbles** under Master Sets.
3. Click **Bubbles Business Card.**

Information for Anderson Pet Mall should be automatically inserted if the Primary Business personal information set has not been modified since Lesson 3. If information for Anderson Pet Mall is not automatically inserted, edit the Primary Business personal information set following the instructions under Creating Personal Information Sets on page 25 of Lesson 1.

4. Click **Color Schemes** on the Business Card Options task pane.
5. Select the **Mountain** color scheme.
6. Open the **Primary Business** personal information set.
7. If the box in front of Include color scheme in this set is *not* checked, click it. (If the box is not checked, the color scheme will have automatically changed to the new color scheme, Mountain. Clicking this box will cause the color scheme to be saved as part of the personal information set.)

If the box is *already* checked, the color scheme will still be the old color scheme. Leave the box checked and click the down arrow under Color schemes. Select the Mountain color scheme.

8. Click **Update.**
9. Save the publication as *Anderson Pet Mall Business Card.*

2 Change font size and print multiple copies of a business card

1. Open the *Anderson Pet Mall Business Card,* if it is not already open.
2. Click **Business Card Options** on the task pane, if it is not already the current task pane.
3. Click **Multiple** under Copies per sheet.
4. Select each text frame on the business card and increase the font size to the maximum size possible for each frame, using the **Increase Font Size** A and **Decrease Font Size buttons** A.

Note   *"Pat Germann" and "Marketing Assistant" should be the same font size, and the address and contact numbers should be the same font size. This will limit how large you can make the font size in those frames.*

Lesson Summary & Exercises

5. Save the business card.

6. Click the **Print Preview button** 🔍 to view how your cards will print.

7. If you will be printing on card stock, load it into your printer.

8. Click the **Print button** 🖨 on the Preview window.

9. Click **Close** on the Preview window to return to the Publisher window.

3 Create letterhead using a design set template

1. Select the **Bubbles** design set on the New Publication task pane.

2. Click **Bubbles Letterhead.**

3. If the logo looks too low or too far from the Anderson Pet Mall name, move it up and/or to the right slightly.

4. Change the font size of the Anderson Pet Mall name to **18.** Resize its frame so that all of the words stay on the same line.

5. Use **Print Preview** to check the position of the Anderson Pet Mall name on the page. Click **Close** to return to the Publisher window. If the Anderson Pet Mall name did not look centered on the page, move its frame as needed.

6. Change the font size of the address and contact information in the lower right corner to **9.**

7. Resize the contact information box slightly, so that all of the E-mail address fits on one line.

8. Save the publication as *Anderson Pet Mall Letterhead.*

4 Create a mailing list using the Mail Merge Wizard

1. Open the *Anderson Pet Mall Letterhead,* if it is not already open.

2. Draw a text box starting about ¼" below the logo and ending at the address box in the lower right corner of the letterhead. The left and right sides of the text box should be the blue margin lines.

3. Click **Mail Merge** on the Tools menu and then click **Mail Merge Wizard.**

4. Under Select Recipients, click **Type a new list.**

5. Under Type a new list, click **Create....**

6. Fill in the boxes on the New Address List dialog box with the following information:
Mr. Kurt Solomon, 1974 Academy Rd., New Castle, IN 47362.

7. Click **New Entry.**

8. Fill in the boxes on the new entry form with the following information: Mrs. Marti Hernandez, 101 E. Liberty St., Anderson, IN 46013.

9. Click **Close.**

10. In the File name: box on the Save Address List dialog box, type Anderson Pet Mall Mailing List and then click **Save.**

11. Click **OK** on the Mail Merge Recipients dialog box.

5 Merge mailing list data and print merged letters

1. After creating the Anderson Pet Mall Mailing List, click **Next: Create the publication** at the bottom of the Mail Merge task pane.

2. Click in the upper left corner of the text box you created earlier and type the current date.

3. Press three times to create two blank lines.

4. Click **Address block...** on the Mail Merge task pane.

5. Click **OK** on the Insert Address Block dialog box.

6. At the end of <<AddressBlock>>, press twice to create a blank line.

7. Click **Greeting Line...** on the Mail Merge task pane.

8. Click **OK** on the Greeting Line dialog box.

Note *At this point, you could also type the body of a letter. Ask your instructor whether or not this is required.*

9. On the Mail Merge task pane, click **Next: Preview the publications.**

10. If everything looks OK on the previews, click **Next: Complete the merge.**

11. Click **Print...** on the Mail Merge task pane.

12. Click **OK** on the Print Merge dialog box to print the merged letters.

13. Save and close the publication.

6 Create a purchase order using a design set form

1. Select the **Bubbles** design set on the New Publication task pane.

2. Click **Bubbles Purchase Order.**

3. Change the font size of the business name (Anderson Pet Mall) to **18.**

4. Change the font size of the words "Purchase Order" to **14.**

5. Change the font size of the rest of the text, including column headings and the address and contact information in the lower right corner, to **8.**

Note *This will cause the text in the Purchase Order #/Date/Vendor ID box to overflow its frame. Resize the frame slightly, using the bottom resize handle, so that all of the text is able to fit in the frame.*

6. After Bill To: type Anderson Pet Mall.

7. After Ship To: type Anderson Pet Mall.

8. In the mailing and shipping address boxes, type or copy Anderson Pet Mall's address from the bottom of the purchase order.

9. In the lower right corner of the form, change "Balance Due" to Total.

10. Delete the last four columns in the first table (the columns with the headings FOB, Buyer, Terms and Tax ID).

11. Resize the table frame so that it is the same width as the table below.

12. Save the form as *Anderson Pet Mall Purchase Order.*

7 Fill in a form

1. Open the *Anderson Pet Mall Purchase Order,* if it is not already open.

2. In the box beginning Purchase Order #, type the following information:
Purchase Order #: P13527
Date: 3/26/02
Vendor ID: v75321

3. Click in the cell under "Req By", type Marti Hernandez, and then press ⟨Tab⟩.

4. Under "Ship When" type 4/8/02 and press ⟨Tab⟩.

5. Under "Ship Via" type Ground Shipping.

6. In the first two rows of the second table, type the following information:

Quantity	Item	Units	Description	Unit Price	Total
3	PT1314	Case	Puppy chew treats	$40.00	$120.00
10	DG1801	Each	Small flea collars	$5.00	$50.00

7. At the bottom of the Total column, type the following information:

Subtotal	$170.00
Tax	Exempt
Shipping	$17.00
Total	$187.00

8. Change the alignment of all of the figures in this table to **Align Right.**

9. Save and print the completed purchase order.

10. Close the publication.

8 Create a table from scratch

1. Open a new blank publication.

2. On the Table menu, point to **Insert** and then click **Table....**

3. On the Create Table dialog box, change the number of rows to **5** and the number of columns to **3.**

4. In the Table format box, click **List with Title 3.**

5. Click **OK.**

6. Move the table to the top of the page.

7. Click the first row in the table and type Product List.

8. Click the first cell in the second row (the header row) and type Item Number.

9. Press ⌨Tab to move to the second cell and type Description.

10. Press ⌨Tab to move to the third cell and type Price.

11. Complete the table with the following information:

    | EB231 | Dog shampoo | $9.99 |
    | EB403 | Hamster wheel | $3.99 |
    | CT502 | Bird vitamins | $8.99 |

12. Save the table as **Anderson Pet Mall Product List.**

9 Insert Rows and Columns and Adjust Column Width

1. Open the **Anderson Pet Mall Product List,** if it is not already open.

2. Click the first cell in the last row and then point to **Insert** on the Table menu.

3. Click **Rows Above.**

4. Fill in the cells in the new row with the following information:

    | EB575 | Cat litter | $5.99 |

5. With the insertion point in the last column, point to **Insert** on the Table menu and then click **Columns to the Right.**

6. Click the first cell in the new column (the cell in the header row) and type In stock.

7. Adjust the width of each of the columns, using the two-way arrow pointer, so that the table fits within the blue margin lines.

8. Save the table.

10 Add borders and shading to a table

1. Open the **Anderson Pet Mall Product List,** it is not already open.

2. Select the entire table.

3. Right-click and then click **Format Table....**

4. Change Presets on the Colors and Lines tab to gridlines (third option).

5. Under Line, change the Color: box to the black option.

6. Click **OK.**

7. Select the rows with Item Numbers that begin with the letters EB.

8. Right-click and then click **Format Table....**

9. Under Fill on the Colors and Lines tab, change the Color: box to the gray option.

10. Click **OK.**

11. Save the table.

12. Close the publication.

Lesson Summary & Exercises

LESSON APPLICATIONS

Complete the following activities in sequential order.

1 Merge Mailing List Data onto an Envelope

You will create an envelope to go with the letterhead you created in this lesson. Then you will merge mailing list data onto this envelope.

1. Open the Axis Envelope template in the Axis design set.

2. Click Page Setup... on the File menu, change Page size to Size 10 (a standard envelope size), and click OK.

3. Change the Personal Information Set to the information set for european travel.

4. Click Mail Merge on the Tools menu and then click Mail Merge Wizard.

5. Under Use an existing list, click Browse....

6. On the Select Data Source dialog box, select *european travel mailing list,* and click Open.

7. On the Mail Merge Recipients dialog box, click OK.

8. On the Mail Merge task pane, click Next: Create the publication.

9. Click the mailing address box on the envelope, and then click Address block... on the task pane.

10. On the Insert Address Block dialog box, click OK.

11. Click Next: Preview the publications.

12. Click Next: Complete the merge.

13. Click Print... on the Mail Merge task pane.

 *If you wish to print onto actual envelopes, load one or two Size 10 envelopes into your printer before completing step 14. (Some printers will only allow you to load one envelope at a time.) If you do not know how to load envelopes into your printer, check with your instructor.*

14. Click OK on the Print Merge dialog box.

15. Save the envelope as *european travel envelope.* Close the publication.

2 Merge Mailing List Data onto a Postcard

You will open the postcard you created in Lesson 1 and add mailing list data to it.

 You must complete Skills Review 4 before you can complete this Lesson Application.

1. Locate and open the *Anderson Pet Mall Invitation Postcard* that you created and saved in Lesson 1.

2. Click on page 2 to view the back of the postcard.

3. Click Mail Merge on the Tools menu and then click Mail Merge Wizard.

4. If you have completed the Skills Review activities for Lesson 6, click Browse... under Use an existing list.

5. On the Select Data Source dialog box, select the **Anderson Pet Mall Mailing List** that you created in Skills Review 4 and then click Open.

6. On the Mail Merge Recipients dialog box, click OK.

7. On the Mail Merge task pane, click Next: Create the publication.

8. Click in the text box that you created in step 3 and then click Address block... on the task pane.

9. Click OK on the Address Block dialog box.

10. Click Next: Preview the publications on the Mail Merge task pane.

11. Click Next: Complete the merge on the Mail Merge task pane.

12. Click Print... on the Mail Merge task pane.

13. Click OK on the Print Merge dialog box to print the postcards with merged addresses.

14. Save the revised postcard. Close the publication.

3 Merge Mailing List Data onto a Newsletter

You will open the newsletter you created in Lesson 3 and merge mailing list data onto its mailing panel.

1. Locate and open the newsletter **Pet Periodical** that you created in Lesson 3.

2. Click on page 4 to view the back of the newsletter.

3. Click Mail Merge on the Tools menu and then click Mail Merge Wizard.

4. Click Browse... under Use an existing list.

5. On the Select Data Source dialog box, select the **Anderson Pet Mall Mailing List** that you created in Skills Review 4 and then click Open.

6. On the Mail Merge Recipients dialog box, click OK.

7. On the Mail Merge task pane, click Next: Create the publication.

8. Click in the mailing address box on page 4 of the newsletter and then click Address block... on the task pane.

9. Click OK on the Address Block dialog box.

10. Click Next: Preview the publications on the Mail Merge task pane.

11. Click Next: Complete the merge on the Mail Merge task pane.

12. Click Print... on the Mail Merge task pane.

13. Click OK on the Print Merge dialog box to print the newsletter with merged addresses.

14. Save the revised newsletter.

Lesson Summary & Exercises

4 Add a Table to a Newsletter

You will add a table to the newsletter you created in Lesson 3.

1. Locate and open the newsletter ***Pet Periodical*** that you created in Lesson 3. (If you have just completed Lesson Application 3, the newsletter may already be open.)

2. Select and delete the Special Points of Interest box on page 1. Also delete the shaded boxes (AutoShapes) underneath the Special Points of Interest box.

3. Click the Insert Table button on the Objects toolbar and draw a table between the black bar and the ANDERSON PET MALL NOW CARRIES CANINECHOW heading. (The table should be the same height as the black bar.)

4. On the Create Table dialog box, change the number of rows to 6 and the number of columns to 2.

5. In the Table format box, click List with Title 3, and then click OK.

6. In the top row of the table, type SPECIALS OF THE MONTH.

7. In the remaining cells, type the following information:
   CanineChow $19.95
   Cat litter $5.99
   Dog shampoo $9.99
   Hamster wheel $3.99
   Bird vitamins $8.99

8. Select the entire table and turn off automatic hyphenation.

9. With the table still selected, right-click and then click Format Table....

10. Change Presets on the Colors and Lines tab to none (the first option). (This will remove the border around the table.)

11. Change the alignment of the price column to right alignment.

12. Change the fill color of the first row to the tan color in the table of contents box.

13. Change the font color of the other rows to the same tan color.

14. Save the updated newsletter. Close the publication.

PROJECTS

1 Exploring Design Sets and Publication Types

Click By Design Sets on the New Publication task pane, if it is not already selected. Scroll down the list of design sets. Besides Master Sets, what are the other design set categories? Click each of these categories and view their contents. Briefly describe how the designs sets in each of these categories would be used. Besides their special purposes, how are these design sets different from the design sets under Master Sets? Choose a Master Set design that you find appealing and list all of the publications in that design set.

Click By Publication Type on the New Publication task pane. Scroll down the list of publication types. Click the categories, such as Business Forms, that have subcategories. (The categories with subcategories have small triangles in front of them.) What publications are available here that are not available in the design sets?

2 My Own Calendar

In Lesson 4, you learned that calendar designs are available in the Design Gallery. These calendars are designed primarily to be inserted into other publications. If you wish to create a calendar as its own publication, more calendar options are available in the design sets than in the Design Gallery. These calendar designs can be accessed either by choosing a particular design set and then clicking its calendar or by clicking Calendars under By Publication Type and then clicking a particular design.

Complete the following steps to create a calendar customized for you and your family.

Open the Blends Calendar or another calendar design that you find appealing. Change the personal information set to the Home/Family information set. Enter your own name, address, and contact information. Enter your family name (for example, "The Smith Family") in the Organization name box. Delete the default information in the tag line or motto box. Click Update.

Click Change date range on the Calendar Options task pane and change the Start date to January and the End date to December. Change the year boxes to the current year. This will create a twelve-page calendar with one month per page. Each month is a table and can be edited and enhanced like other tables.

Click on each page (month) that contains the birthday of a family member. Select the cell with the day of the month that is a birthday and add a fill color to highlight it. Click at the end of the number in the cell and press ⎋Enter◄┘ to move to the line below. Type the name of the family member whose birthday is that day. Change the font size if necessary. Repeat for each family member's birthday. If the Anderson Pet Mall logo appears on your calendar, delete it from each page.

Save the calendar as *Family Calendar* and print it.

3 Happy Birthday to Fido!

The owner of Anderson Pet Mall would like to begin to offer gift certificates to her customers. Because of your expertise in Publisher, she has asked you to create a gift certificate form. All gift certificates are to be redeemable for $10 in merchandise. (If customers wish to purchase more than $10 in gift certificates, they will be given multiple gift certificates.)

Open the Bubbles Gift Certificate. The personal information for Anderson Pet Mall should be automatically inserted.

Click Multiple under Copies per sheet on the Gift Certificate Options task pane. Edit the second text box (the box after "This certificate entitles") so that it reads "to Ten dollars ($10) in merchandise at" Edit the text box under the Anderson Pet Mall address so that it reads "Not redeemable for cash. Redemption value not to exceed $10.00."

Save the gift certificate as ***Anderson Pet Mall Gift Certificate.*** Click Print Preview 🔍 to see how many copies will print on a page and then click Print 🖨.

4 Would You Rather Live on Earth or Venus?

 *If you did not complete Project 5 (Earth to Venus) in Lesson 3, return to that project and complete it. Then complete the following steps.*

Open the updated Venus report that you completed in Lesson 3. Click at the end of the Geology section and insert a table that has five rows and three columns. Choose the List with Title 2 table format.

Leave the first cell in the first row blank. Type Earth in the second cell in the first row and Venus in the third cell in the first row.

In the second, third, and fourth rows, type the following information:

Revolution period	365.2 days	224.7 days
Rotation period	23.9 hours	243 days
Miles from sun	149.6 million	108.2 million

In the fifth row, type Source: *Information Please Almanac,* 1999.

Select the entire fifth row and click Merge Cells on the Table menu.

Select the entire table and add gridlines.

Save the updated Venus report.

5 In the Land of the Little People

During the summer, you are hired by a day care center, Land of Lilliputians, to help with outdoor activities and to assist in the office. Because you mentioned in your interview that you have used Microsoft Publisher, the owner, Mrs. Gulliver, would like for you to create some materials for the day care center, including business cards, letterhead, and an invoice form.

Choose a design set that you think would be appropriate for a day care center. Change the color scheme to one that emphasizes primary colors.

Change the Primary Business personal information set to the following information:

Name:	Greta Gulliver
Address:	789 Travel Lane
	Your city, state and zip code
Phone:	[Your area code]-555-1234

Fax:	[Your area code]-555-5678
Email:	gulliver@lilliput.net
Organization name:	Land of Lilliputians
Job or position title:	Owner

Delete any logos from your publications. When you delete the logo, you will be asked if you want to change to a design that does not include a logo. Click Yes.

Change font sizes as necessary to improve the appearance and readability of your publications.

Save and print each publication. The name of each file should identify the business and the type of publication.

Project in Progress

As the secretary of your Friends of the Library group, you must frequently write letters and attend meetings on behalf of your organization. The previous secretary gave you some old pre-printed letterhead, but you have used nearly all of it, and you have decided to create new letterhead that will incorporate the new logo that you have created for your group. You have also decided that it would be helpful to have business cards that you can take with you to the meetings you attend.

Choose a design set for your organization. Create a business card, using the information from the Other Organization personal information set. (If necessary, edit the Other Organization personal information set, following the instructions in Lesson 1.) Include the logo you created in Lesson 4. Use the same design set and personal information to create letterhead for your organization. Save and print each publication.

APPENDICES

CONTENTS

Portfolio Builder

WHAT IS A PORTFOLIO?

A *portfolio* is an organized collection of your work that demonstrates skills and knowledge acquired from one or more courses. The materials included in a portfolio should pertain to a specific educational or career goal. In addition to actual assignments, a portfolio should contain your self-reflection or comments on each piece of work as well as an overall statement introducing the portfolio.

Two types of portfolios exist. The first, which shows progress toward a goal over a period of time, is called a *developmental portfolio.* Developmental portfolios help you become more aware of your strengths and weaknesses and assist you in improving your abilities. The second type, called a *representational portfolio,* displays a variety of your best work. You can show a representational portfolio as evidence of your skills and knowledge. While you may use either type of portfolio when you are seeking employment, a representational portfolio is more effective.

WHY USE PORTFOLIOS?

Portfolios offer great advantages to you, your instructor, and potential employers. They allow you to reevaluate the work you have created by determining which assignments should be included in the portfolio and analyzing how you can improve future assignments. If the goal of the portfolio is career related, portfolios also help you connect classroom activities with practical applications. A wide variety of genuine work is captured in a portfolio, rather than a snapshot of knowledge at a specific time under particular circumstances. Presenting a portfolio of your work to your instructor and potential employers gives them the opportunity to evaluate your overall skills and performance more accurately.

CREATING A PORTFOLIO

Creating a portfolio involves three steps—planning, selecting work to include, and providing comments about your work.

First, you should plan the overall purpose and organization of the portfolio. After you plan your portfolio, you can begin selecting pieces of work to include in it. Ideally, you should select the work as you complete each document; however, you can review prior work to include as well.

Add one or more documents from the Lesson Applications, Projects, Web projects, and Project in Progress for each lesson. Avoid including too many publications in your portfolio. If two publications demonstrate identical Publisher skills, choose only one for your portfolio. If you apply your Publisher skills in another course or elsewhere, include a sample in your portfolio.

Create a list or log that provides a summary of the contents of your portfolio. (Your instructor may provide a preformatted log that you can complete.) The log can include columns in which you can list the file name, description of the file, when and by whom the file was reviewed, whether the file was revised, and the grade you received on the assignment.

Lastly, you should prepare comments for each piece of work included in the portfolio. As you add work to your portfolio, generate comments about each piece. You may want to reflect on the skills used to create the publication, or you can explain how the publication is applicable to a specific job for which you are interviewing. Your instructor may provide you with a preformatted comments form or you may type your comments.

Perform the steps listed in the Hands On activity on the following page to build your portfolio.

HANDS On

Building Your Portfolio

In this activity, you will plan your portfolio, select the Publisher documents to include in the portfolio, and prepare written comments about each piece of work included in the portfolio.

1. In a word processing document, answer the following questions to help you plan your portfolio:

   ■ What is the purpose of your portfolio?

   ■ What criteria will you use in selecting work to be included in the portfolio?

   ■ What is the overall goal that your portfolio will meet?

   ■ How will you organize your portfolio?

2. Using Publisher, create a log that provides a summary of the contents of your portfolio. Follow the guidelines given by your instructor or provided in this appendix.

3. Remember the purpose and goal of your portfolio and select and print one publication that you have completed to include in your portfolio. Enter information about the document in your log.

4. Prepare comments about the selected publication and attach them to the printout.

5. Repeat steps 3 and 4 to select and prepare comments for other publications to include in your portfolio.

6. Using word processing software, write a paragraph or two introducing your portfolio. Include some of the information considered in step 1.

7. Gather the publications to be included in your portfolio and place them in a binder, folder, or other container in an organized manner.

TOOLBAR AND COMMAND SUMMARY

Standard Toolbar

BUTTON	DESCRIPTION	MOUSE ACTION	KEYBOARD ACTION

Standard toolbar buttons are described in the order they appear on the toolbar.

BUTTON	DESCRIPTION	MOUSE ACTION	KEYBOARD ACTION
	Opens a new publication	Click File, New	Ctrl + N
	Opens existing publication	Click File, Open, click file to be opened	Ctrl + O
	Saves existing publication	Click File, Save	Ctrl + S
	Opens an e-mail document	Click File, Send To, Mail Recipient	
	Searches for specific text in a publication	Click File, Search, enter text to search for	
	Prints a publication	Click File, Print, click options	Ctrl + P
	Previews a publication as it will look printed	Click File, Print Preview	
	Checks spelling	Click Tools, Spelling, Spelling	
	Cuts text or objects and places them on Clipboard	Select text or object, click Edit, Cut	Ctrl + X
	Copies text or objects and places them on Clipboard	Select text or object, click Edit, Copy	Ctrl + C
	Pastes text or objects from the Clipboard	Click at new location, click Edit, Paste	Ctrl + V
	Copies text format and appearance	Select text to copy from, click Format Painter button, select text to copy to	
	Reverses the last action	Click Edit, Undo	Ctrl + Z
	Reverses actions that have been undone	Click Edit, Redo	Ctrl + Y
	Brings selected item to the front	Click Arrange, Order, Bring to Front	Alt + F6
	Rotates selected object to any angle	Select object, click Free Rotate, drag corner of object in direction that you want to rotate it	

TOOLBAR AND COMMAND SUMMARY

Formatting Toolbar

BUTTON	DESCRIPTION	MOUSE ACTION	KEYBOARD ACTION

Formatting toolbar buttons are described in the order they appear on the toolbar.

	Displays styles and formatting task pane	Click Format, Styles and Formatting, make selections	
	Applies styles	Click Format, Styles and Formatting, Create new style, make selections	
	Changes font	Click Format, Font, make selections	
	Changes font size	Click Format, Font, change size	
B	Makes selected text bold	Select text, click Format, Font, change font style	Ctrl + B
I	Makes selected text italic	Select text, click Format, Font, change font style	Ctrl + I
U	Underlines selected text	Select text, click Format, Font, change font style	Ctrl + U
	Aligns text in text box at left	Click Format, Indents and Lists, change alignment	Ctrl + L
	Centers text in text box	Click Format, Indents and Lists, change alignment	Ctrl + E
	Aligns text in text box at right	Click Format, Indents and Lists, change alignment	Ctrl + R
	Aligns text in text box at both the right and left	Click Format, Indents and Lists, change alignment	Ctrl + J
	Inserts numbering in a list	Click Format, Indents and Lists, select Numbered list	
	Inserts bullets in a list	Click Format, Indents and Lists, selected Bulleted list	Ctrl + Shift + L

Formatting Toolbar (continued)

BUTTON	DESCRIPTION	MOUSE ACTION	KEYBOARD ACTION
	Decreases paragraph indent	Click Format, Indents and Lists, change the Indents options	
	Increases paragraph indent	Click Format, Indents and Lists, change the Indents options	
	Decreases font size	Click Format, Font, change size	Ctrl + Shift + <
	Increases font size	Click Format, Font, change size	Ctrl + Shift + >
	Fills text box or object with specified color	Select text box or object, click the Fill Color button	
	Adds or removes line color from text box or object	Select text box or object, click the Line Color button	
	Changes the color of the font	Select text, click Format, Font, select color	
	Changes the line style of text box or object	Select text box or object, click the Line Style button, choose line weight	
	Inserts various dashed line styles	Select text box or object, click the Dash Style button, choose style	
	Inserts arrowheads at ends of line	Choose line, click the Arrow Style button, choose style	
	Inserts shadow around object	Choose object, click the Shadow Style button, choose style	
	Adds 3-D effect to object	Choose object, click the 3-D Style button, choose style	

TOOLBAR AND COMMAND SUMMARY

Objects Toolbar

BUTTON	DESCRIPTION	MOUSE ACTION	KEYBOARD ACTION

Object toolbar buttons are described in the order they appear on the toolbar.

	Selects an object	Click object to be selected	
	Inserts a text box	Click Insert, Text Box, and drag the crosshair pointer	
	Inserts a table	Click the Insert Table tool, drag the crosshair pointer, and select options	
	Inserts WordArt	Click Insert, Picture, WordArt, choose style	
	Inserts a picture	Click Insert, Picture, choose location and type	
	Inserts clip art	Click Insert, Picture, Clip Art	
	Draws a line	Click Line tool, drag crosshair pointer	
	Draws an arrow	Click Arrow tool, drag crosshair pointer	
	Draws an oval	Click Oval tool, drag crosshair pointer	
	Draws a rectangle	Click Rectangle tool, drag crosshair pointer	
	Inserts freeform shapes	Click AutoShapes tool, click type of shape, and choose shape	
	Inserts hot spot in Web publication	Click Hot Spots button, enter information for specific type of link	
	Inserts various elements on forms	Click Insert, Form Control, select type of element to add to form	
	Inserts HTML code into publication	Click Insert, HTML Code Fragment, enter HTML code	
	Inserts an object from the Design Gallery into the publication	Click Insert, Design Gallery Object, select object	

TOOLBAR AND COMMAND SUMMARY

Picture Toolbar

BUTTON	DESCRIPTION	MOUSE ACTION	KEYBOARD ACTION

Picture toolbar buttons are described in the order they appear on the toolbar.

BUTTON	DESCRIPTION	MOUSE ACTION
	Inserts a picture	Click Insert, Picture, choose location and type
	Inserts picture from scanner or camera	Click Insert, Picture, From Scanner or Camera
	Changes color of photo	Click Color button, select the change you want to make
	Increases the contrast in the colors of the selected picture	Click More Contrast button
	Decreases the contrast in the colors of the selected picture	Click Less Contrast button
	Increases the brightness of the selected picture	Click More Brightness button
	Decreases the brightness of the selected picture	Click Less Brightness button
	Crops a picture	Click Crop button
	Changes the line/border style of picture	Click Format, Picture, Colors and Lines tab, make selections
	Changes the way text wraps around picture	Click Format, Picture, Layout, select wrapping style
	Changes picture formatting	Click Format, Picture, select appropriate tab and make necessary changes
	Sets transparent colors in pictures	Click Set Transparent Color button
	Resets picture to its original settings	Click Reset Picture button

TOOLBAR AND COMMAND SUMMARY

Connect Frames Toolbar

BUTTON	DESCRIPTION	MOUSE ACTION	KEYBOARD ACTION

Connect Frames toolbar buttons are described in the order they appear on the toolbar.

BUTTON	DESCRIPTION	MOUSE ACTION	KEYBOARD ACTION
	Links two text boxes allowing text to flow from one to the other	Click Create Text Box Link button	
	Removes link between two text boxes	Click Break Forward Link button	
	Selects the previous text box for the current story	Click Previous Text Box button	
	Selects the next text box for the current story	Click Next Text Box button	

WordArt Toolbar

BUTTON	DESCRIPTION	MOUSE ACTION	KEYBOARD ACTION

WordArt toolbar buttons are described in the order they appear on the toolbar.

BUTTON	DESCRIPTION	MOUSE ACTION	KEYBOARD ACTION
	Inserts WordArt	Click Insert, Picture, WordArt, choose style	
	Changes the style of WordArt	Click Edit Text... button	
	Changes the style of WordArt already in publication	Click WordArt Gallery button	
	Changes WordArt formatting	Click Format, WordArt, select appropriate tab and make necessary changes	
	Formats WordArt to a shape	Click WordArt Shape button, select shape	
	Changes the way text wraps around WordArt	Click Format, WordArt, Layout, select wrapping style	

TOOLBAR AND COMMAND SUMMARY

WordArt Toolbar (continued)

BUTTON	DESCRIPTION	MOUSE ACTION	KEYBOARD ACTION
Aa	Makes all letters in WordArt same height	Click WordArt Same Letter Heights button	
Ab b↵	Changes WordArt to vertical orientation	Click WordArt Vertical Text button	
≣	Changes the alignment of WordArt	Click WordArt Alignment button, choose type of alignment	
AV ↔	Changes the space between WordArt characters	Click WordArt Character Spacing button, choose type of character spacing	

Other Commands

BUTTON	DESCRIPTION	MOUSE ACTION	KEYBOARD ACTION

Commands for which no button appears on the default toolbars are described below.

BUTTON	DESCRIPTION	MOUSE ACTION	KEYBOARD ACTION
	Align or Distribute	Click Arrange, Align or Distribute	
	Arrange (all windows)	Click Windows, Arrange All	
	AutoCorrect Options	Click Tools, AutoCorrect	
	AutoFit Text	Click Format, AutoFit Text	
	Background	Click Format, Background	
	Boundaries and Guides	Click View, Boundaries and Guides	Ctrl + Shift + O
	Cascade (windows)	Click Windows, Cascade	
	Character Spacing	Click Format, Character Spacing	
✗	Close	Click File, Close	Ctrl + F4
	Color Schemes	Click Format, Color Schemes	

TOOLBAR AND COMMAND SUMMARY

Other Commands (continued)

BUTTON	DESCRIPTION	MOUSE ACTION	KEYBOARD ACTION
	Commercial Printing Tools	Click Tools, Commercial Printing Tools	
	Customize	Click Tools, Customize	
	Date and Time	Click Insert, Date and Time	
	Delete Text	Click Edit, Delete Text	
	Delete Object	Click Edit, Delete Object	
	Delete Page	Click Edit, Delete Page	
	Delete Table	Click Table, Delete	
	Design Checker	Click Tools, Design Checker	
	Drop Cap	Click Format, Drop Cap	
	Edit Story in Microsoft Word	Click Edit, Edit Story in Microsoft Word	
	Fill Table Down	Click Table, Fill Down	
	Fill Table Right	Click Table, Right	
	Find	Click Edit, Find	Ctrl + F
	Font Schemes	Click Format, Font Schemes	
	Go to Page	Click Edit, Go to Page	Ctrl + G
	Group	Click Arrange, Group	Ctrl + Shift + G
	Grow Table to Fit Text	Click Table, Grow to Fit Text	
	Header and Footer	Click View, Header and Footer	
	Horizontal Rules	Click Format, Horizontal Rules	
	Ignore Master Page	Click View, Ignore Master Page	

TOOLBAR AND COMMAND SUMMARY

Other Commands (continued)

BUTTON	DESCRIPTION	MOUSE ACTION	KEYBOARD ACTION
	Indents and Lists	Click Format, Indents and Lists	
▢	Insert Table	Click Table, Insert	
	Language	Click Tools, Language	
	Layout Guides	Click Arrange, Layout Guides	
	Line Spacing	Click Format, Line Spacing	
	Links	Click Edit, Links	
	Macro	Click Tools, Macro	
	Mail Merge	Click Tools, Mail Merge	
	Master Page	Click View, Master Page	Ctrl + M
	Merge Cells	Click Table, Merge Cells	
	Nudge	Click Table, Nudge	
	Object	Click Insert, Object	
	Options	Click Tools, Options	
	Page	Click Insert, Page	Ctrl + ⇧ Shift + N
	Page Numbers	Click Insert, Page Numbers	
	Personal Information Sets	Click Edit, Personal Information	
	Publication Designs	Click Format, Publication Designs	
	Quick Publication Options	Click Format, Quick Publication Options	
	Regroup	Click Arrange, Regroup	
	Replace	Click Edit, Replace	Ctrl + H

TOOLBAR AND COMMAND SUMMARY

Other Commands (continued)

BUTTON	DESCRIPTION	MOUSE ACTION	KEYBOARD ACTION
	Rotate or Flip	Click Arrange, Rotate or Flip	
	Ruler Guides	Click Arrange, Ruler Guides	
	Rulers	Click View, Rulers	
	Section	Click Insert, Section	
	Select All	Click Edit, Select All	Ctrl + A
	Select Table	Click Table, Select	
	Send to Back	Click Arrange, Order, Send to Back	Alt + Shift + F6
	Send to Master Page	Click Arrange, Send to Master Page	
	Snap (to ruler, guides, or objects)	Click Arrange, Snap	
	Split Cells	Click Table, Split Cells	
	Status Bar	Click View, Status Bar	
	Symbol	Click Insert, Symbol	
	Table AutoFormat	Click Table, Table AutoFormat	
	Tabs	Click Format, Tabs	
	Task Pane	Click View, Task Pane	
	Text File	Click Insert, Text File	
	Tools on the Web	Click Tools, Tools on the Web	
	Two-Page Spread	Click View, Two-Page Spread	
⊞	Ungroup	Click Arrange, Ungroup	Ctrl + Shift + G

ANSWERS TO *Self* CHECK

Lesson 1

1. T
2. F
3. T
4. T
5. F

Lesson 2

1. T
2. F
3. T
4. T
5. F

Lesson 3

1. e
2. d
3. b
4. a
5. c

Lesson 4

1. d
2. c
3. a
4. e
5. b

Lesson 5

1. hyperlinks
2. navigation bars
3. hot spot
4. Web Page Preview button
5. Publisher window (or publication)

Lesson 6

1. T
2. F
3. T
4. T
5. T

Glossary

A

adaptive menu　A short menu of often-used commands to which a seldom-used command is added automatically once a user selects the command from an expanded menu. Compare with *short menu* and *expanded menu*.

address bar　The place in a browser to enter the Web site address that you want to navigate to.

application　Specialized software program for accomplishing a specific task, such as creating text, manipulating financial information, or tracking records.

application window　A rectangle on the desktop containing the menus and document(s) for an application.

Arial　A common font for headings; a sans serif font.

articles　Stories that appear in a newsletter.

aspect ratio　The width-to-height ratio of an image.

asset　Files that are associated with a Web site and are generally gathered in one folder.

asymmetrical layout　Text and graphics are unbalanced in a publication; generally a less formal layout.

AutoShapes　Simple line drawings you can draw by clicking a button on the Drawing toolbar.

B

best fit　Publisher automatically increases or decreases the size of the type in a text box to fill the text box.

bold　Thick, heavy effect applied to text for emphasis.

border　An edging around a paragraph, page, graphic, or table.

browser　A software tool used to navigate the Web.

bullet　A character, typographical symbol, or graphic used as a special effect.

button　A box labeled with words or pictures that can be clicked to command the computer.

C

callouts　Pulling aside text to highlight it.

caption　A title, an explanation, or a description alongside an illustration.

cell　Single element of a table; a box formed by the intersection of a column and a row.

cell alignment　The combined vertical and horizontal placement of text in cells; e.g., Top Left, Center, Bottom Right.

center aligned　Centered; paragraph alignment in which each line of text is midway between the left and right margins; also, page alignment in which text is midway between the top and bottom margins.

character spacing　The amount of space between characters; e.g., normal, expanded, condensed, or kerned.

choose　See *select*.

click　The technique of quickly pressing and releasing the left button on a mouse or trackball.

clip art　Set of graphics a user can choose to insert into documents. Also called *clip*.

clip art keyword　A word(s) that helps identify clips in Clip Gallery.

Clipboard　Place in memory used by Windows applications for temporarily storing up to 12 pieces of text or graphics to be placed in a new location. Also a toolbar for controlling and clearing items from Clipboard memory; the Office Clipboard.

Clip Gallery　A Microsoft Office folder that has professionally designed images (pictures, photographs, sound, and video clips) from which you can choose an illustration to complement many different subjects.

close　To remove a file from the window and the computer's memory.

columns　Typical arrangement of text in newsletters that places text in two or more columns, thus aiding readability.

command　An instruction given to a computer by clicking a menu option or toolbar button or pressing a combination of keys.

connected frames　Used to allow text to flow from one frame, or text box, automatically to the next frame or text box.

context-sensitive Help   Tips and Help topics related specifically to tasks underway in the application window.

contrast   The difference in brightness between light and dark areas of an image or page.

copy   To place a copy of text or graphics on the Clipboard.

crop   To trim a picture.

customize   To make or alter to individual or personal specifications.

cut   To remove text or graphics and to place it on the Clipboard.

D

data source   the mailing list used to insert addresses into the main publication.

dateline   part of a newsletter that include date, volume/issue number, and may include the company slogan.

default   A preset condition in an operating system or application that remains in effect unless canceled or overridden by an operator.

delete   Remove text or graphics from a document.

deselect   To return an object to its original color or turn off an option, indicating that an item will not be affected by the next action taken or that an option will no longer be in effect.

Design Checker   A Publisher tool that checks publications for design consistency and alerts the user to potential problems.

Design Gallery   A set of predesigned objects that can be inserted into publications.

desktop   The working area of the screen that displays many Windows tools and is the background for computer work.

dialog box   A rectangle containing a set of options that appears when a software program needs more information from the user to perform a requested operation.

double-click   The technique of rapidly pressing and releasing the left button on a mouse or trackball twice when the mouse pointer on screen is pointing to an object.

drag   The technique of moving an object on screen by pointing to the object, pressing and holding the mouse button, moving the mouse to a new location, and then releasing the mouse button. Also called *drag-and-drop*.

drag-and-drop   See *drag*.

E

e-mail   The exchange of messages and computer files through the Internet and other electronic data networks; electronic mail.

embed   To paste text from the Clipboard in the form of a static picture that cannot be edited as text (only as an object).

enumerations   Numbers assigned to listed items or steps to count them or establish proper sequence.

expanded menu   A list of all commands available on a menu that displays when a user clicks the double arrow at the bottom of a short menu. Compare with *short menu*.

F

file management   Operations required to create, copy, delete, move, open, save, and close files and folders.

fill   The inside or main part of an object; also, to color that part of an object.

folder   A named location on a computer hard drive or floppy disk for storing and organizing files and programs.

font   The design of a set of characters. Also called *typeface*.

font size   The size of text characters, measured in points; point size.

font styles   Effects or attributes added to highlight text, such as bold, italic, and underline.

form control   Elements that allow data to be captured and submitted online.

format   A conventional arrangement of text on a page; also, the act of arranging text (aligning, indenting, spacing, etc.)

Format Painter   Allows you to copy the formats and styles of text to other text in the publication.

Glossary

formatting Changing the alignment, indentations, line spacing, margins, and/or paragraph spacing of text.

frames Holds objects such as text, pictures, and graphics in a publication.

G

glossary term A word or phrase appearing in blue (not underlined) on a Help screen that, when clicked, shows the definition of the word or phrase.

graphic Picture, drawing, photograph, or WordArt that can be inserted into a document. Also called *image* and *object*.

gridlines The pattern of regularly spaced horizontal and vertical lines on a table that define the columns, rows, and cells; the cell borders.

group To associate objects together so they can be manipulated as one object.

H

handle Squares that surround an object and allow you to move or resize the object. See also *move handle* and *resize handle*.

Help Information provided on screen by software programs (e.g., Windows Me, Explorer 5, Publisher 2002) to assist users.

highlight An enhancing tool that allows you to place color over text to appear much like a highlighter; can be used to emphasize important text or to mark text to be reviewed.

home page The first page of a Web site, used as a starting point for Web browsing; a Start Page.

horizontal alignment The arrangement of text in relation to the left and right margins.

horizontal scroll bar Scroll bar at the bottom of the screen that scrolls documents from side to side.

hot spot Areas on a Web site that act like hyperlinks.

HTML See *Hypertext Markup Language*.

HTTP See *Hypertext Transfer Protocol*.

hyperlink Text or a graphic inserted in a Help frame, a document, or a Web page that links to another frame or a document, an Internet address, a page of the World Wide Web, or an HTML page on an intranet.

Hypertext Markup Language (HTML) The language for creating World Wide Web documents that contain links to other resources.

Hypertext Transfer Protocol (HTTP) The set of rules that defines the way hypertext links display Web pages.

hyphenate To divide words at line breaks by inserting a hyphen; automatic hyphenation.

I

I-beam pointer Pointer in the shape of the capital letter "I" when moved over text.

icon A small image that represents a device, program, file, or folder.

image See *graphic*.

import Insert a file from another location.

indentation Distance of text from the left or right page margins.

insertion point Blinking vertical line within a document that indicates where text will appear when typing begins.

Internet A worldwide network of computers that connects each Internet user's computer to all other computers in the network and allows users to exchange messages and data.

Internet Service Providers (ISPs) Companies that provide Internet access to users for a monthly or an annual fee.

intranet A network within an organization allowing users to exchange messages and data with other users in the organization.

italic Thin, right-slanted effect applied to text for emphasis.

J

joystick An input device used to control the onscreen pointer; a small joystick is often found in the middle of keyboards on laptop computers.

justified   Paragraph alignment in which both the left and right edges of text are perfectly even. Also page alignment in which text is distributed among the top, middle, and bottom.

K

keywords   Words used to define a search of World Wide Web or Help.

L

landscape orientation   Text arrangement that prints a document on paper that is wider than it is long.

layer   Placing objects on top of each other.

layout   The process of arranging graphics on a page along with text; specifically, the horizontal alignment and the wrap style.

layout guides   The pink and blue dotted lines indicating the margins you have set for a publication.

left aligned   Paragraph alignment in which text is perfectly even at the left margin; the standard (default) paragraph alignment.

letterhead   Paper used to produce written communications such as letters that provides basic contact information for a company.

line spacing   The number of blank lines between text lines; e.g., double spacing leaves one blank line below each line of text.

lines   The outline or edging lines of an object.

M

mail merge   Allows you to enter contact information only once and insert the information repeatedly into publications.

mailing panel   Place on a publication for mailing information, including the recipient's address and the sender's return address.

main publication   The letter or other communication into which contact information is merged from the data source.

margins   Blank areas bordering text on a page.

masthead   The title of a newsletter, usually placed at the top of the first page of the publication.

menu   Displayed on an application screen, a list of options available to a computer user.

menu bar   An area below the title bar of all application windows containing menu names that, when clicked, display lists of commands.

Microsoft Clip Organizer   Contains professionally designed objects that you can insert into publications.

mouse   A hand-held, button-activated input device that when rolled along a flat surface directs an indicator to move correspondingly about a computer screen, allowing the operator to move the indicator freely, as to select operations or manipulate data or graphics.

mouse pointer   See *pointer*.

move handle   A large square with a four-way arrow at the top-left corner of a table, used to drag the table.

N

navigate   To move about on the Windows desktop in a planned or preset course.

navigation bars   Parts of Web sites that allow you to move among the pages on the site.

O

object   Any graphic element inserted into a document, especially graphics created from the Drawing toolbar. See also *graphic*.

Office Assistant   An animated character that can answer specific question, offer tips, and provide help.

Office Clipboard   See *Clipboard*.

online Help system   An onscreen, electronic manual that provides assistance with the features and operations of a computer program.

open   To copy a file from disk into the computer memory and display it on screen; also, to start an application.

Glossary

P

Pack and Go   Publisher feature that allows you to bundle and condense all a publication's files to take them to another computer.

page orientation   The way in which the publication is printed on paper, either portrait or landscape.

paragraph mark   An on-screen symbol (¶) marking the end of a paragraph; also a proofreading symbol indicating begin new paragraph.

paragraph spacing   Space added above or below paragraphs.

paste   To insert cut or copied text from the Clipboard.

personal information sets   Contact information about business or organizations for which you frequently create publications.

point   A unit of measure for text and white space, equivalent to 0.01384 inch.

point size   See *font size*.

pointer   An arrow or other onscreen image that moves in relation to the movement of a mouse or trackball. Also called mouse pointer.

pointing   Moving the mouse pointer over an onscreen object.

portrait orientation   Text arrangement that prints a document on paper that is longer than it is wide; the default orientation.

Publication Gallery   The box to the right of the task pane that displays all the designs available for a publication type.

publications   Print communications such as postcards, flyers, and newsletters that can be created using Microsoft Publisher.

pull quotes   Special text boxes used to draw the reader's attention. Often contains an interesting quote or a highlight from the article.

R

radio button   A small circle filled with a solid dot when selected; only one in a set of radio buttons can be selected.

readability   A rating of text in terms of how easy it is to read and understand, often stated as a grade (school) level.

resize   To change the height and/or width of a graphic.

resize handle   A square at each corner and along the sides of a selected clip or drawing object (or a square in the lower-left corner of a table) that may be used for expanding or contracting the object (or table).

right aligned   Text alignment in which the right edge is perfectly even.

right-click   The technique of quickly pressing and releasing the right button on a mouse or trackball.

ruler   A display of numbered tick marks and indent markers that indicate measurements across a document used to format paragraphs.

S

sans serif   A font without serifs (e.g., Arial); a gothic typeface.

save   To transfer a file from computer memory to a storage disk—either a floppy or hard disk.

ScreenTip   A text box showing the name and description of elements on the screen.

scrollable   Having a scroll bar and scroll box that enable users to look at different areas of the display.

scroll arrows   Buttons at each end of a scroll bar that scroll a window in small increments when clicked—for example, scrolling text line by line.

scroll bars   A bar along the right side or bottom of a window used to bring hidden areas of a document into view.

scroll box   Control within the scroll bars that allows quick navigation within a document.

scrolling   Using a scroll bar; scroll box, or scroll arrows to move through a document.

search engine   An Internet tool that allows a user to search for information on a particular topic.

select   To designate or highlight (typically by clicking an item with the mouse) where the next action will take place, which command will be executed next, or which option will be put into effect.

selection bar The left margin in the Publisher window that responds to the pointer by selecting the line of text.

serif Finishing strokes on the characters of some fonts (e.g., Times New Roman) that form a fine line.

server A computer that supplies data or services to another (client) computer.

shading Color or graduations of gray applied to cells, paragraphs, and pages, often in combination with a border.

short menu A customized menu, listing a user's most-used commands. Compare with *expanded menu*.

shortcut keys A combination of keys to perform an operation or a task.

shortcut menu Context-sensitive menu that appears when selected text is right-clicked.

stacking Placing frames on top of each other.

start page See *home page*.

status bar Bar at the bottom of the document window that indicates information about a command or toolbar button, an operation in progress, or the location of the insertion point.

style A named set of character and paragraph attributes.

submenu Indicated by an arrow on a menu, another list of commands or options.

symbol An object that represents something else by being associated with it or looking like it, especially an object representing something invisible; e.g., ©, ™, ®.

symmetrical layout Text and graphics placed in equally balanced columns creating a formal-looking layout.

T

table A document format having data arranged in columns and rows of cells.

table of contents Listing of chapter and headings and (usually) their page numbers. Also called *TOC*.

task pane A menu box that provides options for designing your publication and previews of those options.

taskbar An area on the Windows desktop that displays a button for the Start menu, icons for commonly used Windows features, a button for each application running, and a button for the clock.

template Master copy of a type of document; a model document that includes standard and variable text and formatting and may include graphics.

text box A box used to hold text (or a graphic) in an object.

text wrapping The way in which text aligns and wraps about objects such as pictures and graphics.

title bar Bar at the top of the screen containing application and document names.

TOC A table of contents.

toolbar A row of icons representing frequently used commands, used to execute commands quickly.

touch sensitive pad An input device used to control the onscreen pointer by pressing a flat surface with a finger; usually found on laptop computers.

trackball An input device that functions like an upside-down mouse, containing a ball that is rolled by the thumb or fingers to move the onscreen pointer.

two-page spread Allows you to view and work on two facing pages at the same time.

U

underline A line under characters added for emphasis; numerous underline style options are available.

Universal Resource Locator (URL) The address of a Web site.

V

vertical scroll bar Scroll bar at the right side of the screen that scrolls documents from beginning to end.

W

Web See *World Wide Web*.

Web page Screens that display information on the Web. Many Web pages contain text, graphics, animation, sound, and video. Also called *home page*.

Glossary

Web site   Specific locations on the World Wide Web, accessible by means of a unique address, or URL. See also *Universal Resource Locator*.

wizard   A document creation tool that is preformatted and offers help with content and organization on the basis of a user's answers to its questions.

WordArt   Decorative text that you can stretch, skew, or rotate to fit a particular shape. See also *graphic*.

World Wide Web   A tool for accessing the Internet that organizes information into easy-to-use Web pages. Also called the *Web*.

wrap text   The way in which lines of text break in relation to an object on the same page; styles include In line with text, Square, Tight, Behind text, and In front of text.

wrapping lines   Black corner points that appear around a graphic allowing you to change the wrap of text around the graphic. Also called *wrapping points*.

wrapping points   See *wrapping lines*.

WWW   See *World Wide Web*.

Index

creating fax cover sheet
using, 293
creating letterhead using,
285–286
previews of, *illus.*, 277
selecting, 276
Design template
creating publications using,
26–33
customizing, 61–65
newsletter from, 96–103
personal information sets
with, 65
postcard from, 27–33
tri-fold brochure from, 55–61
Web site, 210
Desktop
Windows, *illus.*, 8
Double-click, *def.*, 7
Double Spacing button, 17
Downloading
clips, 127
sound files, 249
Drag, *def.*, 7
Drag-and-drop, *def.*, 7
Drag text pointer, 7

E

Edit menu, 11
Editing
captions, 121
tables, 298–299
text in Word, 105
Ellipsis, 11
E-mail
hyperlink for, 221–223
E-mail button, 13
Emboss button, 17
Engrave button, 17
Exiting Publisher, 37
Expanded menu, *def.*, 10
External links
checking, 254

F

Fax cover sheet, 293
Field codes, *def.*, 286
File menu, 11, *illus.*, 36
Fill color
adding to text box, 77
reversing, 162
Fill Color button, 16, 190
Fill Effects dialog box, *illus.*, 188,
191
Find and replace, 22
Folder, *def.*, 34
Font
changing, 74–76
changing design, 72–73
changing size, 72–73
colors, 162
sans serif, 72

serif, 72
Font box, 16
Font Color button, 16
Font size, *def.*, 73
changing, 104
determining maximum size
for frame, 281
increasing size, 281
Font Size box, 16
Font styles, *def.*, 73
rules for applying, 73
Form control, *def.*, 304
Form Control button, 18
Format menu, 11
Format of publication, 140
Format Painter, *def.*, 60
using, 60
Format Painter button, 13
Format Picture button, 117
Format properties, 74
Format Text dialog box, *illus.*, 77
Formatting graphics in newsletter,
171–174
Formatting text in newsletter,
165–171
Formatting toolbar, 16–17, 95
Frames, *def.*, 6
layered, *illus.*, 6
Free Rotate button, 13
Full-color printing, 141

G

Graphical user interface, 6
Graphics, *def.*, 111
adding to newsletter, 164
cropping, 116
editing and formatting,
117–121
formatting, 171–174
importing, 115
importing from Clip
Organizer, 113–114
importing from the Web,
115–116, 126–127
inserting in newsletter,
171–174
text wrapping around, 116,
173
using effectively, 116–117
WordArt as, 111
Greeting line, 290
Greeting Line dialog box, *illus.*, 291
Gridlines
adding to table, 301
Group Object button, 119
Grouped objects, *illus.*, 63
Grouping objects, 118, 221

H

Handles, *def.*, 52, *illus.*, 53
around clip art and caption, 61
Headlines, *def.*, 107, *illus.*, 108

creating, 107–111
Help
Answer Wizard, 22
contents tab, 22
index tab, 22
Office Assistant, 24
online Help system, *def.*, 20
window, *illus.*, 22
Help button, 13
Help menu, 11
Help select pointer, 7
Home button, 39
Home page, 39
creating, 215–223
def., 209
illus., 39
Horizontal alignment, *def.*, 95
Horizontal ruler, *illus.*, 161
Horizontal scroll bar, *illus.*, 9
Hot spot, *def.*, 242
creating, 243
Hot Spot button, 18, 243
Hot Spot frame, *illus.*, 244
resized, *illus.*, 244
HTML, *see* Hypertext Markup
Language
HTML Code Fragment button, 18
HTTP, *see* Hypertext Transfer
Protocol
Hyperlink, 39
between pages, 242–247
checking external, 254
connect pages in Web site, 228
connect to other Web sites,
238–241
deselecting, 212–213
for e-mail, 221–223
search results, 80
Hyperlink select pointer, 7
Hypertext, *def.*, 39
Hypertext Markup Language, *def.*,
186
Hypertext Transfer Protocol, *def.*,
186
Hyphenation
automatic, 74, 299
proper use of, 74
turning off automatic, 76

I

Icons, *illus.*, 8
Image, *def.*, 111
Importing graphics
from a CD, 115
from Clip Organizer, 113–114
from the Web, 115–116
Increase Font Size button, 16, 281
Increase Indent button, 16
Index tab, *illus.*, 23
using, 23
Insert Address Block dialog box, 290
Insert button, 31
Insert Clip Art task pane, 111,
illus., 112

Index

Notes

Notes

Notes

Notes